The Complete YouTube Book

What works for my channel with 8+ million views?

Jerry Banfield

Editor: Michel Gerard

Publisher: *https://jerrybanfield.com/books*

COPYRIGHT

The Complete YouTube Book - Copyright © Jerry Banfield - 2016

All rights reserved. No part of this publication may be reproduced, distributed, or transmitted in any form or by any means, including photocopying, recording, or other electronic or mechanical methods, without the prior written permission of the publisher, except in the case of brief quotations embodied in critical reviews and certain other noncommercial uses permitted by copyright law.

More Books by Jerry Banfield

https://jerrybanfield.com/books

TABLE OF CONTENTS

PREFACE 09

CHAPTER 1: *YouTube* **connected me with a way of living that is awesome. How can you do it?** 13

CHAPTER 2: What to do on *YouTube* **and how to be successful** 19

- You can use *YouTube* to completely transform your life! 21

- The best part about *YouTube* is organic traffic from search! 25

- Ranking high on *YouTube* search is ridiculously easy! 28

- *YouTube* subscribers are the #1 most valuable followers I have online 34

- Do what you love on *YouTube* and you will keep doing it! 41

- Uploading one video is the biggest step you can take today! 43

- What to name a *YouTube* channel and make the videos about? 46

- How can you get people to watch your *YouTube* videos? 50

- The basics of making a viral video on *YouTube!* 54

CHAPTER 3: My video production process from start to finish 67

- See what equipment I use to film all of my videos on *YouTube* 69

- Lighting on a budget 74

- Filming videos in *1080p HD* is easy with *Camtasia Studio* 77

- My new filming system using *iPhone* with *iRig HD* mic + screen capture software 83

- Why I upload *1* or *2* videos at a time and try to do it each day 89

- How to handle copyright claims and avoid getting flagged for copyright 94

CHAPTER 4: The *YouTube* video editor is a powerful tool for making your own videos fast! 98

- Introduction to the *YouTube* video editor and how to get free videos you can use! 99

- How to make a niche topic video using the *YouTube* video editor + add your audio 108

CHAPTER 5: Live streaming on *YouTube* is a big thing that is here right now! 112

- *YouTube* live streaming launched my first viral video! See how to get started 113

- How to setup your first live event or live stream on *YouTube* 119

- Getting the live stream for a video game started with *Elgato* game capture HD 129

CHAPTER 6: *YouTube* thumbnails are key for free suggested video views and search clicks 133

- How to make a great *YouTube* thumbnail with *Canva* based on data 134

- What software to use for your *YouTube* thumbnails and graphics 143

- *YouTube* thumbnail creation simply with *Fiverr* 149

- *YouTube* thumbnails in search ranking for branding consistently and getting clicks 155

CHAPTER 7: *YouTube* SEO: optimizing titles, tags and descriptions for video views 159

- *YouTube* video uploading, title, tag and description walkthrough 161

- *YouTube* title optimization tips for *YouTube* search and *YouTube* suggested video 170

- *YouTube* tagging tutorial in depth for maximizing suggested video views 178

- *YouTube* video description in depth. Long descriptions are way better! 190

- *YouTube* keyword tool for expanding your description and making a better title 200

- Proof these *YouTube* strategies are working rapidly 210

CHAPTER 8: *YouTube* viral video launch process 216

- *YouTube* viral video creation fast tutorial and overview 217

- *YouTube* viral video launch day 2 reviewing the ad campaign and initial views 225

- Results of this video a year later. This made my next viral video happen! 230

CHAPTER 9: *YouTube* analytics are the secret to optimizing your *YouTube* channel for success! 235

- Introduction to *YouTube* analytics including views, minutes watched + top videos 237

- *YouTube* analytics traffic sources explained for *YouTube* search + suggested video 248

- *YouTube* subscriber analytics tab explained for how to know which videos get subs 262

- Optimizing your *YouTube* video tags, title, and description based on analytics 275

CHAPTER 10: *YouTube* video ranking with *Google AdWords for Video* 287

- Introduction to *Google AdWords for video* 288

- My channel is growing today because of advertising my videos 290

- Making your *YouTube* ads with *Google AdWords for video* 295

- Choosing which videos to advertise 299

CHAPTER 11: *YouTube* comments, engagement and community interactions 306

- *YouTube* comments and engagement explained, and why it is valuable for growth 307

- I try to answer every comment on my *YouTube* channel 312

- How to add your biggest *YouTube* fans to a *Google Plus* circle with three clicks 318

- *YouTube* community settings to block spammers and bullies 323

CHAPTER 12: Ways to make money on *YouTube* 327

- Start on *YouTube* and then work your way into making *Udemy* courses 328

- Case study of how to make new viral *YouTube* videos + earn with *Google AdSense* 339

- *$2,500* per sale from *YouTube* tutorial videos with an *"email for more help"* link 347

- *Patreon* allows you to get paid to make *YouTube* videos and more! 352

CONCLUSION 362

LEGAL NOTICE 364

PREFACE

Thank you very much for reading this book! You are reading this now because you want to learn more about *YouTube* and how to have a successful *YouTube* channel. I hope that I will answer all the questions you may have in the different chapters of this book and help you make the right choice for a strategy that will work for you to have success on *YouTube*.

How did you get here with me?

In 2005 while I was in college at the *University of South Carolina*, I tried to start working online. I signed up for an *MLM* program and a survey website. A month later, I had refunds from both and figured working online was not possible because everything was a scam. The truth was I was afraid to fail again.

In 2011, I moved in with my wife and launched an online business focusing on video game addiction in an attempt to avoid dealing with any of my other problems. In a few months, I changed my business to selling T-shirts because I realized there was no money in video game addiction. A year after starting my business, I dropped out of my criminology *PHD* program at the *University of South Florida* to run my business full time, which by then had changed to helping clients with *Facebook* and *Google* ads based on my experience failing to do them successfully for myself.

In 2013, I started sharing everything I knew for free on *YouTube* because I hoped it would help me get more clients. By April 2014, I was nearly bankrupt after failing at *15+* different business models. I was also nearly dead from trying to drink the pain away and fortunately the fear of death motivated me to get into recovery. Being in recovery motivated me to focus more on being of true service to others and less on what I would get out of it. I started making courses online with *Udemy* which soon turned into my first real business. I partnered with as many talented instructors as I could and learned from top instructors how to get my courses the most sales.

In 2015, I tried making some inspirational videos sharing what I learned in recovery and got an amazing response on *YouTube*. To make the background on my videos more interesting, I started making the inspirational videos while playing video games. To make a more helpful website, I hired a freelancer to convert the videos into blog posts. A *Udemy* student named *Michel Gerard* then helped me turn those posts into books.

By 2016, the *Udemy* courses I was teaching had made nearly *2 million dollars* in sales with me receiving over *$600,000* of that. Things went so well on *Udemy* that they decided to launch a new pricing policy in April 2016 that reduced sales by *80%* site-wide which encouraged many instructors to leave. Since I did not take the hint, *Udemy* chose to ban me based on what they said were policy violations despite my best efforts to work within the rules.

Now I am trying out live streaming video games both for the self-help message and the hands on tutorials that I watch when I am playing a new game. Again I take another leap of faith in my business online which I hope is for the right reason of being in loving service here with you.

Thank you very much for reading this and I hope you enjoy the rest!

Jerry Banfield

CHAPTER 1

YouTube connected me with a way of living that is awesome. How can you do it?

I am honored and very lucky that I can start every day off making videos. That's my job now and that's what I do. I have my own company and I work for myself. I make videos every day to put on my online courses at *jerrybanfield.com/shop/*.

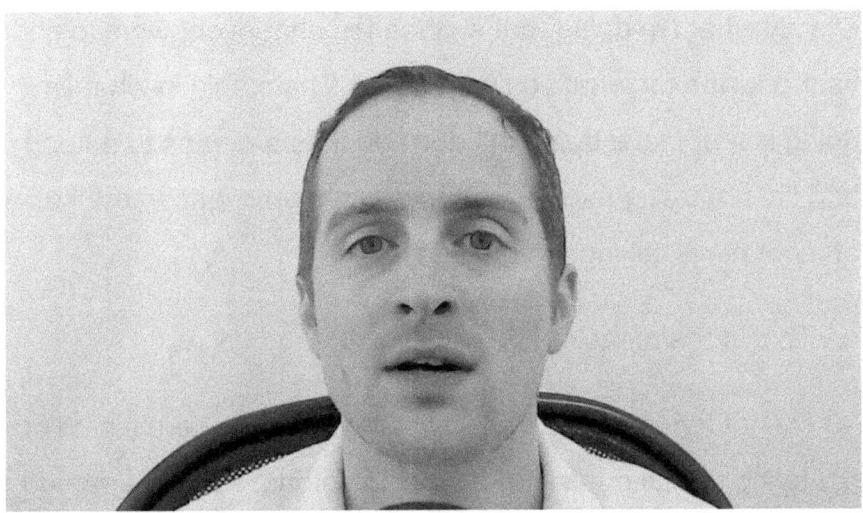

Then, I put some of those videos as free previews on my *YouTube* channel. My *YouTube* channel *(www.youtube.com/c/JerryBanfield)*, Jerry Banfield, has **72,000+ subscribers**, more than **eight million views**, and **922 videos.**

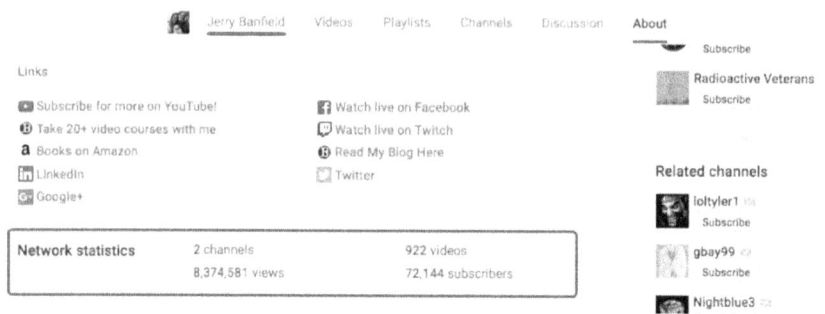

I absolutely love it!

What I'm offering you in this book is not a system to do exactly what I'm doing, but an idea for what might work to find your passion for what you want to do. The magic in what I'm doing is that I love doing it! I don't do it as a means to an end and I'm not trying to go anywhere. I'm happy right where I am at, right here, talking to you today.

That is the miracle.

I'm not trying to use this so I can get somewhere else. I'm not trying to make this into a stepping stone, so then I can do something bigger. This is the big thing I'm doing and I love it! If you want this to be the big thing you are doing, then you have got the basics in this book of exactly what you can do to make that happen.

Ultimately, exceptional things through creativity happen when you love what you are doing, you are present when you are doing it and you are not doing it as a means to an end. You can see a lot of online courses and videos everywhere, where it is just a means to and end and where there is no real passion. You often have to struggle really hard to create things like that too because you have to work against your inner self. You have got to fight by making scripts and forcing everything together somehow.

I make things nearly effortlessly because it comes from the soul. It is passion and I love doing this! There is almost no resistance to it and it just comes out. I don't have to use a script and I don't have to plan hardly anything out. It just explodes out of me into existence online. That's the power I'm offering you by what I share in this book.

I'll give you a lot of the technical details on how you can go through and do some of these things. I'll give you the gateway and the excitement into the world to do this. Now, if you want success with it, it is up to you to find an area that you are passionate about. I haven't seen this covered in other books or online courses.

You can do an infinite number of things, but there is only one thing you are going to do right now, that you would be fulfilling your inner purpose, that you would feel it is the right thing to do, and when you match up with that, everything becomes almost effortless.

That's not to say your whole life is perfect, and you don't have some down times, but your work becomes a flow of creativity and passion. *YouTube* is a great venue to explore this. By doing webcam videos, screen captures or even just putting other videos together. If you love making top ten videos, then give it a try. If you enjoy watching videos on a certain topic, and you have thought: *"You know what, I can make a better video on that."* Then go for it if you enjoy doing it, if you do it as the thing that is the big thing to do and not a means to an end.

What I am giving you is a powerful set of tools, where you can use this to work and make videos at home full time. But if you are doing it to try and get somewhere else, it is not going to work. If you want to do this, find your passion in it. That can be scary and you will have to make changes to your life lots of times to get things to work exactly the way you want them to.

I had to take *50,000* dollars out in loans last year to make a full transition and to doing this that I love, from what I was doing because it paid well of just serving as many clients as I could.

My *YouTube* audience can see and feel that I love doing this! I took a big risk in borrowing all that money in order to make this transition happen. You might need to take some kind of risk to make it happen for you. You might have to quit your job, you might have to move, you might have to buy a whole new set of computer and recording equipment. You might have to take a risk to get the enjoyment and fulfillment you want out of your work every day. This is well worth it!

You can test out all these things usually without taking much of a risk, but if you want real consistent fulfillment in what you are doing, you have got to give your all to it. You have got to commit to it and to trust that whatever you are doing is right and just let it happen. So kind of let go in the mind of all of the thoughts, plans and schemes, and just let yourself do what you are supposed to do. That's what I'm doing now and I just love it!

I hope this book will be useful for you in getting and being where I am because ultimately a place where I am is *now,* and it is the same place you are in a bigger sense. It is all about organizing the practical things around you, and being in the moment, enjoying and doing what you love to do and communicating that.

CHAPTER 2

What to do on *YouTube* and how to be successful

Thank you very much for getting started in the second chapter of this book that covers the essential on how to have a successful *YouTube* channel.

<u>You can use YouTube to completely transform your life</u> and it is what I did. *YouTube* is the foundation of what has allowed me to teach online and it can help you achieve the lifestyle you want to have.

I will show you that <u>the best part about YouTube is organic traffic from search</u> as I find no better source in the world for organic traffic. In fact, it is easier to get good rankings in *YouTube* than it is in *Google* search.

<u>Ranking high on YouTube search is ridiculously easy</u> when you know how to do it correctly and it is what I will show you in this section.

With more than *2 million likes* on *Facebook* and *120,000 followers* on *Twitter*, <u>YouTube subscribers are the #1 most valuable followers I have online</u>.

When you do something you love or do something you enjoy, that is the most value you can give on *YouTube*. <u>Do what you love on YouTube and you will keep doing it!</u> Doing something you hate, as a means to an end, or just to make money won't bring you success.

Making one or two hundred videos for *YouTube* may be intimidating as there is no way you could possibly do it at once, but <u>uploading one video is the biggest step you can take today!</u>

Do not make the same mistakes I made when I started a couple of company channels. I will tell you <u>what to name a YouTube channel and make the videos about.</u> This will save you time and frustration.

<u>How can you get people to watch your YouTube videos?</u> Getting people to watch your videos is hard when you start a channel, but I can tell you that there is an easy way, and I will show you.

Finally, you will learn <u>the basics of making a viral video on YouTube</u> as I share with you how I did it with my best viral videos.

I invite you to read on...

You can use *YouTube* to completely transform your life!

What is possible when you apply the strategies in this *YouTube* book to what you are doing? You can completely transform your entire way of living using *YouTube*.

YouTube is the foundation of what has allowed me to teach online. I show you this as proof of how powerful these things are actually working for me and my life today.

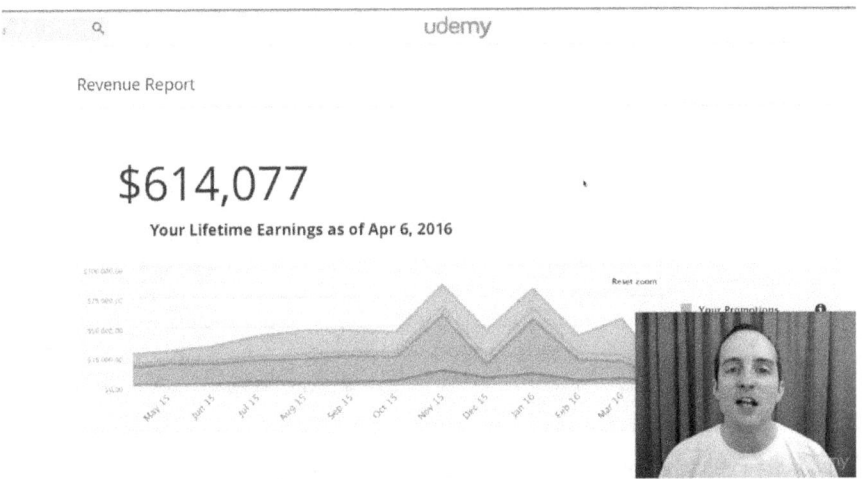

I'm grateful that I have made over *$600,000* to teach on *Udemy* and I hate showing you the income because I know what judgments can come from that, and yet I have to show you this because it is clear proof of how much the things work that I'm showing you.

YouTube has brought me so many students who then have taken so many courses that have allowed me to do what I'm doing on *Udemy*. I'm grateful I'm earning around *$1,000+* a day on *Udemy*. It is *April 6* today and I have got almost *$6,000* already this month, *$53,000* last month, *$39,000* in February and *$78,000* in January.

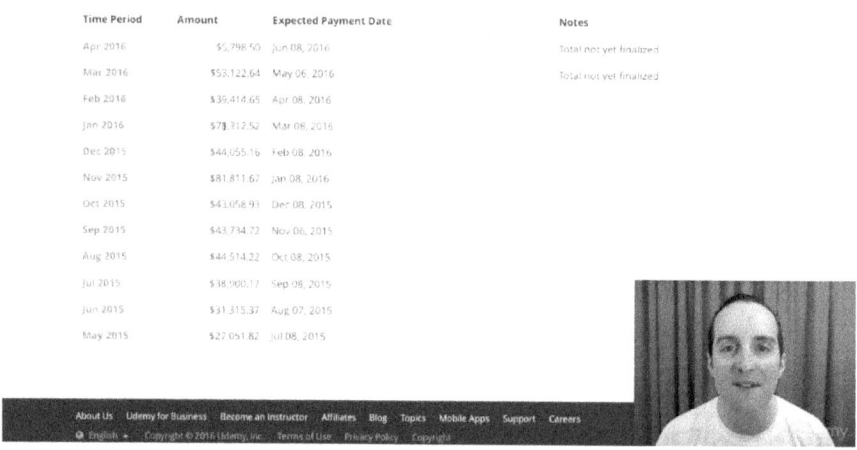

The point is *YouTube* has been the key to this. I make videos on *YouTube*, that then get people to go buy my *Udemy* courses. Now, I literally get paid to do pretty much whatever I want to.

I have a live stream on *YouTube* of playing *League of Legends*, I have helpful books, tutorials, inspirational and animated videos.

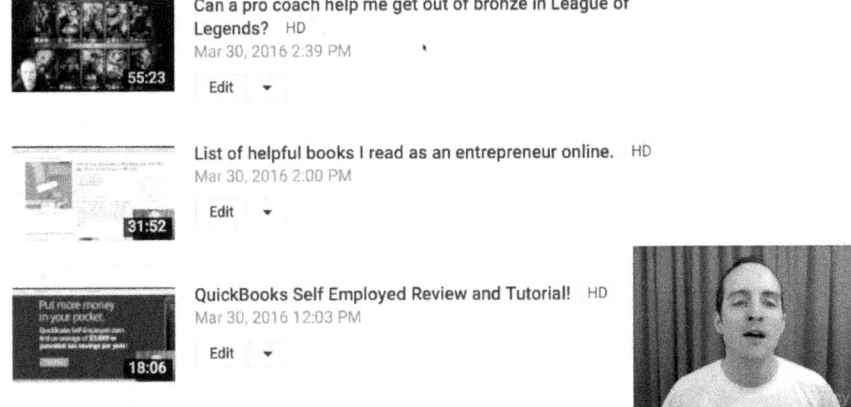

I even spent hundreds of dollars to buy downloadable game content so I can make a video on my *YouTube* channel to show other people whether it was worth it, a video that people actually really enjoy.

Now, this is amazing. I was hustling, struggling, suffering, and trying to just make a dollar here and a dollar there. Doing the work on *YouTube* has been one of the best things I have ever done for my entire professional life. It is more valuable than going to graduate school, more valuable than all of the school and training I did.

YouTube has given me some amazing results in my life. What I hope is that this book allows you to see whether you want to do more on *YouTube* and what you are really capable.

I'll start it out by trying to give you the very best of what I like and what works for me on *YouTube* right up front, and then I trust your judgement to go from there and learn more about what you are most interested in.

The best part about *YouTube* is organic traffic from search!

Organic traffic is the number one value I find on *YouTube* and the reason it is worth doing. I find no better source in the world for organic traffic than *YouTube*, and this is my organic traffic on *YouTube* over the last year.

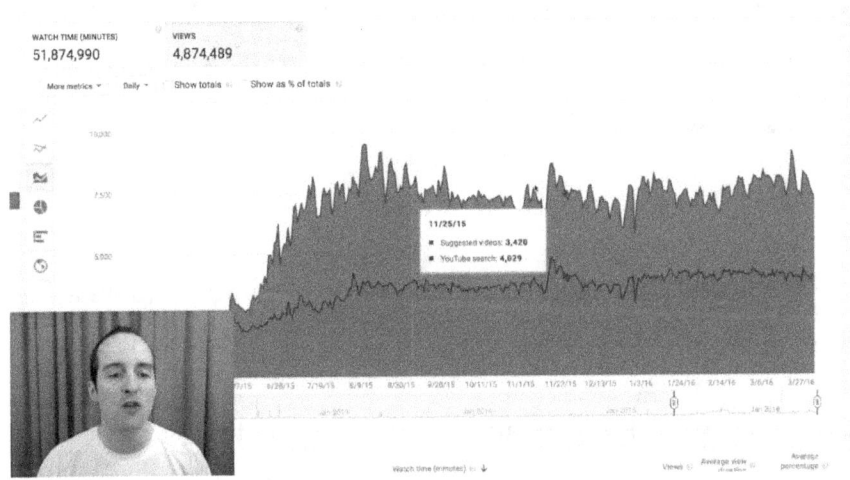

You'll see thousands of views, over *7,500* views most days now that I get from *YouTube*. That traffic is amazing because these are people searching for exactly what I'm doing. You might have even found this book or one of my courses (jerrybanfield.com/shop/) this way as a result of this *YouTube* organic search traffic.

This is the best source of traffic I have found online in years of doing Internet marketing.

Why? It is free!

If I had to pay for this traffic, it would cost me anywhere from *$1,000* to *$10,000 plus* per day to replicate the traffic I get for free, and it is extremely high quality. I get people who watch a video and go straight into a course and buy right after that with me. I have tested a ton of other traffic sources, nothing beats *YouTube*.

Why? It is a combination of traffic.

YouTube is the world's second-largest search engine after *Google* and has low competition.

The competition is absurdly low on many things on *YouTube*. On *Google* if you try and search for various terms the competition could be insane to try and get on that first page of results. On *YouTube* you can pretty easily use what you learn in this book and get on the top of even very competitive search terms.

The reason you see this traffic here is because I used what I show you in this book to take one of the top positions on the one word search term *"Hacking."*

Now, imagine how hard that would be to do that on *Google* search, it would be almost impossible. On *YouTube* it is pretty easy. *YouTube* is exceptional for traffic and I love it.

Ranking high on *YouTube* search is ridiculously easy!

What I love most about *YouTube* is that ranking high is ridiculously easy. There is one simple thing you do in order to rank high. You can literally just pay for it. No other *SEO*, no other ranking I know of is this simple. You can see I have done it on my channel.

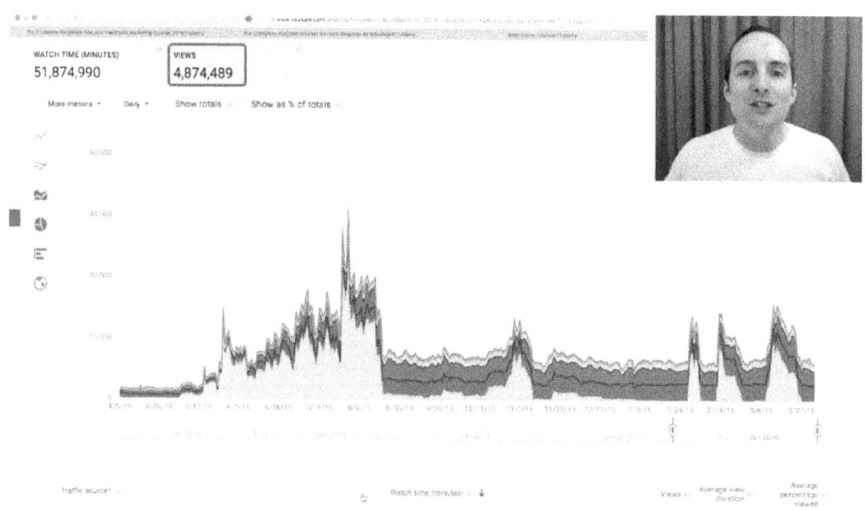

1.5 of the 4.8 million of views I have gotten on my channel came from paid advertising in the last year.

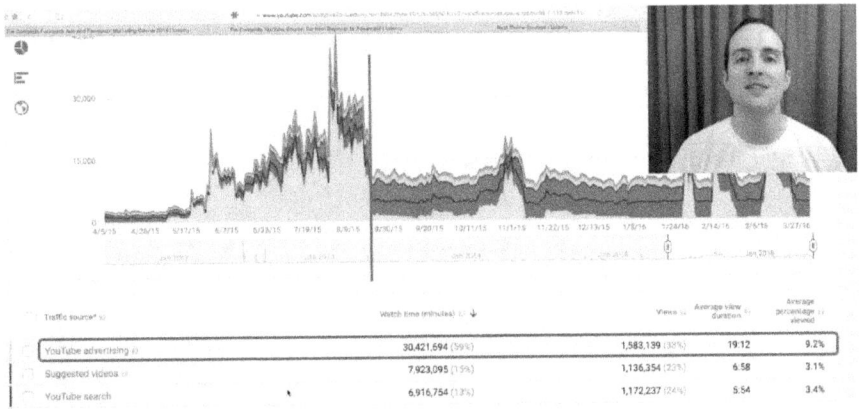

Now, if you look at that, you can see a relation in my organic traffic. Just before the red vertical line on the image above, I spent a ton of money to rank a video up towards the top on a competitive search term, and then what you notice below, after I spent this money on *YouTube* ads and got the video to the top, it stayed on top on its own without advertising.

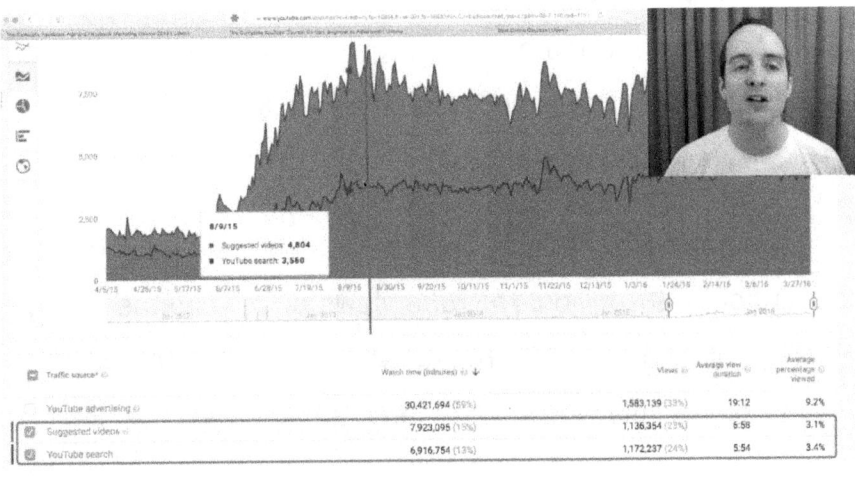

You can see on my traffic stats that I have spent a lot of money on *YouTube* ads. Now you would ask how much money? It is surprisingly small.

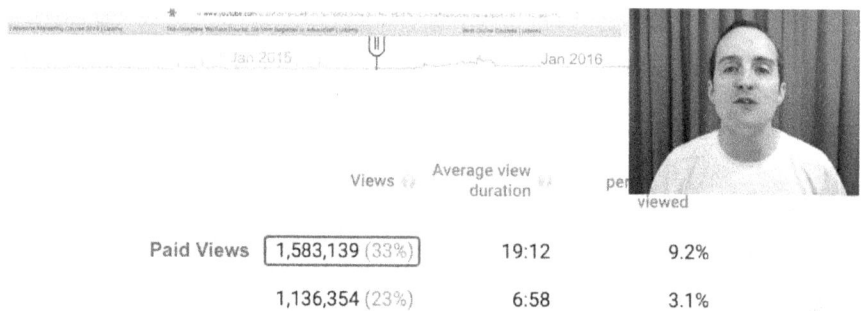

So, for *1.5 million views* how much do you think I have spent to get those views? You might be surprised that I have only paid an average of *$0.01* for each of those views. That means I have spent around *$15,000* on *YouTube* ads.

Now let's put that in context. If I spent that amount on *Facebook* ads, I would have no organic traffic out of it. On *Google Adwords*, just doing search ads, after I spent my *$15,000* I would get nothing.

I spent the *$15,000* on *YouTube* ads and that has been the foundation of *8+ million YouTube* views on my channel today. So, I spent the money on *YouTube* ads, I got *1.5 million paid views* from people who saw the ads, and then another *3+*

million views that have come for free as a result of the ads.

There is nowhere else I know where you can get that. If you want to be number one position on *Google* search, you can't just pay to be up there, unless you continue paying all the time. With *YouTube* ads, the ads themselves rank the video.

So, how does that happen?

Let's look at the average view duration.

I don't know exactly how *YouTube* goes about it. Whatever *YouTube* does in the backend of their advertising greatly artificially inflates the amount of average views on a video.

So, that means when you have got more minutes watched on your video *YouTube* thinks it is a better video and ranks it higher. Let's look at organic traffic, the average percent watched is about *3%* on millions of views. Meanwhile, almost *10%* watched from *YouTube* ads. This is way higher than the organic traffic and this then gives the video a huge artificial boost in ranking.

Now, if your video stinks, it is not going to stay ranked high. You can guarantee the greatest possible position for your video. You can force your video with the *YouTube* ads up to the very top of the rankings, and if your video is actually good, it will stay there.

You don't have to build back-links to your videos and you don't have to do anything fancy, all you have to do is use *Google AdWords for video (*<u>adwords.google.com/video</u>*)*, which I'll show you in detail in chapter 10.

When you use *Google AdWords for video*, target all countries in the world, set the bid to *$0.01* per view, and go on a dollar per day budget. You will get a hundred views guaranteed as long as you don't target to narrow every day for your video. The beauty of it is that it is scalable. If you can spend *$10,000/month,* you can build a gigantic audience for whatever you are doing on *YouTube*.

I love this strategy, where else can you simply pay this easily to get organic traffic? There is nowhere I have found in Internet marketing that is this easy. You make videos, you pay to advertise, and they go straight up to the top of the rankings. If the video is good it stay there, if the video is bad, you stop advertising it and try another one.

I have done this with a bunch of videos on my channel and that's why today I am crushing it with all this organic traffic every day, which then turns into subscribers.

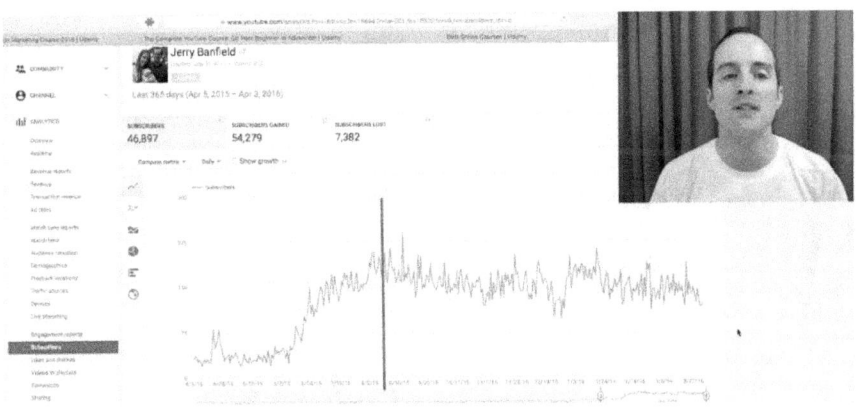

The real gold on *YouTube* is subscribers.

YouTube subscribers are one of the most valuable things I have ever found in Internet marketing.

YouTube subscribers are the #1 most valuable followers I have online.

YouTube subscribers are absolute gold out of all the followers I have online. I have got over two million likes on *Facebook* and over *128,000* followers on *Twitter*, but the *70,000+* subscribers I have on *YouTube* are more valuable than all the likes on *Facebook*, and all the *Twitter* followers combined.

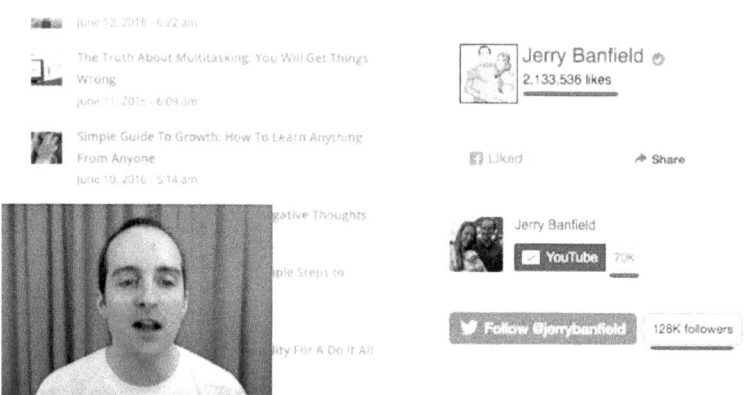

Why?

Because of this:

What's the hardest thing to do on *YouTube*? It is to get people to watch your videos, love your videos, like and comment on the videos, and share the videos.

That's what's really hard. Subscribers are generally avid fans.

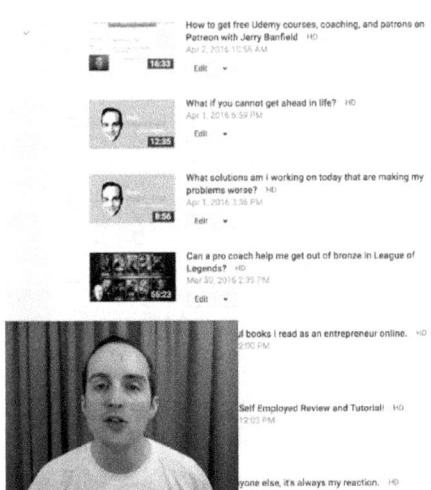 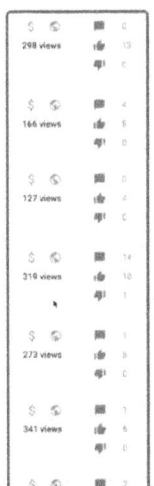

Subscribers tend to like almost everything I do today. So, what does that mean?

What you will notice is that people engage almost on any video I put up on my channel. I get hundreds of organic views by hundreds of people watching every single video. Most videos get anywhere from five to ten likes and get comments.

Every video I upload starts from scratch, and gets views and engagement. What does that tell *YouTube*? That tells *YouTube* that every video I upload is worth watching and obviously there are different amounts. This one for example got *4* likes, *2* dislikes and *110* views, and is probably not the best I have made.

This *1:49* minute video already has *733* views, *16* likes and *6* comments.

This one has *1,200+* views right away, *22* likes and *16* comments.

What I have got now is an audience. I don't have to email them or do anything, but to upload a new video and my existing audience gets it.

YouTube tries to give the right person the right videos. So, if people just watch my *Call of Duty* videos or my *League of Legends* videos, *YouTube* tries to give them the right videos out of what I make. All I have to do now is make videos.

How does this prove so valuable? What happens is, the more subscribers you get, the more views and engagement you get for free automatically. I have got about over *70,000* subscribers now and subscribers have a lot of churn.

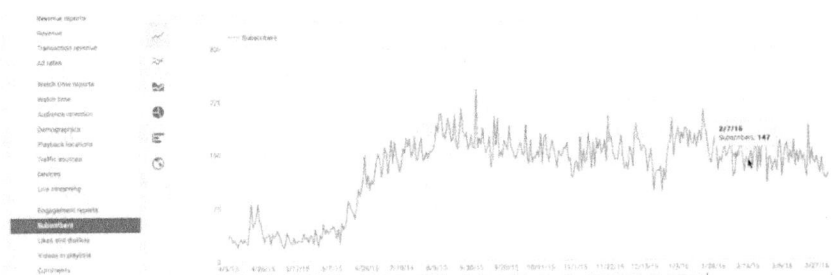

I will make a video that will make people unsubscribe, but overtime my subscribers continue to become more and more avid fans. As this continues to grow even just getting the same number of subscribers every day, I already am to the point where almost every video I make gets *100* views for free and good engagement.

We just talked about how valuable the organic traffic is on *YouTube* and when you hit a certain threshold of subscribers you can pretty much guarantee a number one or a top ranking on almost every one of your new videos.

This happens very glamorously in the video game niche.

If I search for something like *"Black Ops 3 Zombies Easter Egg Shadows of Evil"* which is often the kind of thing I look for, these guys up there have gigantic amounts of subscribers.

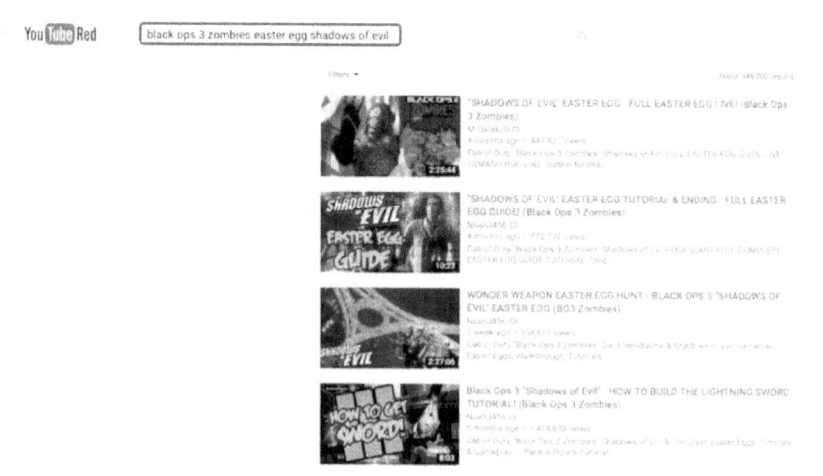

Their videos almost automatically jump to the top.

With a lot of subscribers, you don't even need to run *YouTube* ads anymore. *YouTube* ads are initially necessary to get the original views and build your subscriber base. When you get enough subscribers you can just throw out new videos and lots of them will go straight to the top of the rankings automatically.

This seems to happen really well and it started for me at *50,000* subscribers. When you get over *100,000,* it can in some niches be enough to take first place on every single video. On lots of Internet marketing kinds of things like I do, I have enough subscribers that I can throw my video right up towards the top just by making a new video.

Where else do you know where you can just do what you like to do, make videos showing what you are doing, and that will almost guarantee top position for organic traffic? I don't know any way you can replicate this using anything else. Even with a popular blog, it is not that easy to just take the top of *Google* search rank. If you have something like *Forbes.com* you can't just right away take the top searched rank either.

Subscribers are the most valuable thing I have ever found online in terms of a follower, and I show you what has worked for me to get so many subscribers in this book. Most importantly, I have given a clear objective once you know what the most valuable thing is you can go after it. If you go after *YouTube* subscribers, you will get them.

All you have to do, and all I have to do probably the rest of my life is to post more videos on *YouTube*. At some point, just the *YouTube* income alone from running ads will give me the ability to do whatever I want.

Now, that's even just without using anything outside of *YouTube*. I'm grateful I already have the ability to do this because of tying *YouTube* in with my online courses.

So, no matter what you are doing today, you can literally use *YouTube* to do it for the rest of your life.

Do what you love on *YouTube* and you will keep doing it!

This is my *YouTube* channel, *Jerry Banfield*, and what you'll notice is that I have **72,000+ subscribers**, more than **eight million views**, and **922 videos.**

I am showing this to tell you one key thing, do what you love and you will keep doing it. If you figure out what you'd like to make videos on, you will keep doing it and that's where all the good things happen on *YouTube*. I didn't get to having *922* videos doing something I hated, doing something as a means to an end, or doing something just to make money.

I do videos I love on topics I'm passionate about and care about just like this book or my online courses. I have a lot of passion for teaching *YouTube* successfully *(jerrybanfield.com/product/youtube/)* and I'm doing this because I love it. When you watch my videos, you can feel that coming through, and everyone watching your videos can feel that coming through too.

When you do something you love or do something you enjoy, that is the most value you can give on *YouTube*. Then, if you want to have lots of subscribers and views, you will be willing to go through all of the learning and challenges necessary, all of the time and effort to make all those videos in order to build your audience, and get the help out there you are trying to give to people.

I'm grateful that I learned this lesson on *YouTube* early on. I started out making dating videos because I had a lot of passion about dating, and the dating videos didn't go hardly anywhere on *YouTube*, and yet all of the work doing those videos helped me learn and learn. I'm writing this book now because I have learned a lot about *YouTube*. I have made a lot of mistakes and I have gotten through a lot of things on *YouTube* that I never would have gotten through if I didn't love doing all these videos.

I appreciate you reading this and I hope this is motivational and inspirational for your journey on *YouTube*.

Uploading one video is the biggest step you can take today!

The biggest step anyone can take today on *YouTube* is to upload one more video. I'm grateful that after a few years on *YouTube* I have learned the most I can do each day is to just uploaded one video. One video adds up to a lot over time. It might not seem like much, the biggest difference on *YouTube* is having 0 videos on your channel to having 1, and then *1* to 2, 2 to *3*.

I didn't get more than *900* videos on my channel by uploading them all at once that's for sure. What I try to do is just do one or two a day. I uploaded two videos right before writing this chapter because I do what I tell you to do. I offer you the chance to do it yourself, if you want to get the same results I have.

When you upload a video each day, you learn a little bit each day too. I have learned a lot on *YouTube* by learning a little bit each day, not all at once. The beauty of this is that no matter where you are at it is the same step. If you have got *0* videos and if you can upload a video today, that's a huge step. If you have got *705* videos, uploading another video is a huge step.

Each day one video at a time over a few years adds up to an amazing *YouTube* channel, and one video is manageable. You look at it and say, *"I can't do 900 videos."* If you told me when I started on *YouTube* that I would have more than 900 videos, I would have thought that was crazy because I would have only pictured uploading them at once. When you say that you can do a video or two every day, that's not very much, and yet it adds up to a lot.

If you get anything out of this book, I hope it is motivation to upload one new video and take that next step. That's something concrete that you can do here and you can go to *YouTube.com/upload* to make that happen.

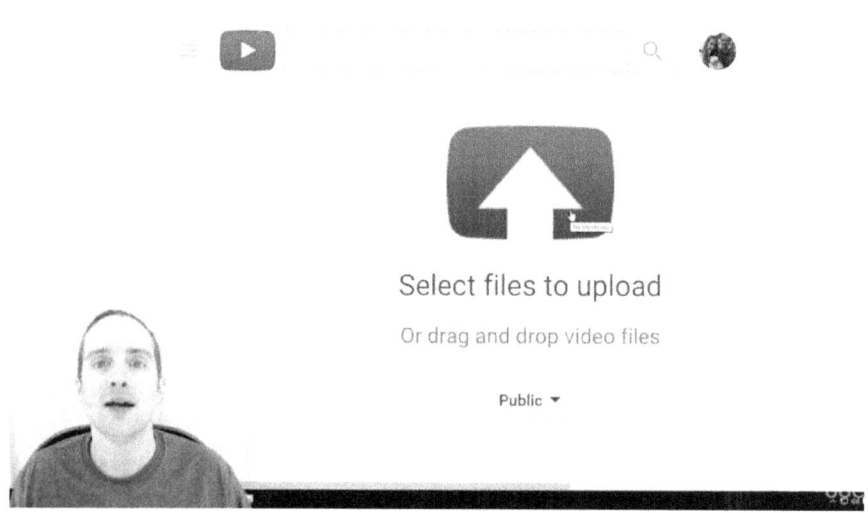

Now, the key thing often is fear. When you go to upload that first video there may be fear, I know even still uploading my videos there is fear. What are people going to think of this? What if people don't like it?

I'm here to tell you that the first video I uploaded was on different ways to say the *"F word."* Yes, I'm serious. That was my first video on *YouTube*, I made it private now because I'm kind of embarrassed about it, and yet I got that video uploaded on *YouTube*. I took that first step, and if I hadn't taken it there wouldn't be the *900+* videos after it.

I learned, improved and made better videos. Almost anything you upload has got to be better than the first video I uploaded, and if you have already got videos up there just continuing on with that next upload will add up so much. The biggest channels I generally see have thousands of videos on them. They give their audience something new every day and you don't have to worry about who watches your videos, you don't have to worry about anything, you upload the video, you do your best, and you keep going forward doing that each day, or as often as you can.

I hope that this gives you motivation and inspiration to use that upload button on *YouTube*.

What to name a *YouTube* channel and make the videos about?

What have I used to name my channel and organize the videos I make? What do you want to make videos about and how should you brand your channel? I have branded mine as you can see below with **Jerry Banfield.**

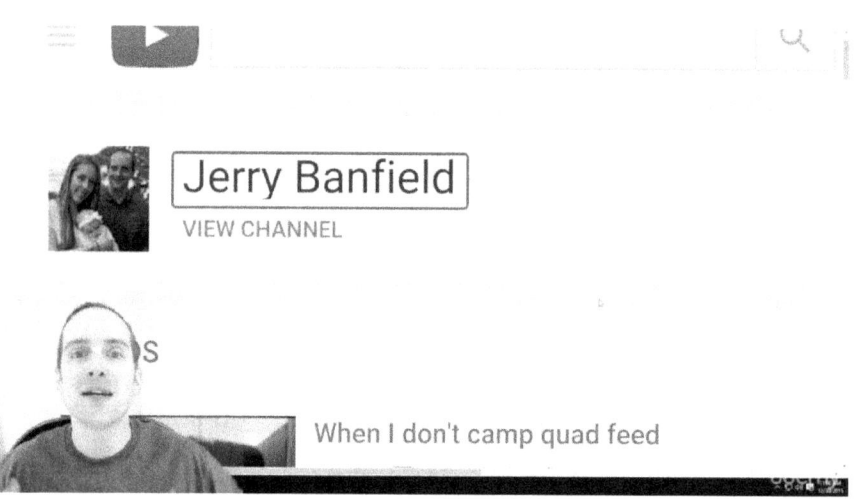

The reason I have done this is because I can make videos about anything and that's what I'm doing. If I show you some of my videos, you can see I have videos on all different subjects.

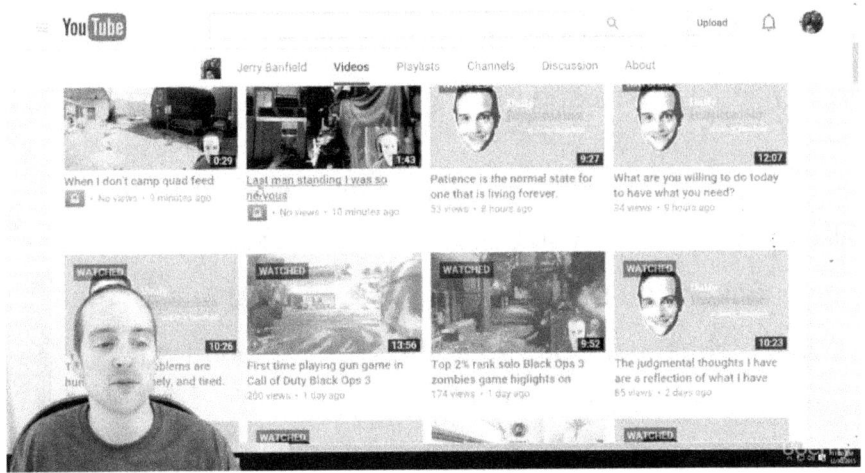

I have *"Call of Duty Black Ops"* videos, daily inspirational videos, and tutorial videos. This allows me then to put anything I want on my *YouTube* channel all in the same place. I made the mistake of trying to make a couple of company *YouTube* channels. The problem is that it is so hard to get an audience on *YouTube*, especially that initial audience. If you are trying to go through and make two or three different channels about too specific of a theme, then it is really hard to get any audience for each of them.

It is also hard to keep doing the same thing over the long term. On my channel, I started off doing videos on how to cuss, it was terrible and I stopped doing them. Later, I did videos about dating, I don't do many dating videos anymore. Then I started doing *Facebook* ads videos, and I moved into more tutorial videos on all kinds of subjects. Today, I do daily inspirational videos and gaming videos.

The beauty of this approach is that you can do everything all in one place and you build an audience around you. You can count on you or your name to stay the same over the course of what you do in your life. This is a long-term approach on *YouTube*.

If you are looking for a *10* or *20* years plan essentially on *YouTube*, setting things up the way I have got them set up with my name allows me to know that no matter what I'm doing, I can keep putting it on my *YouTube* channel.

People often will subscribe for any specific person and the branding matches what people subscribed for. It is harder to get people to subscribe to a company or generic entity. People are used to subscribing to a certain musical artist or a certain person's videos on *YouTube*.

When you brand your *YouTube* channel with your name from the very beginning, then you can have the easiest time growing your channel and you don't have to worry about changing topics. People have tolerated me making videos on all kinds of different subjects, and sure I have lost some subscribers over it, and yet I have built a really deep relationship with the subscribers who watch dating videos, gaming videos, tutorial videos, and inspirational videos.

When you can show people all sides of yourself on your *YouTube* channel, you then have the best chance to build a deep and lasting relationship with your viewers on *YouTube*. It ultimately is how you build a great audience on *YouTube* with a small group of people who are really enthusiastic about your channel, talk to their friends about you and share your videos.

I hope in sharing this with you that I have helped you to avoid making the mistake that I made setting up a bunch of different *YouTube* channels to start, and shown you straight to what I have learned that works best.

How can you get people to watch your *YouTube* videos?

Once you have got at least one video on your channel, or maybe even before that, the big question often is how am I going to get people to watch my videos? This was one of my biggest struggles for the first two years on *YouTube* and I have got an incredibly simple and effective solution that has worked wonders for my channel at *www.youtube.com/c/jerrybanfield/*.

Here it is, *YouTube* advertising.

It is crazy simple and really effective. *1.5 million views* in *2015* on my *YouTube* channel have come from *Google AdWords for video,* which is *Google's* advertising product for

YouTube, since *Google* owns *YouTube*.

All of these minutes watched and all of these views led to the majority of the other organic views. The ad views themselves aren't that helpful often, what the ad views do is get minutes watched on your video. When people spend minutes watching your video, *Google* figures out that it is a good video and that it should rank higher in search results and on suggested videos.

The suggested video views is where *YouTube* recommends a video for you to watch on another video, and then *YouTube* search is where people are searching in *YouTube* for a video. These are the two best places to get organic traffic on *YouTube*.

YouTube advertising	30,275,389 (66%)	1,514,927 (39%)	19:59	9.6%
Suggested videos	5,766,237 (13%)	837,620 (21%)	6:53	3.1%
YouTube search	5,186,136 (11%)	874,293 (22%)	5:55	3.7%

These are the two places that have given my channel the majority of the value it has, and these views are easy to get if you advertise your video, and the more effective job you do of making good videos, the more effective the ads will be.

I have a video now with *1.2 million* views and it is because I advertised it a lot, and yet now it has gone viral all on its own. *Google AdWords for video (www.google.com/intl/en/landing/awv/)* is incredibly effective and I will teach you everything in this book.

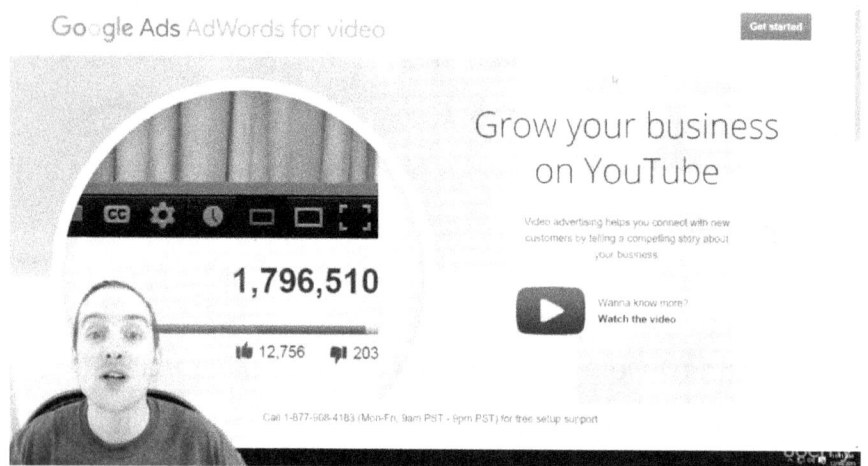

I will show you how to get views for just *$0.01* each using global traffic, and if you want your ads in somewhere like in the *US*, it is as low as *5* or *6* cents a view, *Canada* is around *3* or *4* cents, the *UK* & *Australia* have comparable cost. *Google AdWords for video* is incredibly effective at everything you want to accomplish on *YouTube*, and for me it is peace of mind.

I know when I upload a video that I can get thousands of people to watch it for just *$10* or *$20* in the *Google* ads, and then I know it will rank high enough to get organic traffic which is what I really want. You don't have to worry, or struggle, or be concerned about traffic as long as you make videos that are compliant with the *Google's* terms and conditions that *Google* shares with you, then you can get traffic to your videos.

I hope this gives you relief and confidence that you can get people to watch your videos no matter what, using *Google AdWords for video*.

The basics of making a viral video on *YouTube*!

Here are the basics of making a viral video on *YouTube* based on my experience making several viral videos. These are the most viewed videos I have here in my channel. You can see this *Complete Free Hacking* course has over *1.5* million views, tens of thousands of likes, hundreds of dislikes, and thousands of comments.

I have several other viral videos like this one where I used the same strategy on several different categories:

I have a *Google AdWords* tutorial, a *Linux* tutorial, a variation of the same hacking video, a different *Linux* tutorial, a dating video, three *Facebook* ads tutorials, another *Google AdWords*, *Ubuntu Linux*, *Wireshark*, then two gaming videos.

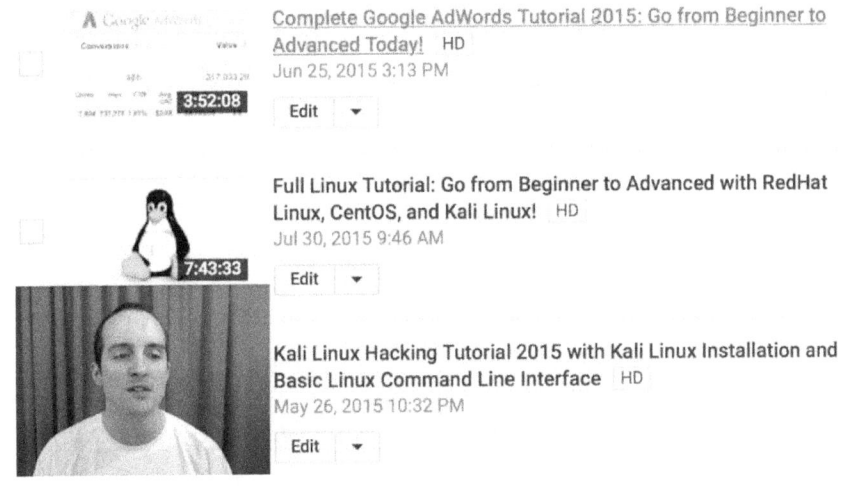

Now the cool thing is that I learned these strategies on these gaming videos and on the *Facebook* ads videos, and then I actually applied them better to the hacking video.

Let's look at my top video on *YouTube*.

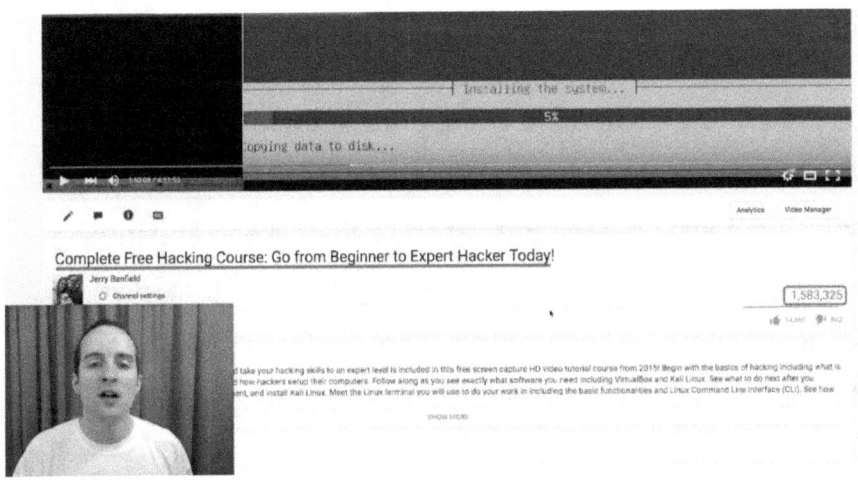

The number one most important thing is having a video with something that's high quality in it and matched with what you are doing.

What do I mean by high quality?

This is a hands-on nearly five hour *getting started hacking* video *(youtu.be/7nF2BAfWUEg)*, and then this makes sales on my best selling course *(jerrybanfield.com/product/hacking/)* now since this video came out. If I hadn't put this video up, it wouldn't have made a fraction of what it did. I didn't even make this video except for the beginning.

You might need to collaborate with someone like I did to get a viral video. I made most of the other videos myself, except for a dating one and this very best one where I simply worked with someone else to get it made.

You often will need to collaborate with others to get your best viral videos made. However, you can learn and try these things out just yourself to start more than likely. The most powerful things on *YouTube* are longer videos that have a full in depth tutorial. That's what my best video is, a long hacking tutorial including actual installation and getting started with hacking.

Now, think about what you watch as a user. Those gaming videos I got viral are the same kind of gaming videos I watch. I make the same kind of videos I watch. If you are struggling to figure out what you should make, just make videos like you already watch. The *hacking* video is also like what I watch. I like long in-depth tutorials. The longer the video is, the more effective the *YouTube* advertising strategy is, and this video was easy to rank high on an extremely competitive term.

If you go search *"hacking"* in one single word, very competitive term, there are five million results according to *YouTube*. The video is a little bit out of its prime as I haven't run ads on it, but it is still on the first page.

When you search for *"hacking for beginners,"* you'll see that this video actually comes up number one on this search term.

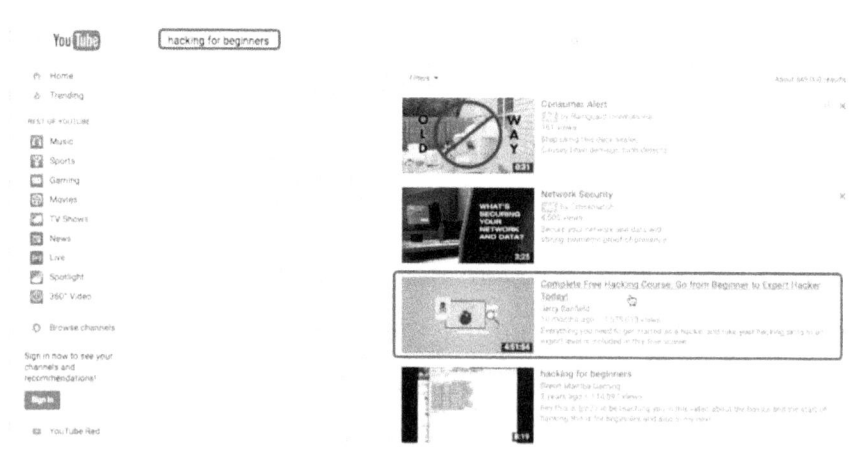

Understanding your audience is critical, which is why it's easy to make a viral video when you know your audience, and that means making a video often on something you already know about. If you know about video games and that's what you want to do, make a video like the one you watch so it is easier.

I had a decent understanding of what people wanted out of hacking on *YouTube* just by looking around. You make the video and that's a whole thing in and of itself, you could go on for hours and hours about video production. Screen capture videos often are the easiest to make and they work the best.

Then here's where you do the real *SEO* work. The title is very both clickable and search friendly, as I'm thinking of what people are looking for, and it must be like a *"complete free hacking course beginning to expert hacker."*

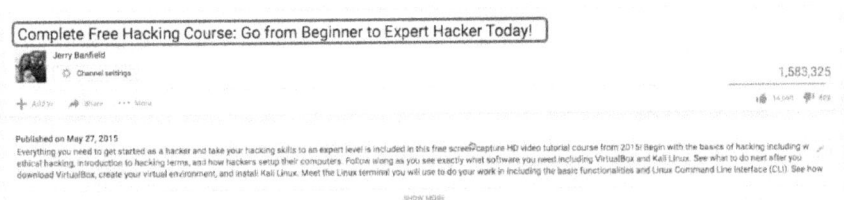

Now what's the point of watching the video, you can't become an expert hacker simply by watching the video, but it is both *search engine optimized* and *a call to action*. Obviously the title is critical and often the easiest way to figure out the title is to do videos on whatever you want to, and then see the search data that comes in, and then try more videos based on that.

Then the key thing for search, especially on *YouTube,* is to have a naturally written description that helps people navigate. I have got all these little time points here, this both helps people navigate and it helps *Google* understand what exactly is in this video.

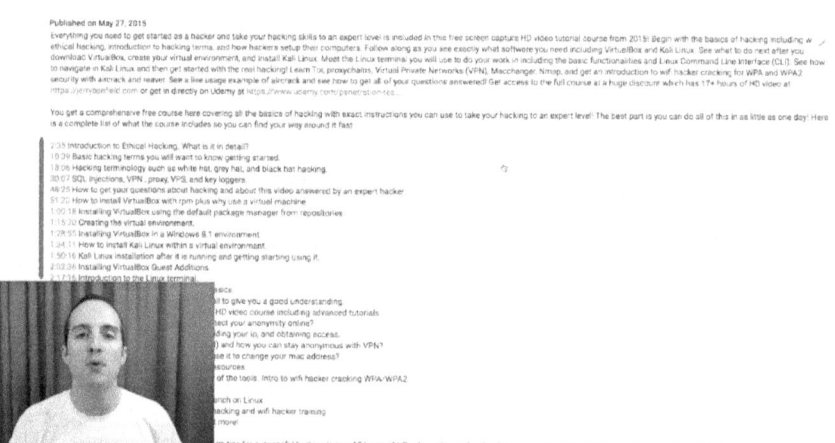

When I was first trying to learn and take it to the next level on *YouTube* I wanted shortcuts. I wanted to just throw keywords out there and rank high. The shortcut I will give you to doing great on *YouTube* search is to write a real description explaining exactly what is in the video.

When you go write a description that is just keyword spamming or isn't very helpful, then that's not going to get you anywhere. When you just spam keywords and throw all these keywords you want to rank on, that's not going to work.

This is what works: write out a full description.

I often use a transcript of everything that is said in the entire video because you can help *Google* fully get ok with the video.

With terms like *VirtualBox, Windows 8.1, proxy servers, private net, Aircrack or Reaver*, you can get in on the suggested videos, which is similar in traffic levels to *YouTube* search. You can get in on all the suggested videos and on all these search terms by putting it this way.

Also, people can just click on the time stamp link and it skips to that point in the video. Since it is a really long video, this encourages higher watch times. If someone comes onto the video and it is five hours, they often will just complain directly in the comments that it is too long.

If they click on the links in the description they can go to the section they really want to know about like *"Linux command line basics."* Then, they can skip straight to it and watch maybe three percent of the whole video, which is just the *Linux command line basics*. Whereas if you don't have this navigation in place, the user often will just click around a little bit and abandon the video.

```
2:35 Introduction to Ethical Hacking. What is it in detail?
10:35 Basic hacking terms you will want to know getting started.
18:05 Hacking terminology such as white hat, grey hat, and black hat hacking.
30:07 SQL injections, VPN , proxy, VPS, and key loggers.
45:25 How to get your questions about hacking and about this video answered by an expert hacker.
51:20 How to install VirtualBox with rpm plus why use a virtual machine.
1:00:18 Installing VirtualBox using the default package manager from repositories.
1:15:20 Creating the virtual environment.
1:28:55 Installing VirtualBox in a Windows 8.1 environment.
1:34:11 How to install Kali Linux within a virtual environment.
1:50:16 Kali Linux installation after it is running and getting starting using it.
2:02:36 Installing VirtualBox Guest Additions.
2:17:16 Introduction to the Linux terminal.
2:26:52 Linux Command-Line Interface (CLI) basics.
2:40:55 The Linux CLI explained in greater detail to give you a good understanding.
2:56:22 How to get full access to the 17+ hour HD video course including advanced tutorials.
2:58:41 What is Tor? How can you use it to protect your anonymity online?
3:09:39 ProxyChains for using proxy servers, hiding your ip, and obtaining access.
3:21:41 What is a Virtual Private Network (VPN) and how you can stay anonymous with VPN?
```

This description does really good for both search engine ranking and for helping users watch the most of the video.

Then you don't have to guess what keywords to use, all you do is look at the description you already wrote and grab keywords from there. You can see the keywords I just took out of the description and some of the main points.

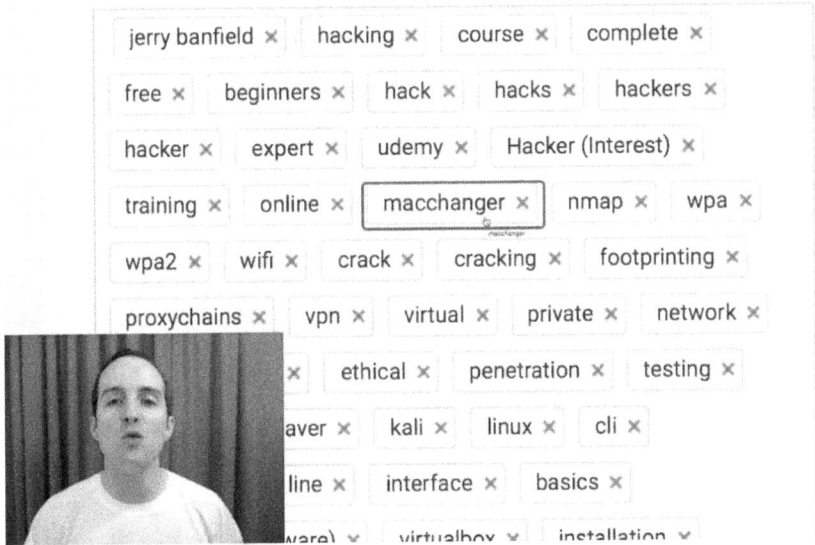

So, for example, I have *"macchanger,"* which is a specific term someone might search for a tutorial on, and then I have *"macchanger"* right here in the description.

This is a simple keyword strategy. When you have written out a good description, you just grab the keywords anywhere out of it and throw them in the keyword section. It is so much easier than trying to fool around with anything else.

The thumbnail is very important too and there are lots of different thumbnail strategies that can work. I have got lots of different thumbnails on my channel, and these are the most viewed.

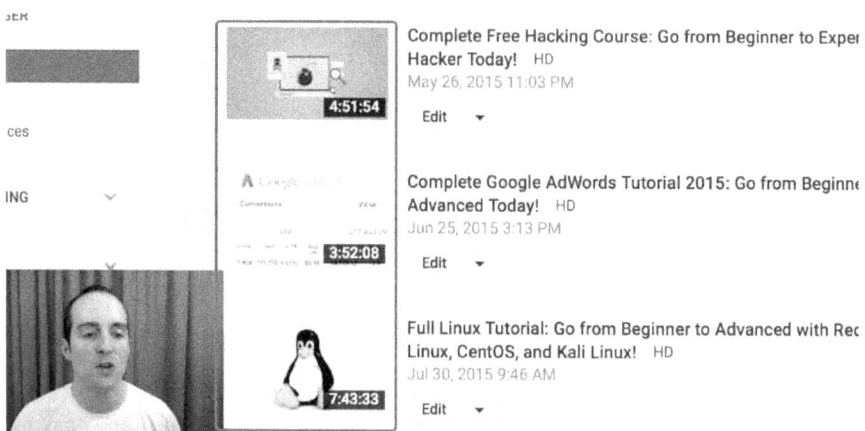

I took the image from the course as it was on *Udemy*, for the first thumbnail. Then, on the second one, I have got showing a bunch of conversion on *AdWords*. Then I have the *Linux* penguin.

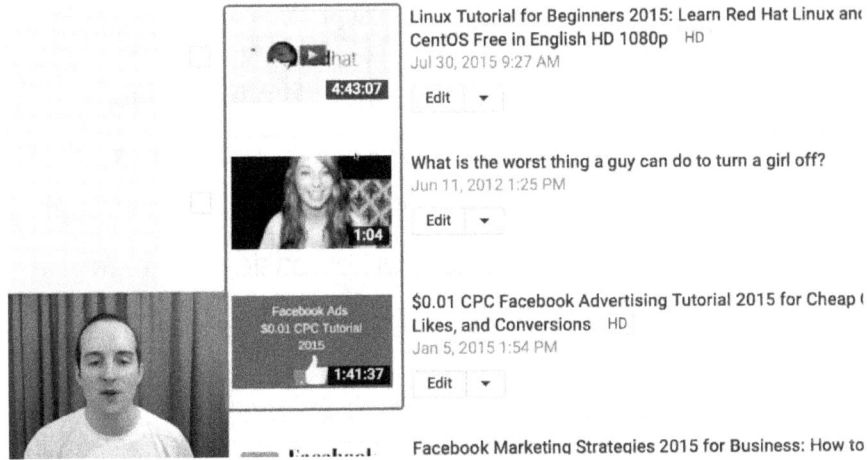

Then I have got *Red Hat*, an automatic thumbnail, and some words on the last one. There isn't an exact strategy that always works on every single video.

Call to action thumbnails can work good like this one, *"Watch the number one new Google AdWords tutorial."*

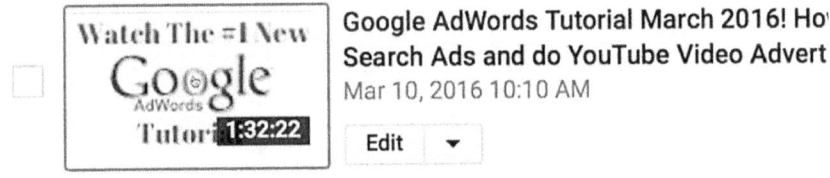

They can work good or can backfire too if you don't get the font exactly right and it doesn't show up good, or if you put the wrong words on it and people don't want to watch it.

Sometimes just doing something with only an image like my course image or the *Linux* penguin, something people recognize, can work better. If you can just quickly throw a text thing up here or if you can just pull image generated straight from something else you have, it will be easier, and then you can test things out over time.

CHAPTER 3

My video production process from start to finish

In order to film videos for *YouTube* you need to have a set of tools. There are so many options available that I want you to save some time and <u>see what equipment I use to film all of my videos on YouTube</u>.

As you are starting your studio set-up, you may not have a big budget to buy expensive lighting equipment. You still can film talking head videos at a very low cost and it is what you will learn in this <u>lighting on a budget</u> section.

If you are doing screen capture tutorials, it might be challenging to publish high definition videos, but <u>filming videos in 1080p HD is easy with Camtasia Studio</u>.

It is always good to have more than one way to record your videos and I want to show you <u>my new filming system using iPhone with iRig HD mic + screen capture software</u>.

You might have a surge of creativity and want to upload ten videos at once, but I will show you <u>why I upload 1 or 2 videos at a time and try to do it each day</u>.

Finally, you may occasionally come across a copyright notice, especially when filming gaming videos. You will learn in this section *how to handle copyright claims and avoid getting flagged for copyright*.

Read on...

See what equipment I use to film all of my videos on *YouTube*

In this section I'm going to show you my complete professional *Webcam* home filming studio setup:

Logitech HD Pro Webcam C920, 1080p Widescreen Video Calling and Recording

Blue Microphones Yeti USB Microphone - Silver

Foam Windscreen for Blue Yeti, MXL, Audio Technica, and Other Large Microphones - Black

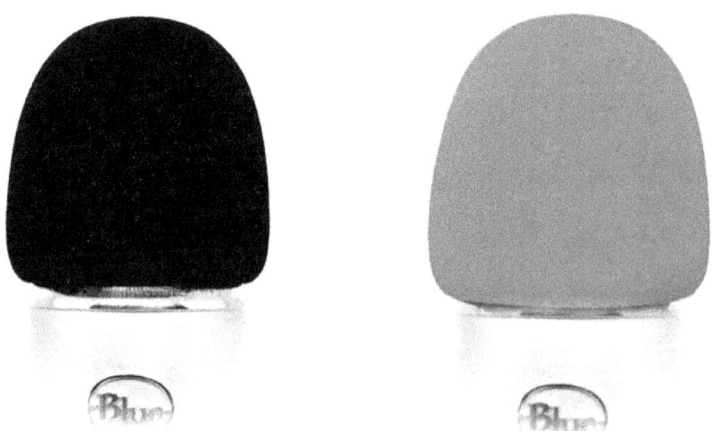

CowboyStudio Photography/Video Portrait Umbrella Continuous Triple Lighting Kit with Three Day Light CFL Bulbs, Three Stands, Two Umbrellas, and One Carrying Case For Product, Portrait, and Video Shoots

Square Perfect Background Stand with 6 x 9 White & Green Screen Muslin Backdrops

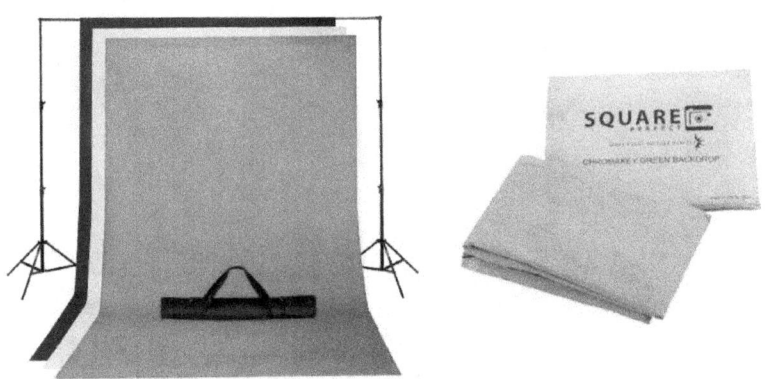

IK Multimedia iRig Mic HD high-definition handheld microphone for iPhone iPad and Mac

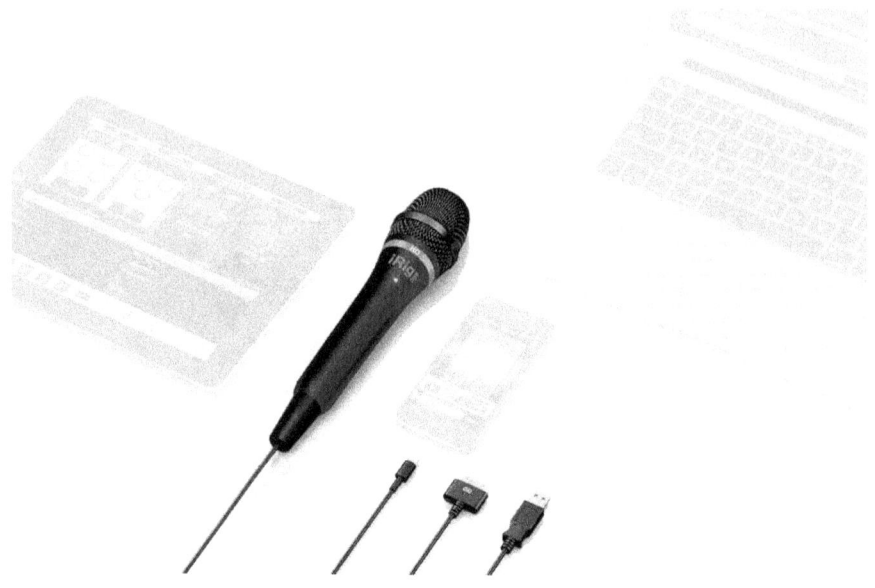

Hamilton Nu-Era Tabletop Mic Stand and On Stage Foam Ball-Type Mic Windscreen, Black.

Elgato - Game Capture HD60

Lighting on a budget

If you do not have the budget to invest in professional lighting, what you can do is to use the following:

Spiral Daylight bulb 23 Watt x 2

Clamp Lamp x 2

White polyfoam boards x 2

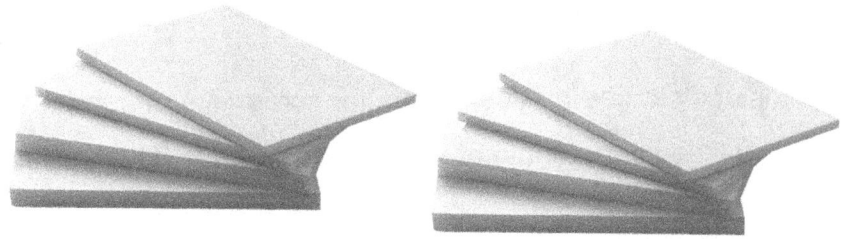

If your desk is against a wall and you are using the webcam on your computer, you can secure the clamp lamps on your table or nearby cabinets and direct the lights on the wall *(if it is white)* or on *polyfoam* boards to reflect back on your face.

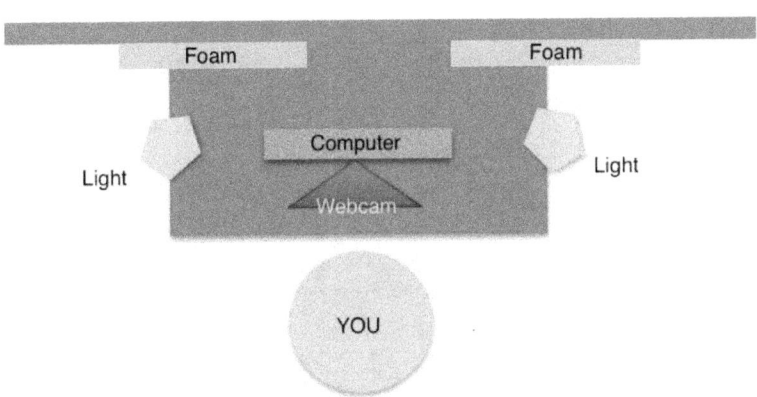

Turn on the ceiling lights, they should also be daylight, to fill in the background/backdrop you have.

It is easy to see on your computer screen if you need to adjust a little bit the angle of your lamps so as to have perfect lighting.

It is often not necessary to have very powerful lights if the whole room is not very bright. Do not allow light to come from outside and brighten the room as it will be very difficult to match it with the 2 bulbs you have.

Try to keep the lighting of the whole room down by closing curtains and the two 23 watt bulbs should do the trick.

Filming videos in *1080p HD* is easy with *Camtasia Studio*

How do I use *Camtasia 1080p screen capture recording* from start to finish?

This has been challenging for me in producing my videos. I hope by sharing my system for recording and capturing my screen in *1080p* that it can help you out.

I have struggled a lot to get my videos down into a good format and find a system so I can quickly record high quality content fast and then share it with my audience.

Let me show you exactly how I make all of this with *Camtasia (www.techsmith.com/camtasia.html)*.

On my desktop I have a *Camtasia* icon that I click to open *Camtasia Studio* up. Then, I hit **"record the screen"** on the top left menu.

Now this little screen recording pops up on my monitor and I am ready to record all that I do on the screen.

The Complete YouTube Book

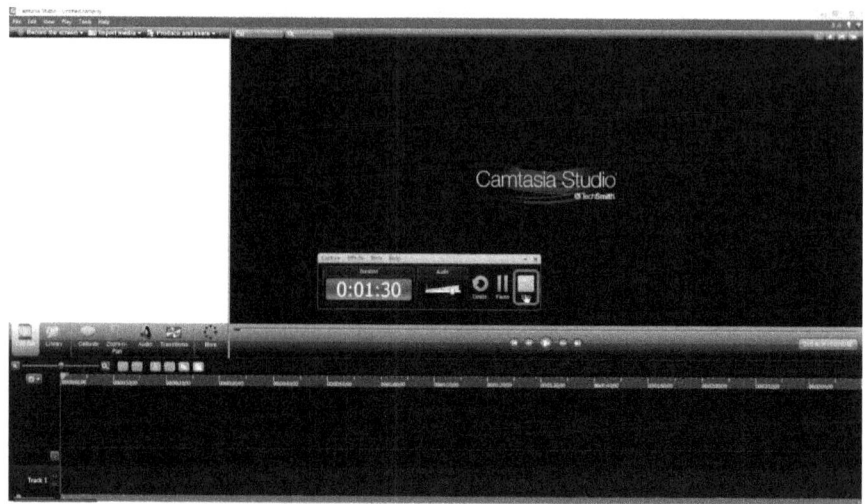

Once I have finished recording, I hit *"stop."* Then, this window comes up to save and edit what I have just filmed.

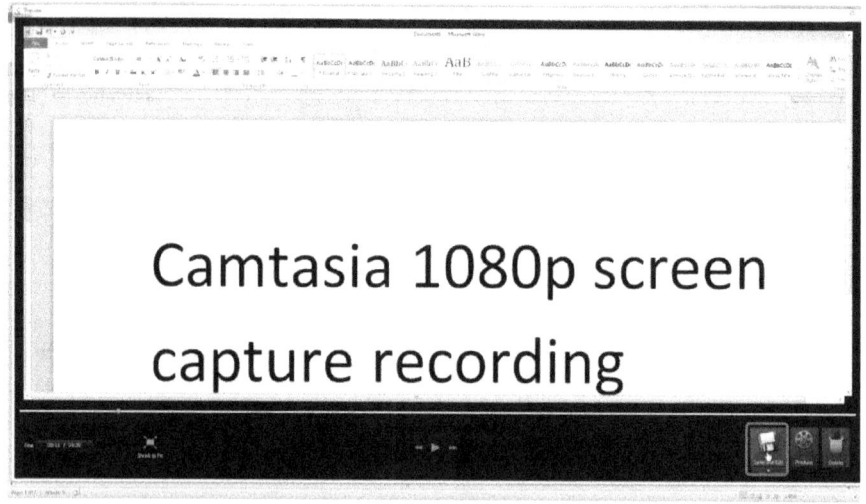

I hit *Save* and *Edit*. *Camtasia* puts the capture in a location and I hit *Save*.

This window comes up and you can see that the default editing dimensions are *1920 x 1080*, which is *1080p*.

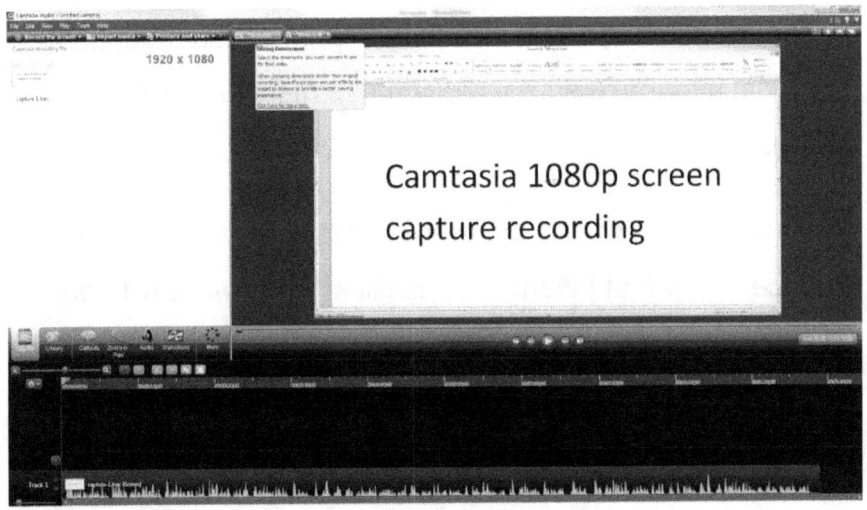

The next part of this is to edit the audio because I'm likely to have noise in the background. What I want to do is enable *"noise removal"* and then I go to manual noise training on selection.

I select this beginning part to manually train on that. Then I play it back to make sure it didn't make me all *Artificial Intelligence* sounding.

Once I have got that done, then what I do is go in and produce this. What I want to do is click *"produce and share."*

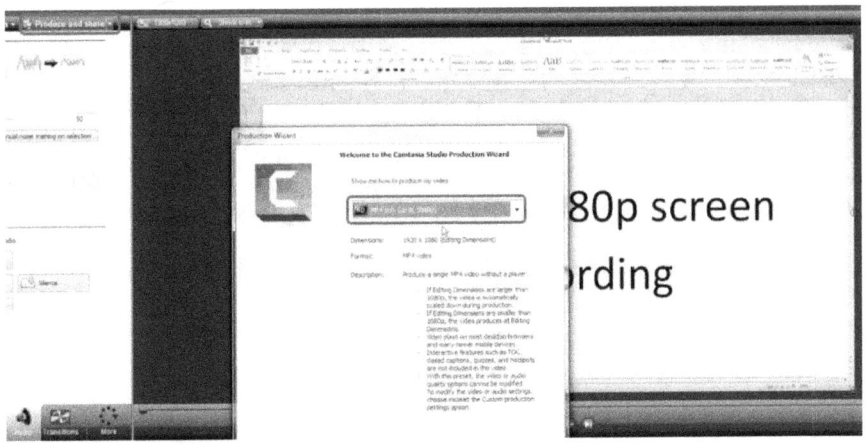

I want the *mp4* only in the editing dimensions, which is *1080p*. I do that then I hit *next,* and then I have to put this into a folder.

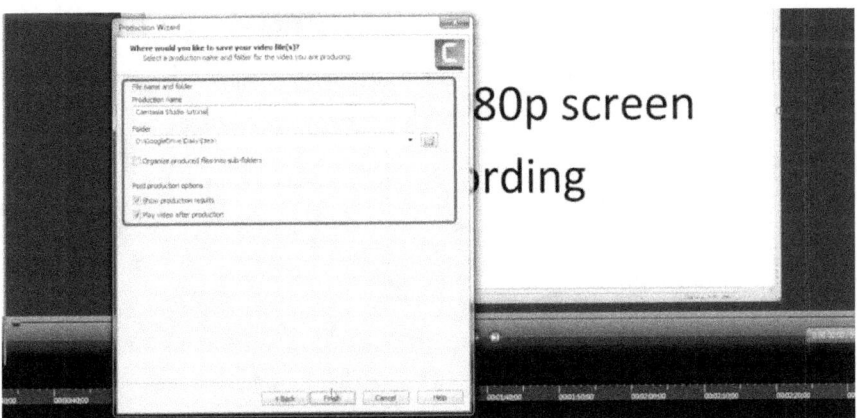

I uncheck *"produce files in the subfolders"* because I don't want a whole bunch of different files coming in and folders created. I name it *"Camtasia Studio tutorial"* and I hit *finish*.

Now, it will render the video and then when the video is done, it is going to play it. This is so much easier than the nightmare I was doing before. I used to use *Snag it* to capture the screen and use *Audacity* to edit the audio, and then put that together in *Windows Movie Maker*. That took a long time and *Camtasia Studio* made it now so much easier.

My new filming system using *iPhone* with *iRig HD* mic + screen capture software

For filming videos, it is important to have a system that works really well to make high quality audio especially and to do screen capture. What I do is what I'm showing you exactly in this section.

One way I do it is to straight up use *Camtasia* screen capture with my mic that I have connected to my computer, but that doesn't always work good. Sometimes the audio doesn't come out good, so I have got another way I do it where the audio consistently comes out excellent.

The main thing is to have multiple methods to record, so that no matter what's going on, or where you are at, or what you are doing, you can record successfully.

Now step one, I have a screen capture program called *Camtasia* and this is what it looks like.

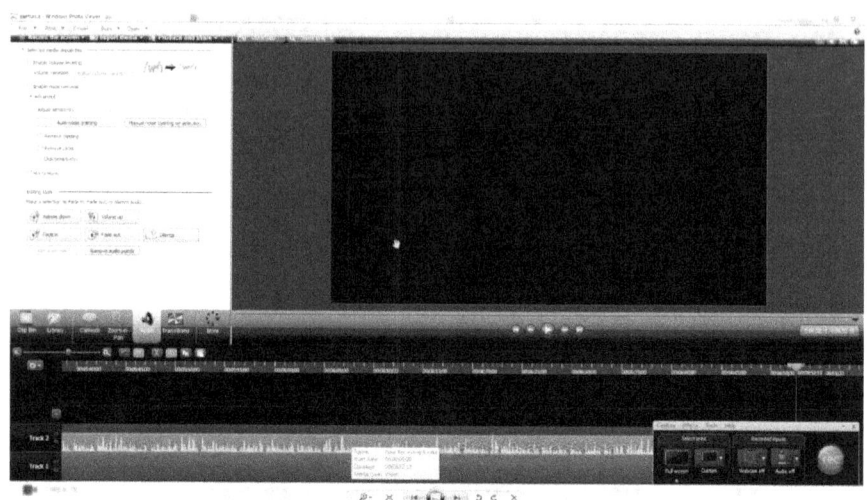

The important thing is that you can substitute nearly any screen capture program into this system. You can use it with almost any free editing software to put your audio and video together. That's what is really cool about this strategy.

I start Camtasia and you will notice the webcam is off and the audio is off too because I'm actually only recording the screen. I'm not recording the actual audio in *Camtasia*.

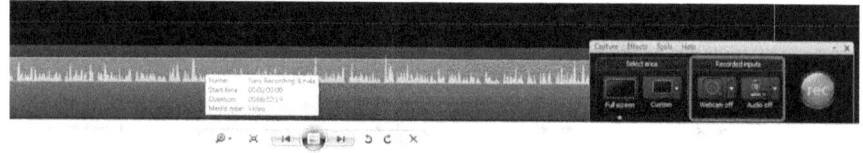

So then you wonder, how are you recording the audio?

What I'm actually doing is using my *iRig mic HD* plugged into my *iPhone* because the audio quality comes out really good that way, compared to using my computer microphone, and especially compared to plugging the *iRig* into the computer.

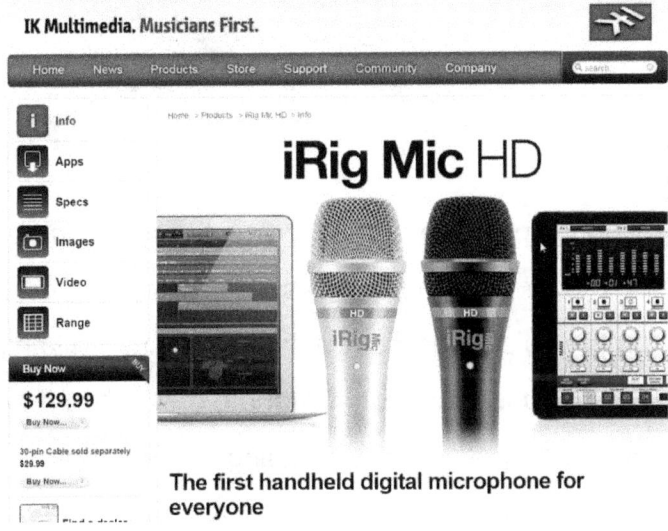

The first handheld digital microphone for everyone

For some reason the *iRig* does not work as well with the computer. It gets distorted.

So instead of trying to fight it, I just work around it and the easiest thing to do when you are filming is just do what does work. I have got feedback from people and found out that the microphone I was using before echoed a lot. So I am using this new system: I use the *iRig mic HD* with a foam windscreen to put on it, which helps a lot.

What I do is I plug the *iRig HD mic* into my *iPhone* and as soon as I hit *Start* on *Camtasia* to start recording my screen, I hit *Start* on the voice recorder on the *iPhone* at the same time. So what I'm doing is recording the audio only in the *iPhone* with the *iRig Mic HD* and then I'm using screen capture to record the actual picture.

The cool thing is that you can use this with almost any screen capture program and just by having an *iPhone* with the *iRig HD* microphone.

Then I use Evernote premium to share the file over on the voice recorder.

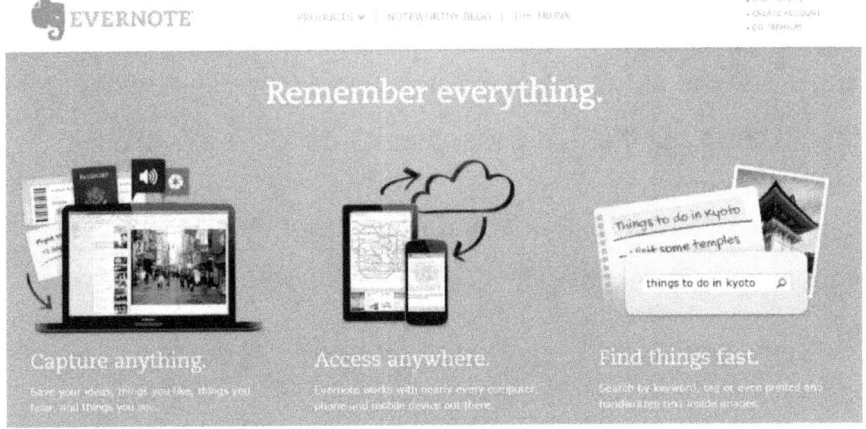

When the voice is recorded, I click *Done* and use the share option to share it straight to *Evernote*. When it is in *Evernote,* all I have to do is sync *Evernote* on my *iPhone* with my desktop. I pull the file off of *Evernote* and then I bring the audio up into *Camtasia*.

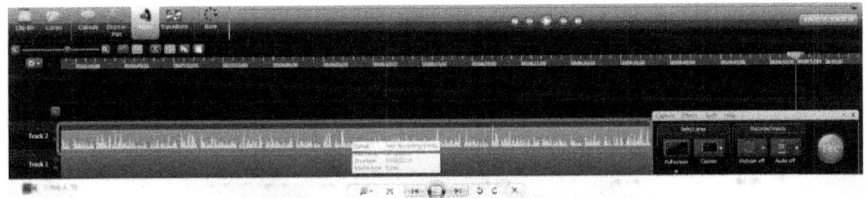

I just have then to produce the video with its screen capture and the added audio on *Camtasia*.

This is my preferred method for doing straight screen capture because I know the audio is going to be good when I record it through my *iRig HD* mic and through my *iPhone*. I know that the computer is not going to distort the audio and then when I put the audio together it sounds really good.

I also still record image and sound together as I showed you in the last section with *Camtasia Studio*, and that works too.

I hope this section has been helpful for you, in giving you some ideas on how you can film beautiful *1080p HD* videos with excellent quality audio using almost any software setup.

Why I upload 1 or 2 videos at a time and try to do it each day

Are you wanting to know how to get as many videos uploaded on your *YouTube* channel as possible? Here is a little trick I used that helps me get many more videos uploaded.

It is to not leave videos unpublished on my channel.

All of my videos are published.

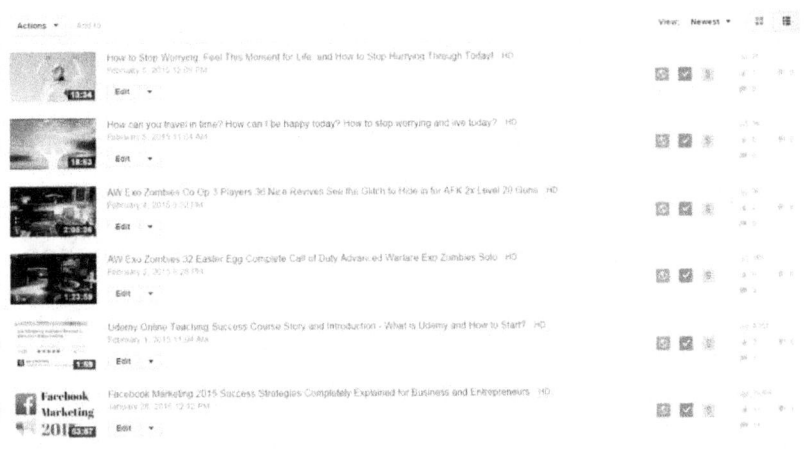

Anytime I have put a bunch of videos up at once, I tend to have a bunch of unpublished videos. Then, it is a big roadblock to me putting more videos up. You don't want to upload a bunch of videos at once because it starts to feel unmanageable. Then my *YouTube* channel gets all backed up, I start feeling guilty that I haven't finished my videos and it discourages me from uploading more videos.

If you want to have a successful *YouTube* channel, upload one or two videos every single day or every other day and then publish them immediately.

If they are not just perfect for *SEO*, or the transcription is not just perfect, that's ok. Just get the videos actually uploaded and published on *YouTube*.

I wanted a better *Easter Egg* video and a better video with commentary on my two *Zombies* videos, and they are not perfect, but I at least got them uploaded. Just getting them uploaded makes a big difference. It is better to put any video at all in your channel, than to put no video on your channel.

You can always delete videos that are crappy, delete or edit certain things from the titles, descriptions or tags. You can change thumbnails if you don't like it. The bottom line is that it is much better to have something than nothing. It is much better to do a little bit every day than to have a big period of time when you don't do anything.

One of the big reasons for this is the views you get from subscribers. If I go to *traffic sources*, and you see the subscriber views, you will notice that my subscriber views tend to be pretty consistent.

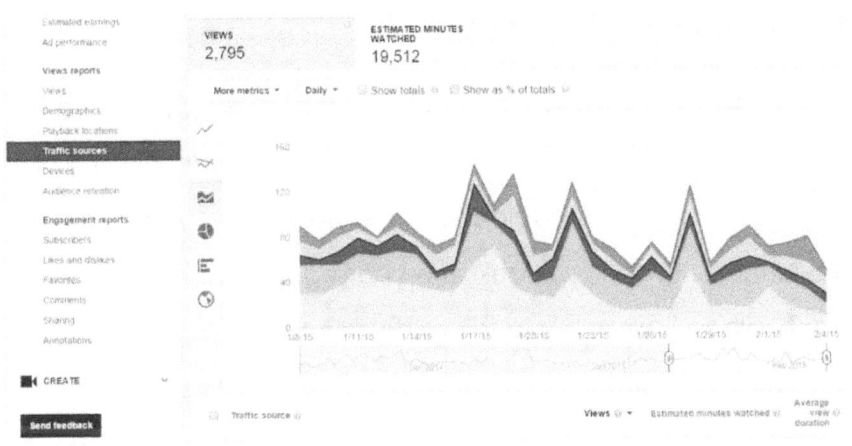

These are some of your most valuable views because these are from subscribers that already like your videos and give you free traffic. So you will note that I'm getting from *80* to *100* views a day from my subscribers. The thing is that if you have periods when you don't get new videos uploaded, your views from subscribers will drop.

You do not want your views from subscribers to drop and if I show you the last *365* days you will note that I'm pretty consistently having views from subscribers every single day.

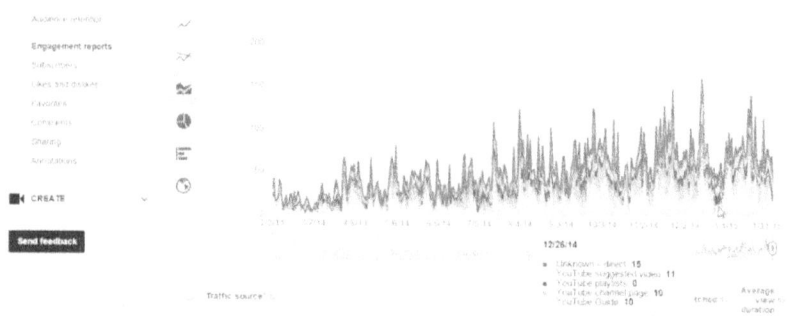

You will note at some points that when I didn't upload a lot of videos, my subscriber views took a big dive. You'll note also that the more videos I uploaded, the more views I have from subscribers. When you look at a year ago, at the left of the graph, when I wasn't uploading that many videos and I didn't have as many subscribers, I have a lot less views.

The idea is to keep uploading more videos all the time consistently, so that your subscribers always have more. You don't want to do big bulk uploads on your channel. I have done this several times, I put *10* to *20* videos on at once and when you do that your subscribers get overwhelmed and you get overwhelmed.

Try to just do what I am doing, two videos yesterday, a video a day before that, one day without one and a video that is a little imperfect and not the way I wanted it, but I still got *184* free views on it and likes. So it is a lot better than nothing.

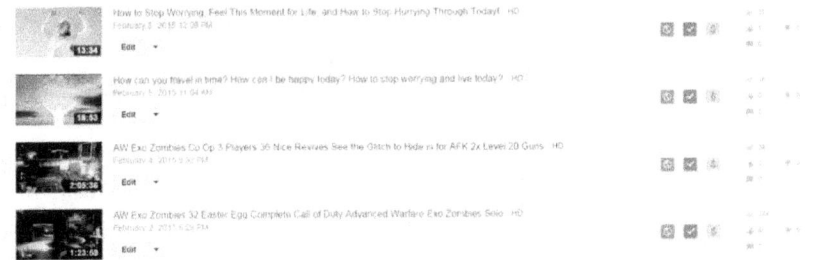

I consistently upload videos every few days and my subscribers consistently have new videos to watch. Even uploading three videos at a time gets to be a bit of a chore. So consistently uploading new videos all the time, just one or two a day is ideal.

This is my uploading strategy for *YouTube* that works for me to get the most new videos uploaded on a daily basis and to not get a backlog of videos I need to publish.

How to handle copyright claims and avoid getting flagged for copyright

How do you deal with copyright notices on your *YouTube* videos? This is the one video I have that does have a copyright notice. Copyright notices usually come from music in your videos.

This video was filmed on a *Zombies* map where I played a song that popped up on copyright notice. A video with a copyright notice can't be downloaded and I can't show ads on it. It makes it very inconvenient and not ideal to use at all. People have watched this video and it got some likes, so I just left it up.

Usually if I get a copyright notice as soon as I upload it, what I will do is find where the copyright issue is in the video. You can see below that it tells me exactly, which point of the content has the issue.

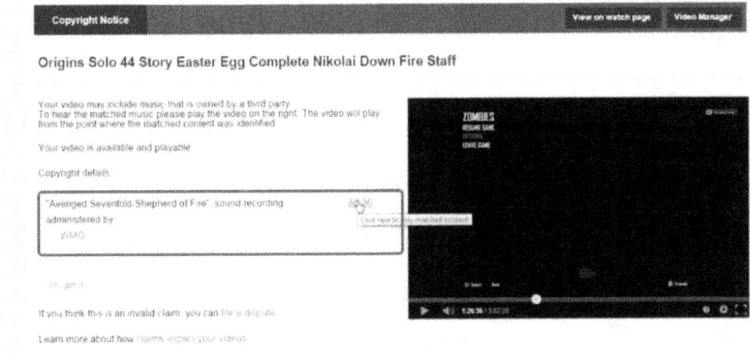

What I will do then is to go back into my video. I will delete it off *YouTube* after I figure out where it is, and then I will edit the video in *Camtasia* or whatever software I am using to edit the video.

I will silence that part of the audio track so that I can re-upload the video and it won't get a copyright notice. I didn't notice this one right when it came up and it was the first time I had a copyright notice. I learned my lesson after this first one and then I made new videos that do not have copyright notices.

Now, when I upload a video and a copyright notice pops up, I find where it is and silence the audio in that portion of the video. With experience you know that will happen before hand and figure out where the issue may be, silence the track and upload the video.

You can do the same thing If you are in a game, you can just turn the game sound off, but in some of the things you do songs will pop up. If you know exactly where the song pops up, then you can figure out where you are likely to get a copyright notice in the video and edit it.

Then you will be able to use *Adsense* or anything else to monetize your videos or use the editor, anything you want then is possible.

You don't want a lot of copyright notices on your account because there is a little good standing green dot as you can see below.

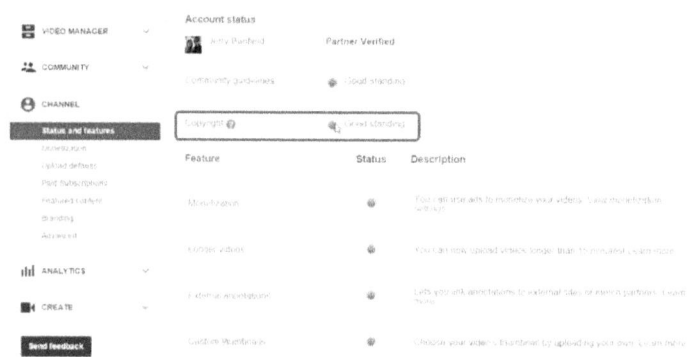

You want to be in good standing on the copyright and community guidelines. One or a few copyright notices will not give you a problem all by itself, especially if you get your account verified, but you don't want to have a lot of copyright violations on your account because then some of these green features you see like monetization, fan funding, and others can get disabled.

You don't want to get anything disabled on your account by *YouTube*, so do your best to keep all these things green. The best way to do that is just to see when you get a copyright notice, delete the video immediately off *YouTube*, silence the audio and re-upload it.

CHAPTER 4

The *YouTube* video editor is a powerful tool for making your own videos fast!

In this chapter you are going to learn how you can make videos with the *YouTube* video editor without having to film anything yourself.

Read this section for an <u>introduction to the YouTube video editor and how to get free videos you can use!</u>

Have you seen these *Top Ten* channels? They use the videos licensed as *Creative Commons* so they can be re-used to make new videos that can go viral very fast.

In this section I will show you <u>how to make a niche topic video using the YouTube video editor + add your audio</u>.

Read on…

Introduction to the *YouTube* video editor and how to get free videos you can use!

There are two basic ways to do videos on *YouTube*. One, you upload your own. Two, you use existing videos to make new ones. Using existing videos to make new ones is a gigantic resource, especially if you want to make viral videos that get a lot of views on *YouTube* very quickly and easily. All you have to do is go to your *YouTube.com* dashboard and then click on *Create*.

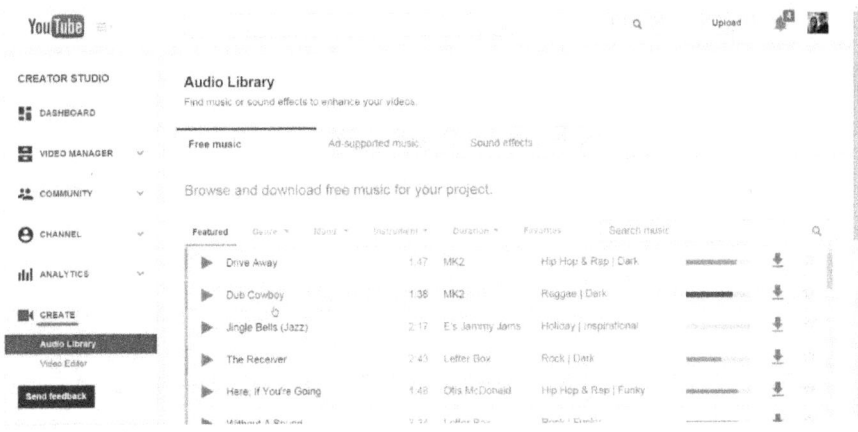

You then get to the **YouTube Video Editor**, which has an **Audio Library** and a **Video Editor**. The video editor is very sweet for putting your own videos together. These are my videos you see below and I can remix them quickly.

One of my top videos is a remix video of two of my videos put together.

The real power of the video editor is to pick up *Creative Commons* videos, especially if you don't have any of your own videos. So for example, you might have seen popular *YouTube* channels like top ten channels that just have tons of top ten videos on them. This is exactly how you are able to make those.

You can search for niche topics like *"funny dog video"* or anything similar to that, and you can then drag these funny dog videos into your timeline.

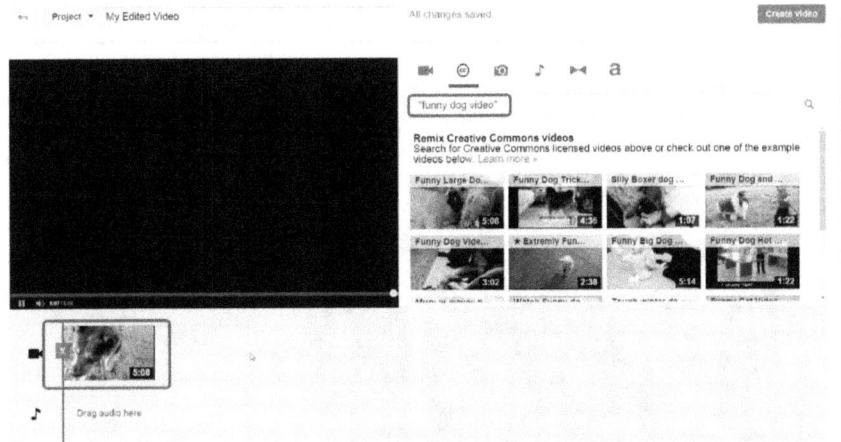

You don't want to use anything in the *Creative Commons* without changing it because if you use someone else's video exactly, then *YouTube* will not allow you to monetize it. You need to make some changes to it.

This is the *YouTube.com/editor* and where the *Creative Commons* video tab is located.

YouTube channel creators have licensed their videos to be used by anyone who wants to use them. You can do that yourself too.

First select the video you want to modify the license and click the *Edit* button.

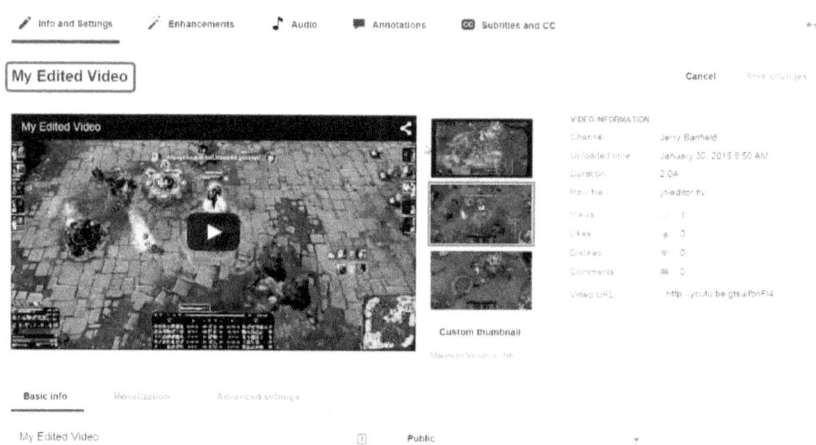

You will be in the section where you can modify different settings for the video, and you have to click on the *"Advance Settings"* tab.

It is right in the *"License and rights ownership"* section.

There you can select *"Creative Commons - Attribution"* and share your video with the world.

Most videos are on the *Standard YouTube License,* which make them just like any other standard creative endeavor. You own the copyright to the video. In this case above, I own the copyright to this video, so other people just can't use it.

Some *YouTube* creators will go there and put *Creative Commons - Attribution* on their videos so that they have a chance to get watched and shared a lot more often. When you use a *Standard YouTube License*, it is a lot more restrictive in terms of sharing.

The *Creative Commons* library in the video editor is looking at *Creative Commons* videos where creators of the videos have given you permission to reuse and remake their videos however you want to.

Look at how sweet this is, you can take existing videos people have allowed you to use and put them together into a new video. I could call this *"Top Ten Dog Tricks Videos."*

All I'm really doing is dragging other people's videos into my timeline. So now I have 5 different dog tricks videos that other people have filmed that I can use now to make my own video. I just have to hit the *Create Video* button to make this video pop up in my channel.

The idea of this is you want to make videos people enjoy using videos other people have already made. Sometimes putting things together in a new video can be a lot more fun than just using the original. Things like *America's funniest home videos* are often just getting other people's video and putting them in context.

A really powerful thing to do is to create a video, and then download that video to put your own audio on it because all of these videos are likely to have a lot of different audio, and then re-upload it. Audio is one of the biggest factors for video satisfaction because if you have inconsistent or low quality audio, it really detracts from the experience.

You can't do this within *YouTube,* which is pretty frustrating, but what you can do is use this audio track option that *YouTube* gives you.

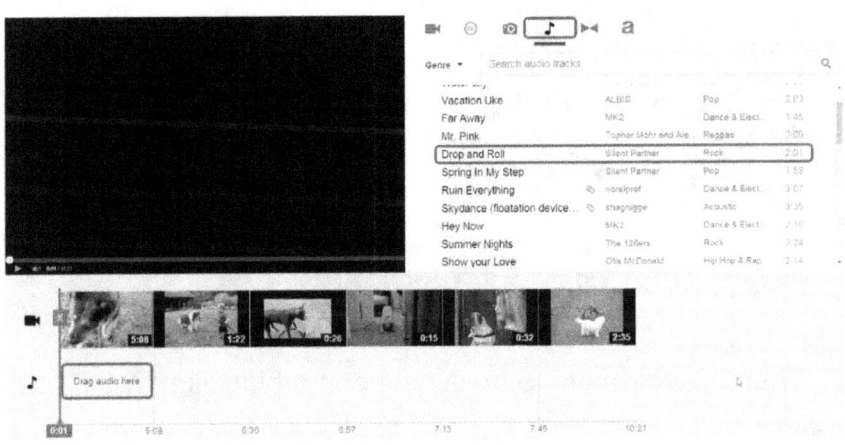

You can drag free music into the audio area so you can put music over the existing audio. What you don't want to do is use something with the tag on it where the owner of the song will be able to monetize your video.

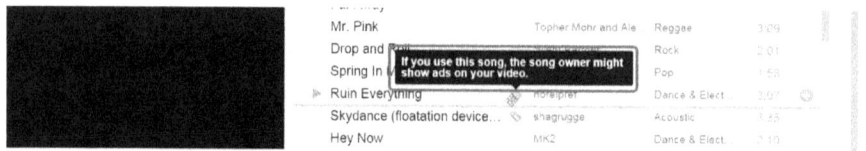

You want to be able to have all your ways to make money open in this.

If you want to do some simple things like introducing the video, what you can do is drag a little centered title and put it up at the front of the video into your timeline.

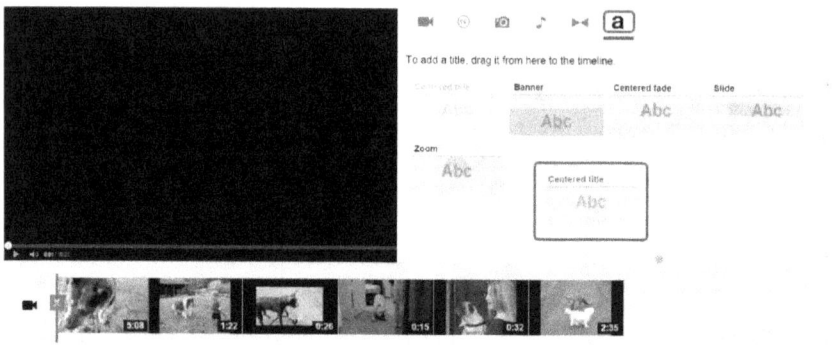

Then, all you have to do is type something like *"Top Funny Dog Videos."*

This will introduce my series of videos and give it unique exact purpose.

I hope showing you how to use the *YouTube* editor just as a general introduction is really helpful for you in giving you the ability to make some sweet new videos out of existing videos.

How to make a niche topic video using the *YouTube* video editor + add your audio

If you want to see how to use the *YouTube* video editor quickly to make a viral video on a popular topic here is how you do it. You don't even need to actually have the footage yourself, all you have to do is find it.

I'm into the *League of Legends* and one of the big things that you can do is get a *Pentakill*. There are lots of videos if you just search for *Pentakill* on *League of Legends*. There are tons of videos and there are videos with tons of views on *Pentakill*, so it is a popular niche topic.

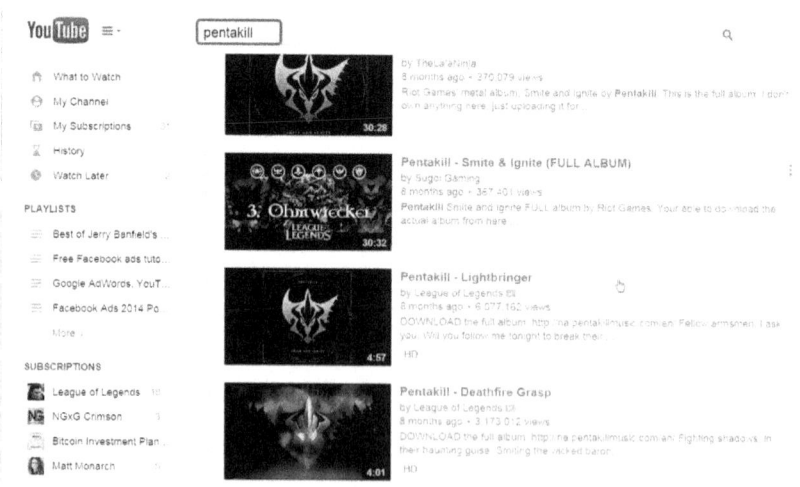

If I want to make a *Pentakill* video, I can even pick the most popular current champions to make a video with. So when I type in *Pentakill Olaf*, I can see that there are lots of these *Pentakill Olaf* videos, all of which in the top half at least have 20,000 views.

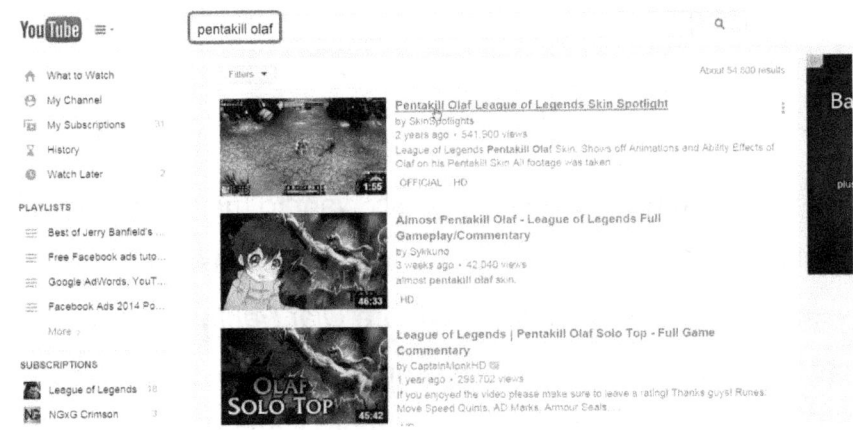

So what I can do to actually make my own is go to the *YouTube* video editor: *YouTube.com/editor*.

Then I click on the *Creative Commons* tab and search for *"Olaf Pentakill"* or *"Pentakill Olaf,"* in quotes. I have now found a video that has an *Olaf Pentakill*, so I can drag that down to my timeline.

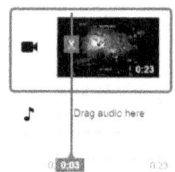

There are more videos if I really want to make a sweet *Olaf Pentakill* video. I can look through all of these other videos and see if there are anymore *Olaf Pentakill* hidden. I can then edit just the *Pentakill* out of the video. I can also try searching with other terms to find more videos.

Finally I click *Create Video* and then it comes up as *"My Edited Video."*

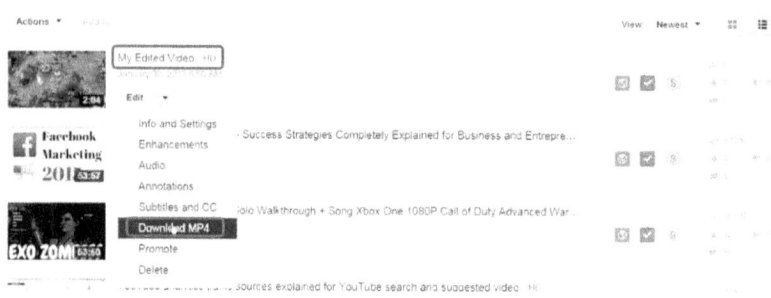

You can then download the video in *mp4* format to edit the audio, which is likely to be inconsistent containing other people's commentary, sound or background music.

Then, I can use a video editor like *Camtasia Studio* where I can silence the existing audio, put my own audio on it and re-upload it. That will make for a sweet experience because it is consistent with my channel then. It has my audio on it with commentary and music, and it has some sweet video footage to go with it.

The idea is that *YouTube* wants as much good content as possible. The people who have listed their videos as *Creative Commons* are open to having their videos used in other videos, and then the benefit for them is that they get cited and linked back to in the *YouTube* credit section.

CHAPTER 5

Live streaming on *YouTube* is a big thing that is here right now!

One big opportunity you have to be successful on *YouTube* is to do live streaming. When you broadcast live, you have the potential to reach and engage audiences in a new level.

I will show you how <u>YouTube live streaming launched my first viral video! See how to get started</u> and how to enable live streaming in *YouTube*.

Setting up a live stream event can be challenging and it is preferable to do a test event to make sure your equipment is working well with *YouTube* before the actual event. I will show you <u>how to setup your first live event or live stream on YouTube</u>.

If you are a gamer and want to stream live, you must not miss this section: <u>Getting the live stream for a video game started with Elgato game capture HD</u>.

Read on...

YouTube live streaming launched my first viral video! See how to get started

One big opportunity you have to be successful on *YouTube*, and more generally with your videos online, is called live streaming, or live events. A live event is where you actually broadcast live, the same as when you watch a live sport on *TV* or even online.

When you broadcast live, you have the potential to reach and engage audiences in a new level. The demand for online live video is growing rapidly, which is why *YouTube* has added the new live event section on the website.

Now you have to have setup this on your profile. You have to enable live events and you have to agree to *YouTube's* terms and conditions for live events. You also need to have a verified profile.

In order to enable live streaming you have to go to this page: *www.youtube.com/my_live_events*

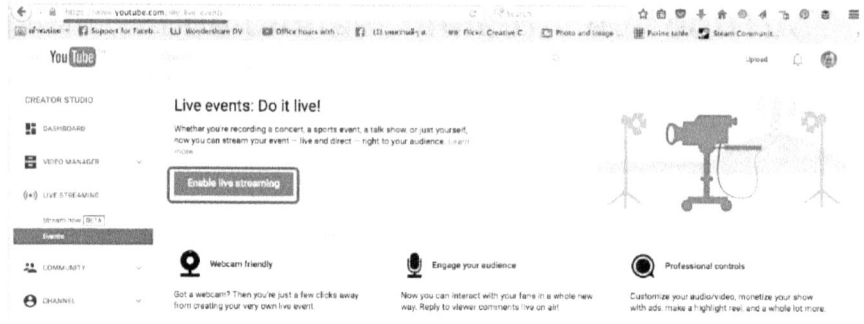

Then, click on the *"Enable live streaming"* blue button. You will be shown *YouTube's* terms and conditions.

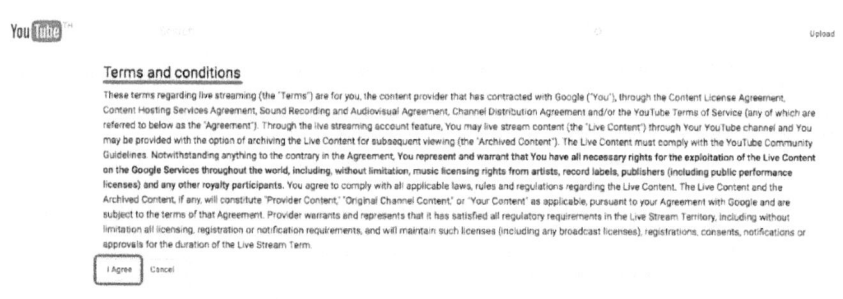

Click the *"I Agree"* button.

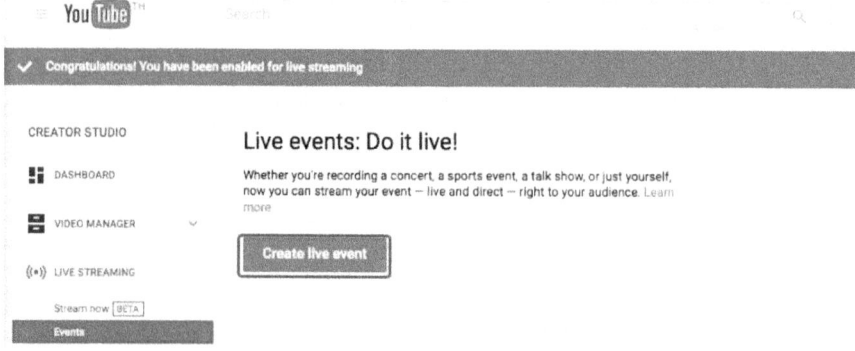

You are now all set-up to start live streaming and you can have new videos that will upload straight on your channel. This has been very successful for me in making viral videos. About half of my best videos in terms of views were live events.

These videos were all live events consistently successful getting organic views on *YouTube*.

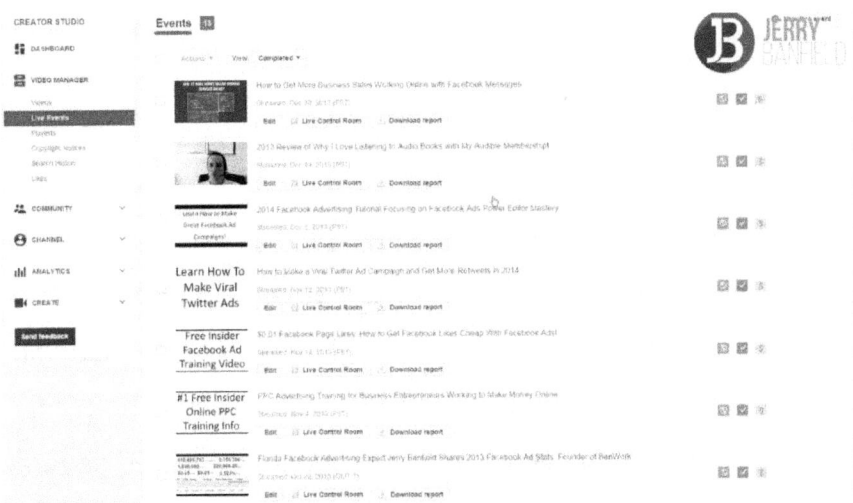

Live events have an advantage especially if you have an established channel, *YouTube* gives you options to put a notification on all of your videos to find all people into the live event. What I'm seeing a lot of now are people that are going to create a new live event, and what they do is use a *Google+*

hangout.

That's what I did to make the live events I have shown you before.

You use *Google+ Hangouts On Air* to make the event, you go live and then it is automatically added to your channel. Not only that, but then you can send people the link to the *Google + event*, which is really good for *SEO* and it is much better than using something like *"Go to Webinar,"* that I used several times to do webinars.

The thing is that *Go to Webinar* gives me no long term *SEO* benefits and no long term benefits for my channel. I advertise the live events as well as the video afterwards, and you can see this video then did very well on my channel.

It got hundreds of thousands of views and that has been a huge success for me. This is the video analytics, in the last *28 days* this video got *1,600* free views. It was uploaded a year and a half ago, and it has got *129,487* views lifetime. It is not even of good quality.

Live events have huge potential on *YouTube*, so you definitely want to go to the *Video Manager* and if you don't see live events setup there, apply for it. It may not be available in every single country, but I do know that it is available in my country in the *US* and many others.

I challenge you to figure out a way to do a live event on your channel and to create one of your next viral videos.

Have you been wanting to do a webinar? Have you been wanting to just sit down and talk about something? If you want to reach out to your existing audience, try having a live event.

Make sure you get everything tested out beforehand because live events can get tricky to get right. The easiest type of live event is to do a *Google+ Hangout*. If you try to stream a game that can be challenging and you should test in advance.

The live events feature on *YouTube* is extremely helpful for making viral videos and extremely helpful for the long term growth of your channel.

How to setup your first live event or live stream on *YouTube*

One of the newest methods for getting tons of views and attention online is *Live Event* viewing, especially on video games. Sites like *Twitch* have gotten very popular especially off of live events. What you want to be able to do is know how to make a live event on your *YouTube* channel.

Here is how you do it. You go to *Video Manager* and then there is a live events tab if your account is in good standing.

If you have everything setup right, there shouldn't be too much to do.

If you have applied for live events before and your account is in good standing, you should be able to create a new live event.

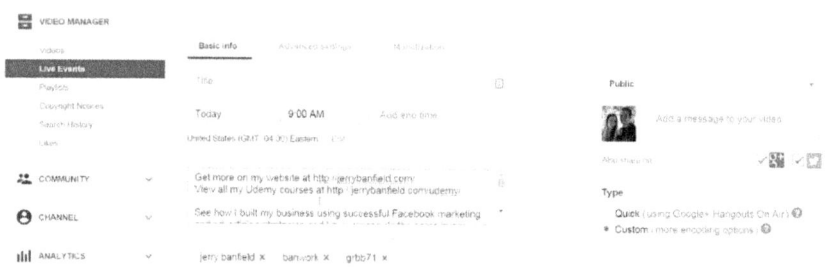

Tomorrow I'm going to try one of these live events on my channel. I'm going to try when the new *Zombie map* releases for *Call of Duty Advanced Warfare*. I will try to do a live event on my channel to see what people think of it and see how it works.

I would love to be able to do more live events on my channel because I have the advantage of getting all the people actively watching my channel into the live event with the *promoted through featured content* advanced setting.

You have the settings in this page, where you can drive all of the people into actually interacting with you in an event.

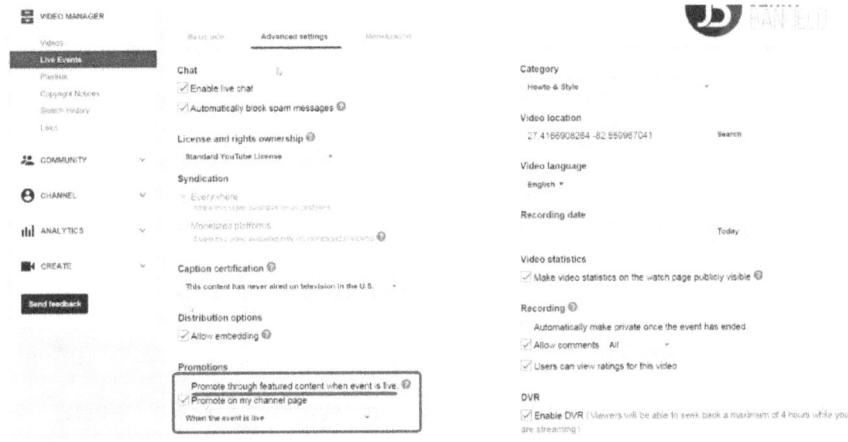

I have seen a lot of people who have big success with a live stream audience and this is where you do it. It is just like setting a *YouTube* video in terms of getting the information up.

There is the title, the description and keywords. Then you have got the message you can share on *Google+,* and you can either do a quick event using *Google Hangouts* or you can do a custom one that has more encoding options.

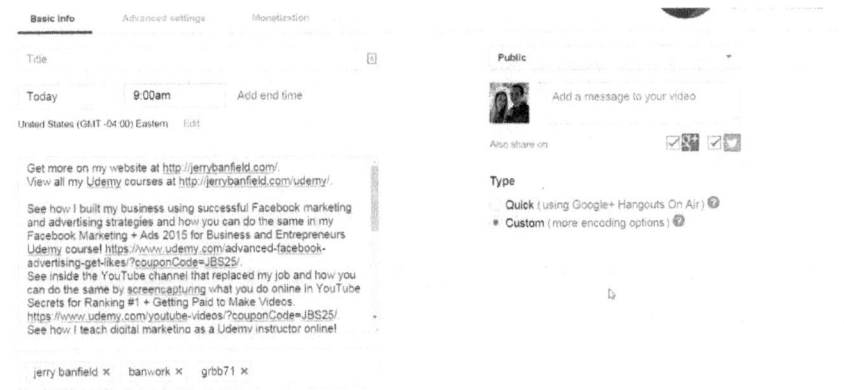

If you have something like I'm doing tomorrow, that is going to be a live stream with a new *Zombie map* release, that is scheduled, it is very important to be able to test out how things work on *YouTube*.

You want to try and do it before the actual event is live to make sure everything works, the same as doing a webinar or anything else similar, once you have got it all set up before your audience actually is sitting there watching.

I did a video before and I thought I had the commentary on, and then after three hours of video, no commentary on, *whoops!*

You want to test this out beforehand and I will just create a quick title and description, I will run through the advanced settings and I will click create an event. I will get this event started and just run it for a little while as I want to see how the entire event comes out for real. I'm going to actually play the *Zombie maps* the day before to test this out and make sure it actually comes out right.

Live events upload straight on *YouTube*, so it is a lot faster than trying to stream something on your own or record it on your own, and then upload it.

Now you can see that I have gone through, added the description and the basic info of the same as I would for a regular *YouTube* video.

I have set up my *Google+* to share and now I'm going to *Advanced Settings*.

I want to enable *live chat* where I can actually interact with people while they are watching, and I want to switch my category to *Gaming*.

I put the recording date on today and make the video stats available. I allow comments and users can view ratings. I enable *DVR* so that people can go back. Broadcast delay is the amount you see in the player and the amount the viewers see to help ads inserted, but as I am not running ads, I'm not going to be worry about putting a delay on it.

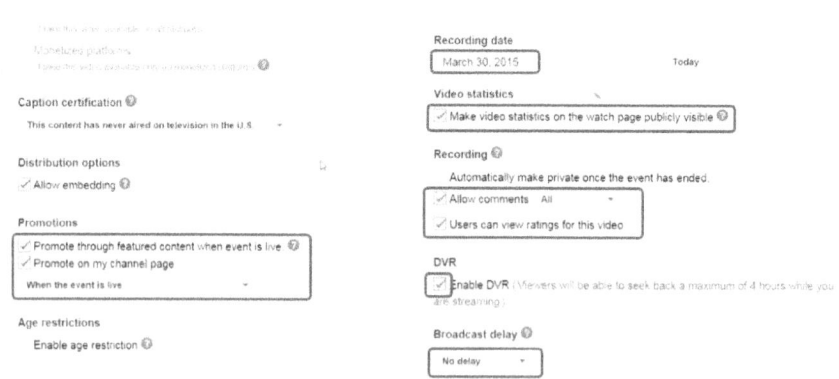

In the *Promotions* section, I can promote on my channel page when the event is live and through featured content.

I created the event to start at *9:00 a.m.* and it is *8:24 a.m.* now. I'm going to give this a test run to see how it comes out. I'm not clicking on *Monetization* and I go straight to the *"Create event"* button.

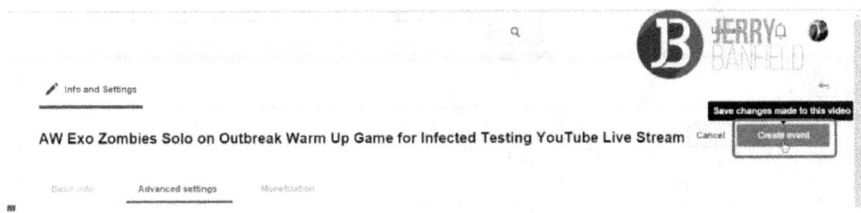

Now, what *YouTube* let me know is how exactly I can get an actual video feed. *YouTube* calls it *"Ingestion Settings"* and I have different options to select.

What I can do then is select the bitrate and get an actual thumbnail working on my live stream.

What I have got already is my *Elgato* game capture *HD*.

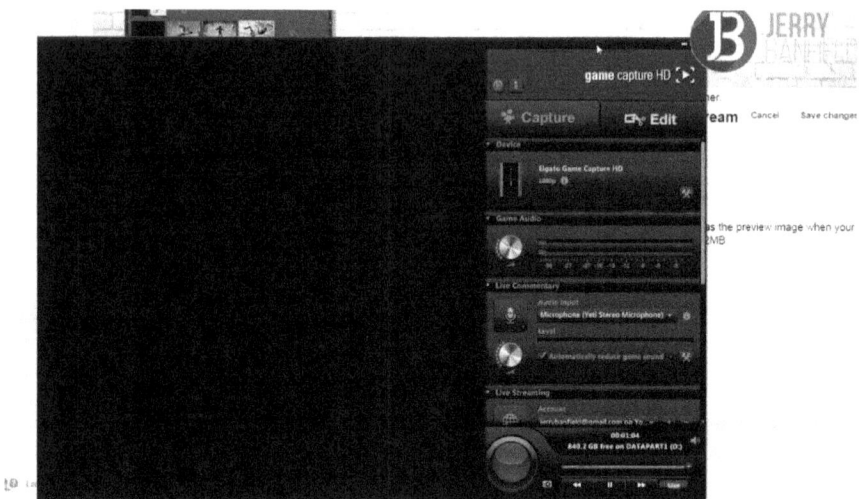

Then, what I want to do is set a *"Custom Ingestion"* so that *YouTube* will create the stream.

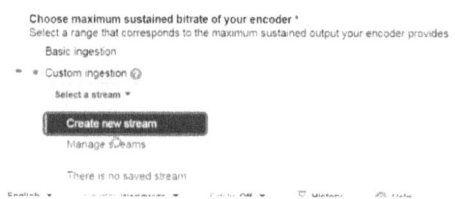

I can now enter the title: *Test Elgato game capture HD*. Then, add a description for the stream.

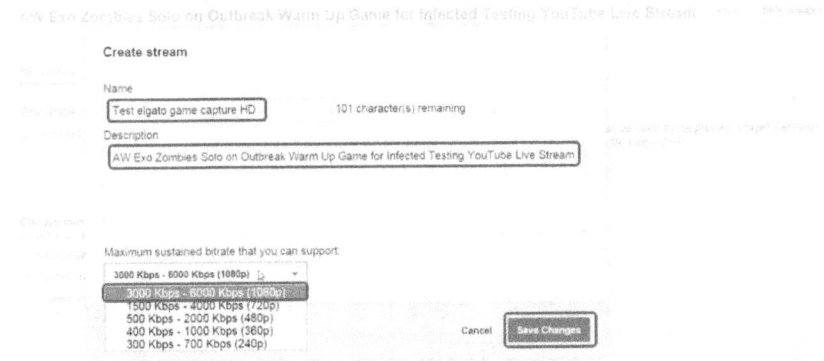

The bitrate for *1080p* is *3000 Kbps - 6000 Kbps* so I select that and hit *"Save Changes."*

It is now showing as a *"Custom Ingestion"* and I have to look at setting the encoder. *YouTube* has a program called *Wirecast* and that might work good, but as I am using *Elgato* I have to select *"Other encoders."*

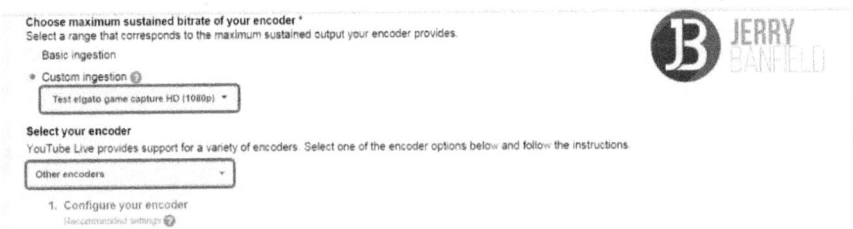

When I go to my *Elgato* game capture *HD*, I have to click on the little live stream button, then it has got the event setup in the menu.

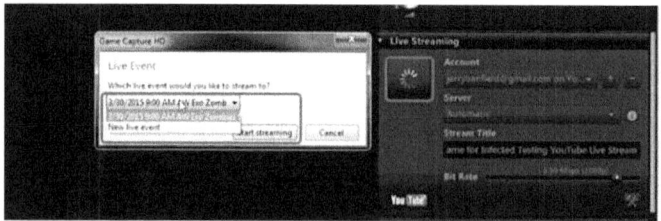

All I have got to do now is click the *"Start Streaming"* button. How sweet is that! That's the nice thing if you are doing this for video game capturing.

Now at the same time, you can always just use your camera to do this if you are trying to do a webinar, or you could use any other thing you have got setup for. You can set up a screen capture, but how ever you do it, this is how you get your live event setup on *YouTube*.

If you want to set up some kind of video game streaming or streaming from another device like a *TV*, then this *Elgato Game Capture HD* works really good for that.

Getting the live stream for a video game started with *Elgato game capture HD*

On my *Elgato game capture HD*, this is how I start the stream. First, I have got to get everything setup and I want to enable live commentary which is using this microphone.

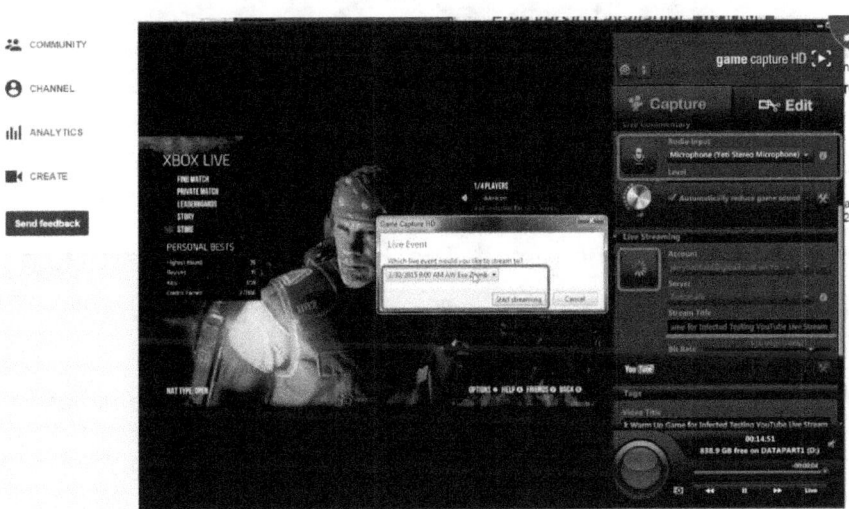

I have all the rest of it set up and configured already. I have got the title ready and I click on the *"Live Streaming"* square button, which open a small window. Then, I have *"Advanced Warfare Exo Zombies"* showing up. I can hit *"Start streaming"* now and I make sure it gets synced up.

So in the live streaming you would definitely want to get everything good and tested. Then you can do things like turn on live commentary like I have got now.

This is my Live Stream test and what I want to do is figure out exactly how it looks like on *YouTube*.

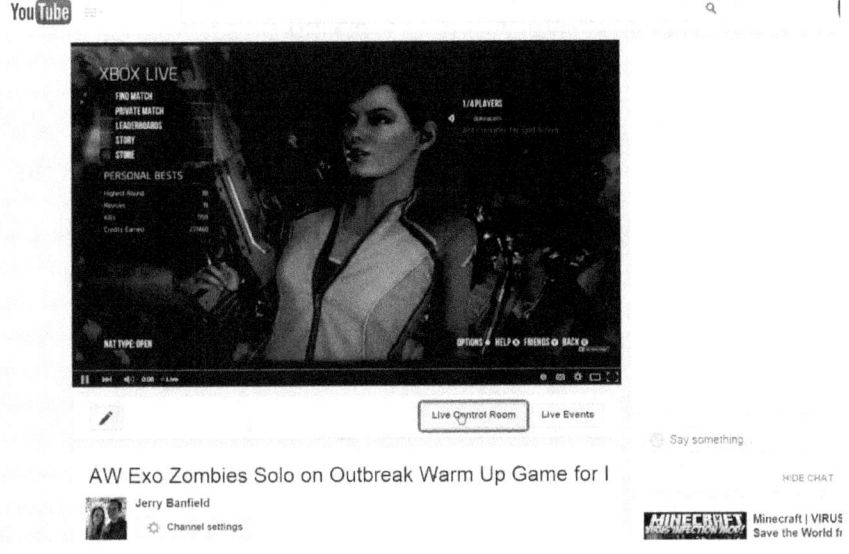

I want to go to *Live Control Room* and it says that I'm live, so that's good!

I have got the event setup and I have got it connected with my *Elgato game capture HD* and *YouTube* says in the *Live*

Control Room that everything is working good.

Since this is just a test what I want to do is just try this and see how it actually works and what I will actually do is create another event, then stream that for real and see how that goes.

CHAPTER 6

YouTube thumbnails are key for free suggested video views and search clicks

Thumbnails on *YouTube* are critical to get more views for your videos and I will show you how to make a great YouTube thumbnail with Canva based on data.

There are many software that you can use beside *Photoshop* and I will share with you what software to use for your YouTube thumbnails and graphics.

If you are not a graphic designer and don't want to go through the trouble to try to do it yourself, you may want to consider YouTube thumbnail creation simply with Fiverr.

YouTube thumbnails in search ranking for branding consistently and getting clicks is a little trick that can help you get more views for your videos.

Read on...

How to make a great *YouTube* thumbnail with *Canva* based on data

Thumbnails on *YouTube* are critical and I will quickly share with you what works to make a good thumbnail. You have to look at your *YouTube* analytics and see where you are getting views on suggested video. If you are getting views on suggested video, that means the thumbnail is good.

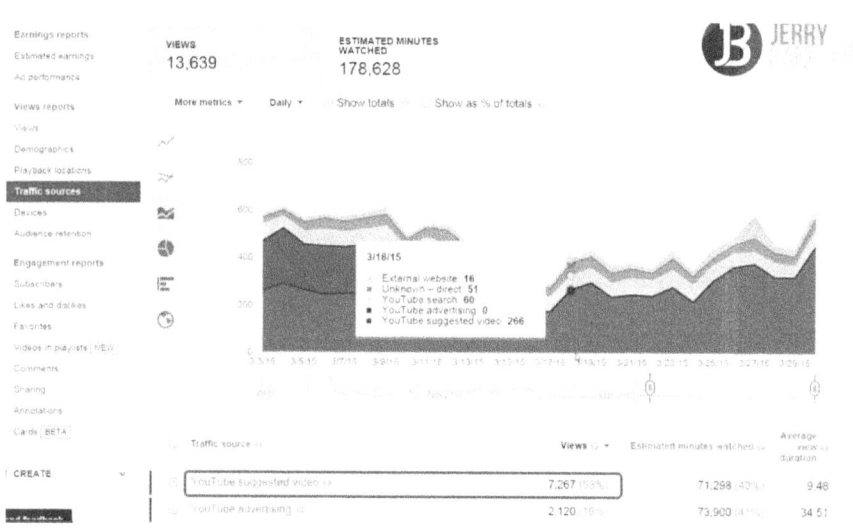

The title can be important, but the thumbnail is the key for suggested videos. I can see on this video that my thumbnail is really good.

Good thumbnails are very simple. It has some words and a recognizable logo that matches what the video is about.

When your video is doing well on search, but not so much in suggested video, it is usually the thumbnail.

This one is doing well in suggested video as well. You can see it has the same type of design as the last one. It is straightforward with some words and a couple of related symbols.

Now you can see that this thumbnail is not working well in suggested video.

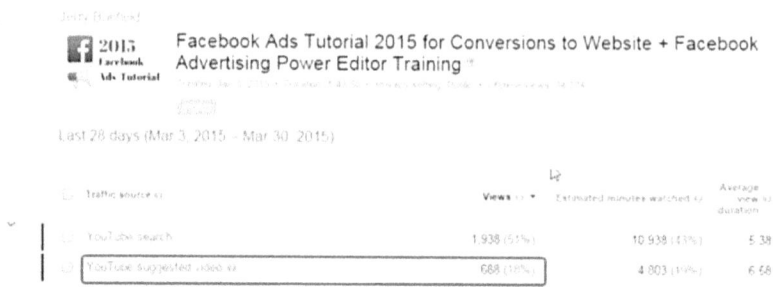

It is showing up on *YouTube* search so I know it is ranking well on keywords. It is not getting clicked on in suggested video, the issue is probably not the video itself or the words, but the thumbnail. The main thing to do then is to improve the thumbnail based on what's already working.

I use *Canva.com* to manage my thumbnails because there is easy availability of additional designs and stock photos.

I have all my thumbnails here and I have got this *Facebook* ads thumbnail which is working really good.

All I'm going to do is copy it.

If you don't have a thumbnail to start from, what you need is a custom dimension of *1280 x 720*, that's the size you want to use for a thumbnail.

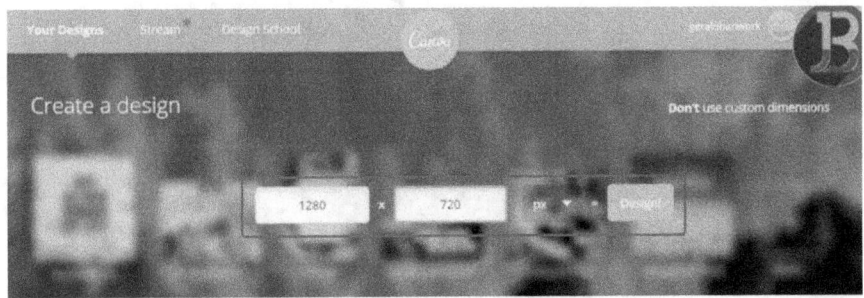

What I want to do now is change the thumbnail I just copied.

This is the original thumbnail.

What I want to do is change this thumbnail into something more like this.

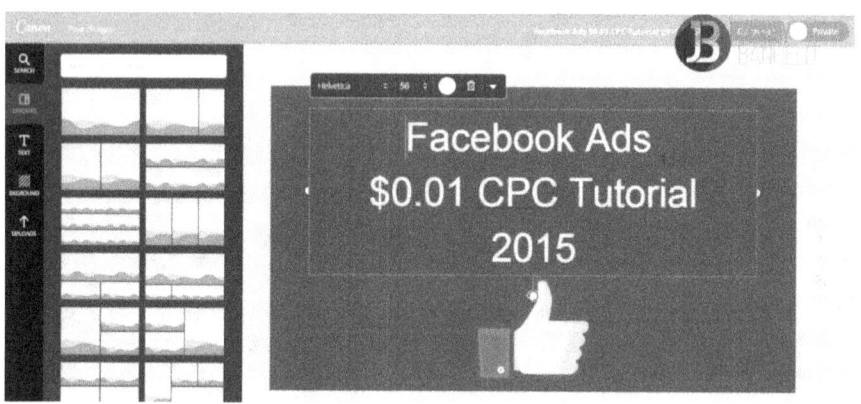

So, what people are showing they want is some recognizable *Facebook* brand symbol and what I can do is actually shrink the text on this. *"Facebook Ads,"* and then I could put something like *"for conversions."* I can put the *2015* somewhere else and make the font a little bit bigger so that it shows up more clearly on the thumbnail.

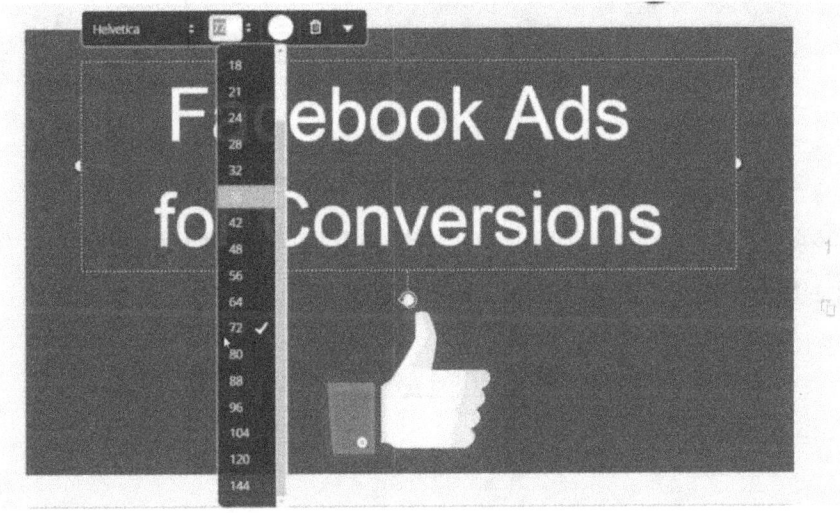

I can then add the year, align the text left and move the *Like* symbol to the right a little bit. *2015* is important to let the viewers know that it is a new tutorial and it is not something that's old school. It is risky sometimes to use a lot of text, but what I saw in my other videos is that the thumbnail with a lot of text is working.

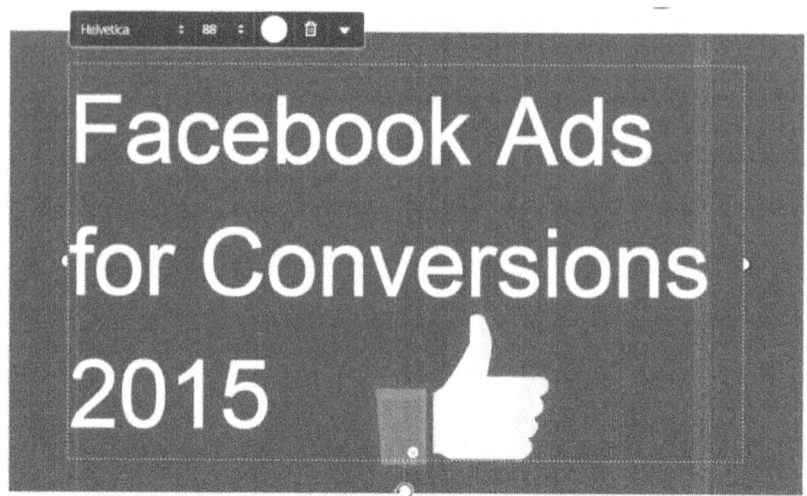

Now I have got a new thumbnail that should work better based on what the last thumbnail is doing. Whether it will work better or not, the analytics will say.

All I have to do with *Canva.com* now is to download the image from it.

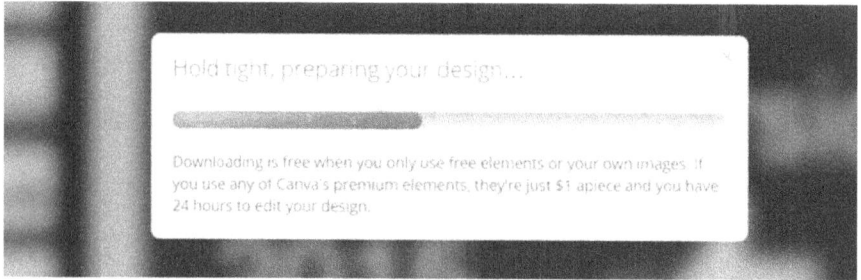

When it is downloaded, I go back to edit the video in *YouTube* and change the thumbnail. Look at that thumbnail *"Facebook Ads for Conversion 2015."*

It is very clear what value you get out of watching this video in the thumbnail now, so I hit *"Save changes."*

So now, I have got my new thumbnail and the timestamp doesn't overlap the Like symbol.

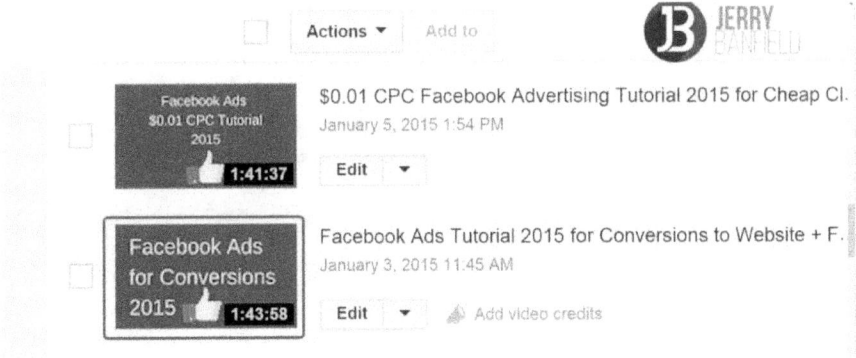

This is how you look at what's working on your existing thumbnails, and then optimize them with what's proving to actually work.

What software to use for your *YouTube* thumbnails and graphics

When it comes to creating graphics, the first software that everyone thinks about is *Photoshop*. If you have it on your computer and already know how to use it, well it is great.

If you don't know how to use *Photoshop* and don't have the budget to buy a license, don't be disappointed as there are other options. *Photoshop* is overkilled for making thumbnails anyway.

Paint for *Windows* is useless and what you need is a simple software that can handle different layers, so you can make a nice graphic easily.

These are my suggestions, I have used all of them.

www.gimp.org

Gimp for *Mac*, *Windows* and *Linux* is an *Open Source* software and is free. It is very similar to *Photoshop* and you can do very complex image manipulations with it. You can add layers, text, effects and all the things you will need for your *YouTube* graphics.

Getpaint.net for *Windows* is a free software which is very easy to use. It is an improved version of the *Paint* program in *Windows*, and you can work with different layers, apply special effects and make titles. The software also has many other powerful tools to edit your images and photos.

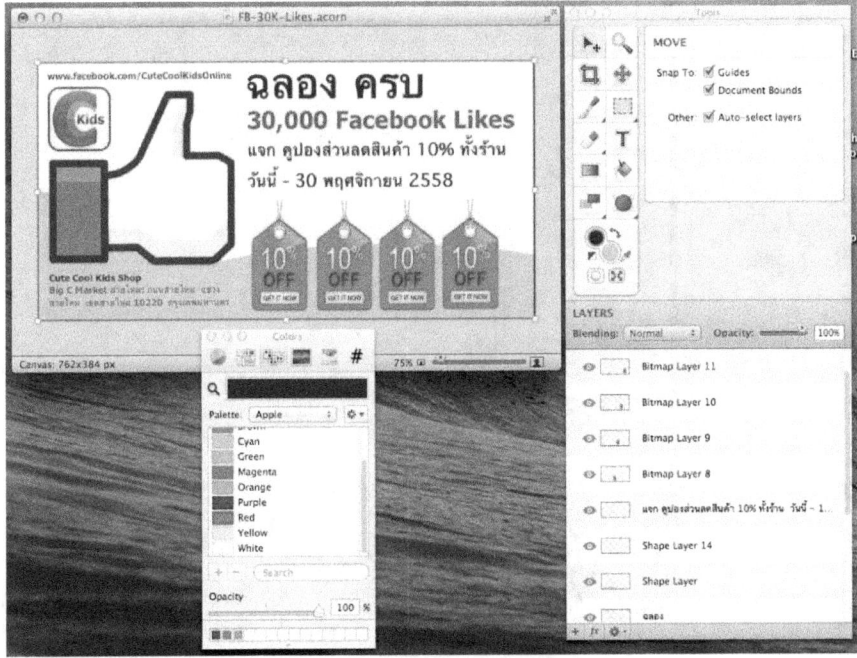

flyingmeat.com/acorn/

With *Acorn for Mac* you will be able to do all you need to do with graphics. You can add layer masks, add vector shapes, use custom brushes and non-destructive filters, add text and do instant *Alpha* to remove backgrounds.

It is an excellent alternative to *Photoshop* and it is what I use the most now. There is a *14* day trial and a license is $29.99.

The Complete YouTube Book

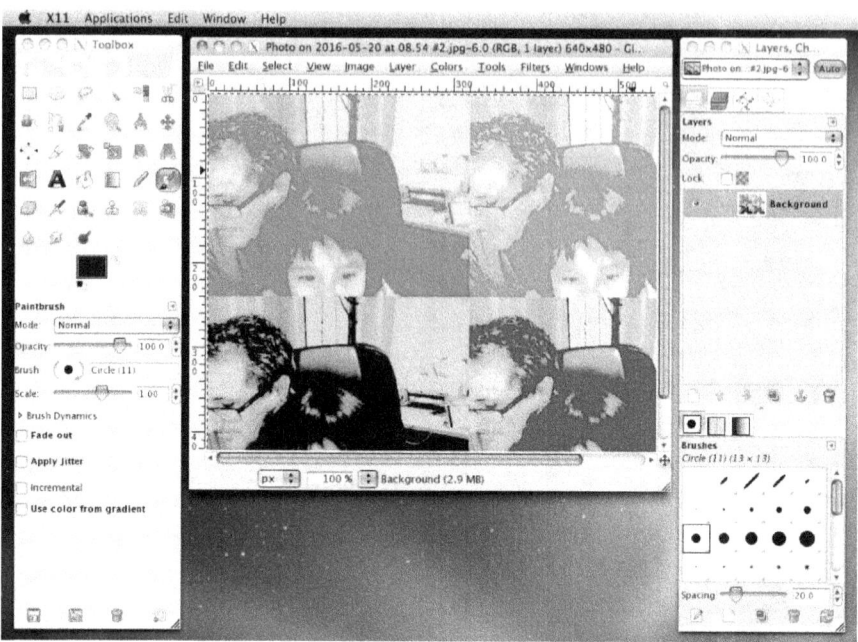

I prefer to have a software installed on my computer so that I can re-use previous work to make new images, but there are also other image software on the cloud that you can use.

Canva.com is a free software that can help you to do your _YouTube_ graphics very easily. It is on the cloud and you need to be connected to the Internet to use it, nothing to download on your computer, except the image you have created with the application. It can be used to easily make your _YouTube_ thumbnails as described in the previous chapter.

You can do all the things that the other software above can do and it is very intuitive. You can use their free images, upload your own or buy one for $1.

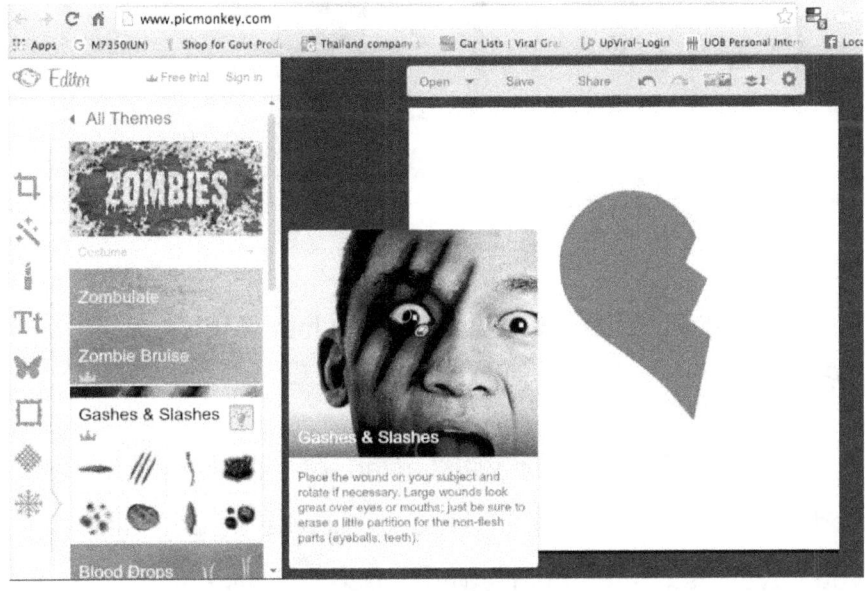

www.picmonkey.com

If you like effects in your thumbnails, *PicMonkey* is maybe what you need. You can do all the image manipulations you can do in *Canva* plus very specific effects like *Zombies* effects.

Or maybe you like vampires...

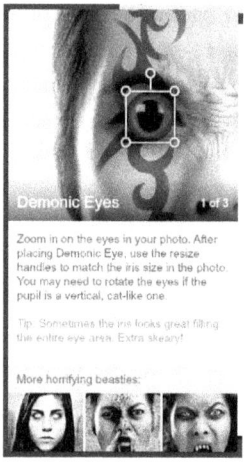 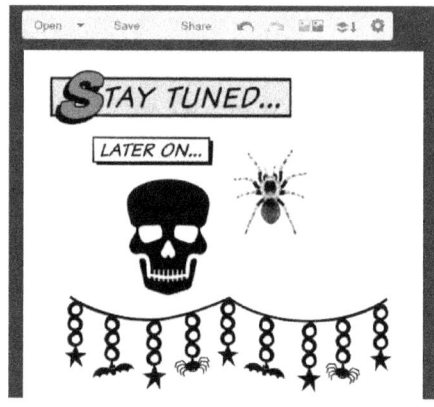

Definitely a fun software to use with lots of themes and graphics.

There is a free version with limited tools and annoying ads, and a paid version at *$4.99* a month. Maybe a good idea if you have lots of thumbnails with effects to make.

YouTube thumbnail creation simply with *Fiverr*

Your *YouTube* thumbnails are really important for getting clicks on your videos, especially in suggested video and search. If you are not good at doing thumbnails, all you need to do is get someone to make you a good thumbnail.

Go to *Fiverr.com* and type *YouTube* thumbnail. You can easily find people who will make you a very good thumbnail and I usually sort by high rating to see who is doing the most.

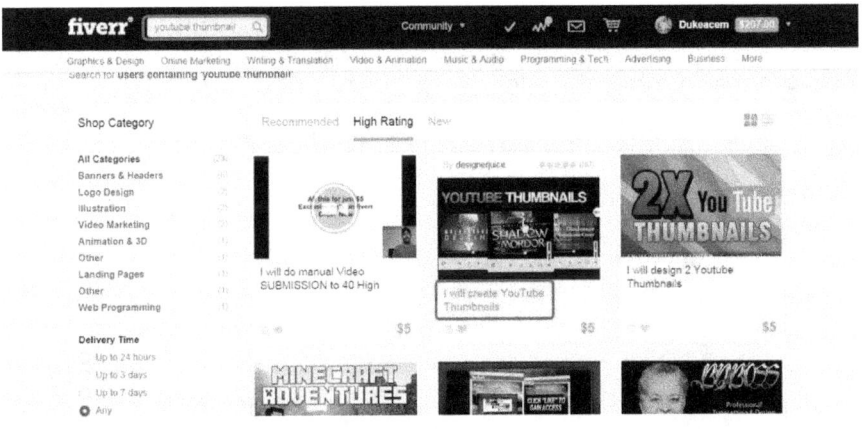

This one right here looks like a good gig for *YouTube* thumbnails and you don't have to guess either, you can just try ordering one from different gigs and see which freelancer does the best work for your videos.

It is that easy, you just go through, pick a gig and order a thumbnail. However, if you have *400* videos, you may not want to do that for every single one of your videos to get started.

What I'm going to do now, because I have some videos that need some thumbnail help, is to order a couple of thumbnails for videos that are getting views. If your video is getting views and you want it to get more views, doing a thumbnail is a good way to do it. How do I decide which video needs a new thumbnail?

I did some basic thumbnails and what I want to do now is find where my thumbnails are not very good, and where I am getting views. On the analytics tab, I'm figuring out which videos need new thumbnails.

Video	Views	Estimated minutes watched	Average view duration
Facebook Ads Tutorial 2015 for Conversions t...	20,250 (20%)	279,026 (33%)	13:46
$0.01 CPC Facebook Advertising Tutorial 201...	11,680 (12%)	204,143 (24%)	17:28
Buy bitcoin with cash at your local bank and s...	5,566 (5.6%)	26,587 (3.1%)	4:46
Flippa selling process overview: how to sell yo...	4,720 (4.8%)	25,666 (3.0%)	5:26
How I Created 5 Udemy Courses in 45 days!	4,224 (4.3%)	25,497 (3.0%)	6:02
YouTube SEO tutorial after you upload the vid...	3,753 (3.8%)	16,816 (2.0%)	4:28
How do you tell a girl you love her?	3,239 (3.3%)	2,265 (0.3%)	0:41
YouTube analytics traffic sources explained fo...	3,229 (3.3%)	9,113 (1.1%)	2:49
2014 Facebook Marketing and Advertising Tip...	3,073 (3.1%)	26,397 (3.1%)	8:35
Complete Facebook Advertising Tutorial: How To Get Cheap Clicks with Facebook Ads + Power Editor	3,024 (3.0%)	20,502 (2.4%)	6:46
	2,979 (3.0%)	26,383 (3.1%)	8:51
	2,213 (2.2%)	20,209 (2.4%)	9:07
	2,132 (2.1%)	12,688 (1.5%)	5:57
Complete Facebook Advertising Tutorial: How...	1,941 (2.0%)	18,705 (2.2%)	9:38

I'm checking out which videos I have here that got views recently and are actually getting suggested video views, and then I can figure out what I want to order a new thumbnail for.

I go down to the *Traffic sources* for this video, which is a *YouTube SEO* tutorial, and I'm getting views in *YouTube* search and suggest video. So, I would like to get a new thumbnail for this video.

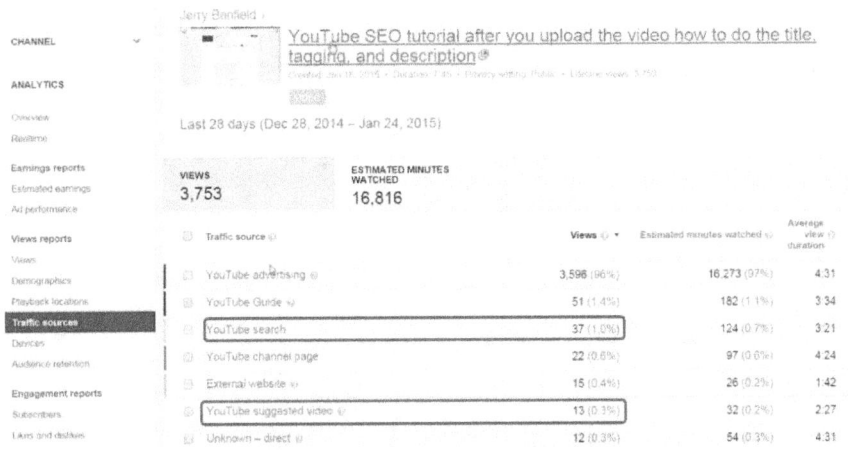

On this video, my face could definitely use a new thumbnail. I am getting a few views and also suggested videos.

The Complete YouTube Book

I would definitely get a new thumbnail instead of my face.

The problem again with thumbnails like this one below is that they are so bland it is hard to get clicks.

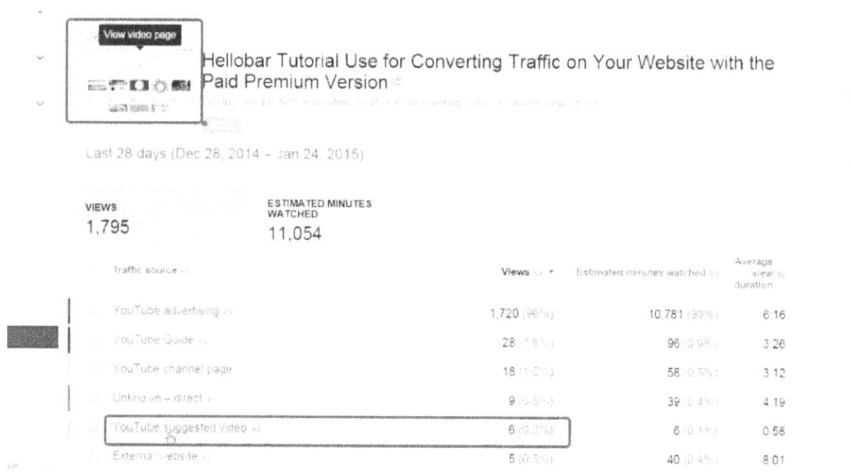

The suggested video is not very good but I'm coming up in the YouTube search for *Hellobar*, so I do need a thumbnail for this video.

All I do now is I go through and pick a gig on *Fiverr* and the thumbnail on that one looks really good.

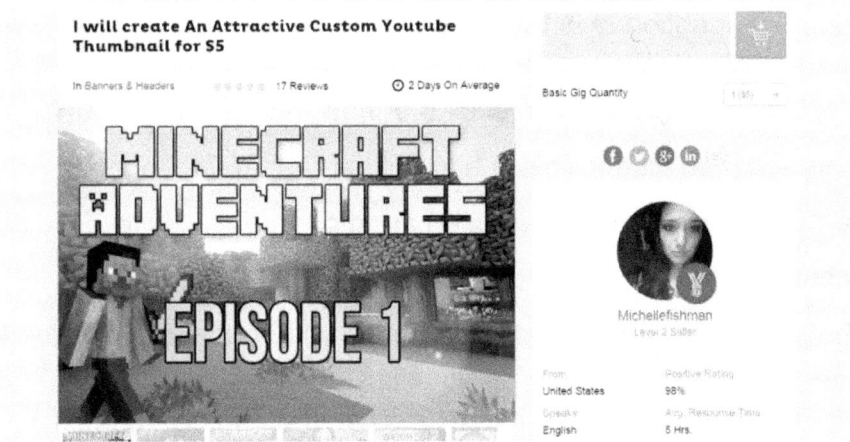

So I just click *"order now"* and I'll see what the order instructions are. I have already a *$207* balance, so I copy the *YouTube* link and then I paste it in this window.

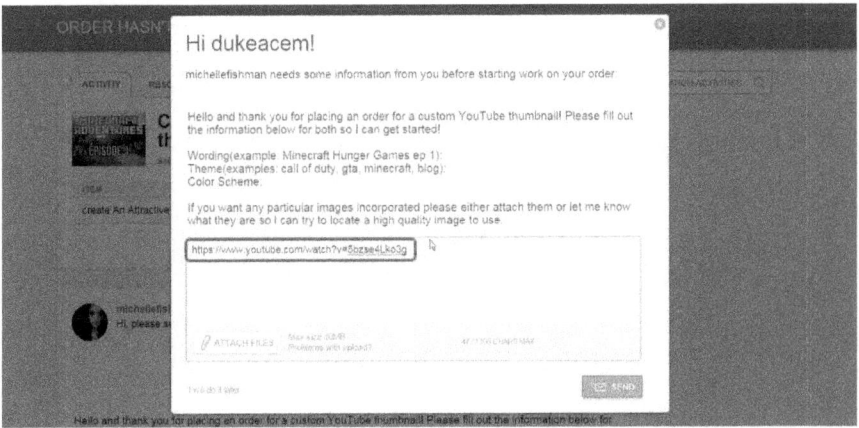

I need to tell this freelancer now the wording, the theme and the color scheme I want for the thumbnail. I don't want any particular images incorporated and I can just make a little short description of what I want.

When it's done, I can stick that new thumbnail straight in the *YouTube* video. This is a lot easier than trying to mess around with it myself because I am more than likely to consistently get good thumbnails out of this. That will look better than anything I would try to do, with much less effort.

There are ways you can try and do thumbnails yourself, but if you are not a graphic designer, just get someone else to make your thumbnails. If you have only a few videos, get thumbnails for all of them. If you have a ton of videos, pick out the videos that most need a new thumbnail.

YouTube thumbnails in search ranking for branding consistently and getting clicks

Do you want to see how to use your thumbnails on *YouTube* to rank higher and get more views. Here is a sweet little trick I'm going to show you now.

I want to look at a search term I'm ranking on and working to be top on. If I search for *"Facebook ads"* and scroll down past the ads, I have the third and fourth video down there.

If you just look at the thumbnails, you can't tell exactly that I have made both of these videos. What I want to do is take advantage of having two videos in the top and brand them so they all stand out as mine. What can be more impressive than having two branded videos in the top? No one else has two videos in the top, and in fact I have three videos in the top ten.

Here is how I'm going to do it quickly with *Canva.com*.

I go to my previously created thumbnail and I copy it to make a new one. The original is for *2015* and what I want to do is change the year to *2014* like this.

Now that will perfectly line up with my existing thumbnail. So when you see this on the results, you see one is newer and one is older, but both of them are obviously from me. So if you take a look again, that will make my branding consistent between these two.

Now all I have to do in search for my *"#1 2014 Facebook Ad Tutorial"* video and change the thumbnail.

Then, I have a nice new thumbnail up there that's consistent with the other one instead of looking different. The thumbnail size should be exactly *1280 x 720* pixels so it looks good.

What I can do is actually do it again with my third video on the first page results.

I will then see if I get a better ranking with the new thumbnail in the analytics and I can repeat this with other search terms. That's a little trick you can do with your thumbnails to help you get more clicks because when people see consistency, then they are more likely to have higher amounts of trust, and a higher likelihood of wanting to go straight to you.

CHAPTER 7

YouTube SEO: optimizing titles, tags and descriptions for video views

YouTube SEO is essential for the success of your channel. Doing it properly will help you to have your videos rank higher in *YouTube* search, and will help you to get more views from suggested video.

In this first section, I'm going to show you my <u>YouTube video uploading, title, tag and description walkthrough</u>.

The title of your video is very important and I have <u>YouTube title optimization tips for YouTube search and YouTube suggested video</u> in this section.

If you think that tags are not important, think again! Read this <u>YouTube tagging tutorial in depth for maximizing suggested video views</u> and see fast improvement.

"A short video is fine!" Really? Learn about <u>YouTube video descriptions in depth. Long descriptions are way better!</u> I show you why.

There are different keyword tools that can help you in your *SEO* effort. Use this <u>YouTube keyword tool for expanding your description and making a better title</u>.

Don't take my words for it! See my results for the last *28* days of my channel in this final section: <u>Proof these YouTube strategies are working rapidly</u>.

Read on…

YouTube video uploading, title, tag and description walkthrough

Having a good process for uploading videos on your *YouTube* channel is important. I will show you my actual process to upload a video and I will start with this. First, I want to have a mindset of uploading one video at a time. If you see all these videos that are published on my channel, even having one video that is not published starts to hold me back and slow me down.

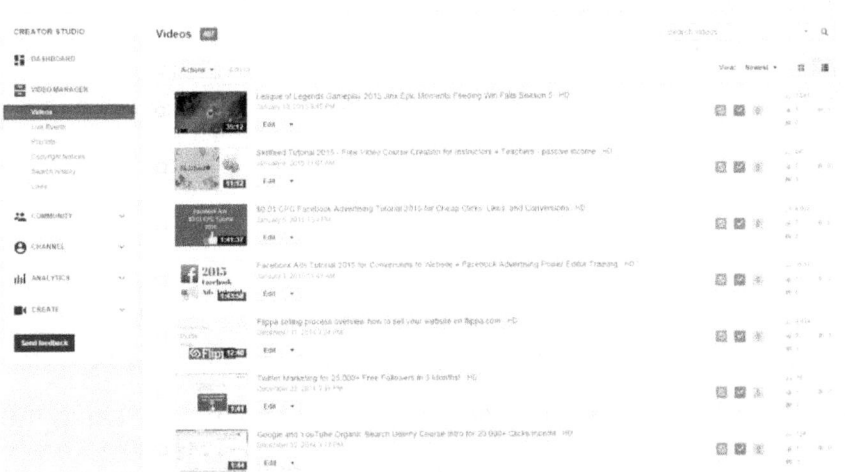

What I want to do is to just do one video at a time, getting it actually published and uploaded without doing anything else besides that. I get this video uploaded and what I want to do now is figure out how to give it a good title.

One of the things that I found for *SEO* that works good is to highlight things people are searching for, such as **"Hello Bar Premium"** because *"Hello Bar"* is a specific service that people will look for exactly. I can use this title: *"Hello Bar Tutorial Used for Converting Traffic on Your Website with the Paid Premium Version."*

This is a very clear thing I'm doing with this video. I'm giving people a quick *Hello Bar Tutorial* on my website, then what I do is add at the end of the title the *Paid Premium Version* because I know lots of people will search for using the paid version and want to see that specifically.

What I need now is a description. A quick description reiterating the title is ideal for *SEO*. I want to start right away with *"How to use Hello Bar"* and give a basic description. Then what I could do, when I get it transcribed, is edit it and put a longer description in.

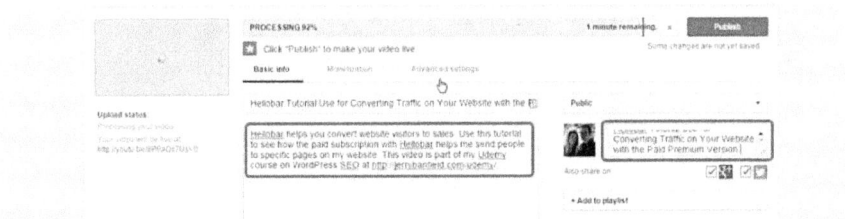

What you want is to have a very good description on your videos and the longer the better. Since I have a transcriber, I can put then the text for the video they transcribed into the video itself. I have got this short description with all of the essentials that goes back over the *SEO* terms and different specific terms. It is written to get clicks so I want to communicate immediately why people should watch the video, what they will get out of it, and then what they should do for more, which is going to my website.

I use this same thing to put it in the message on *Twitter* and on *Google+*, which is important to get the video indexed and shared.

I go over to **Advanced Settings** to make sure every field is filled out at least.

A nice little option is to notify subscribers, but if you are putting something up that's different from usual, you don't want to notify subscribers. When I upload video gaming videos, I don't notify subscribers because people mostly want *Internet Marketing* stuff on my channel.

Now that you filled the *Advanced Settings* in, filled the details of the title and the description in, and the sharing option at the right, then what I want to do is start tagging.

Most of my videos have *Jerry Banfield* and *Banwork*, which is my company tag. This helps me appear in more suggested videos next to my own videos because if you are watching one video, I want you to watch more videos.

Now I go through and tag other things that are related to this video. *Hello bar* is exactly what I want to rank for, *hello bar tutorial* and things like the year *2015*. Then, *hello bar premium, hellobar subscription, hellobar paid, website, traffic, converting* and *clicks*.

What I can do now is some keyword research with Keyword tool IO *(keywordtool.io/youtube)* in the *YouTube* section.

I type *hellobar* and see what keywords it recommends so that way I can get an idea to what to try to rank for, based on what other videos are already up on.

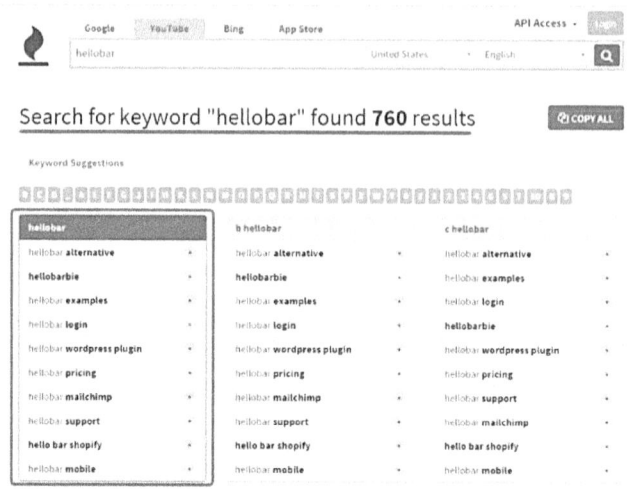

These are good suggestions to put in the tags. When there are specific phrases, I can put those in the description as well.

So now that I have got *hellobar* up, I can see exactly what some of the top keywords are for it: *hellobar examples, hellobar login, hellobar wordpress plugin, hellobar support,* and *hello bar* separately, *hellobar mobile* and *hellobar alternative.*

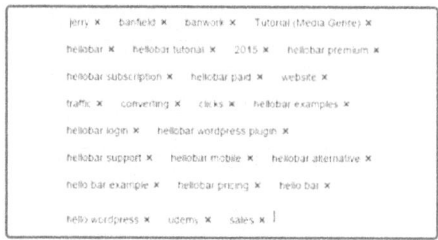

Now, I got all these different tags in and that will help me get the ideal amount of clicks on it.

Even though this may not perfectly relate in what my video is, it will help get people to click on it and watch it, because if no one clicks on my video and watches it, it is already useless to even have it uploaded. You want to tag as many related terms as you can and you want to tag things that are not as much common sense all the time either.

You want to make sure that you get your video in front of as many places as possible and give *YouTube* as many options for sharing your video as possible.

I don't have a thumbnail now for this and will add one later. I want to get this video published as it is taking a while to process.

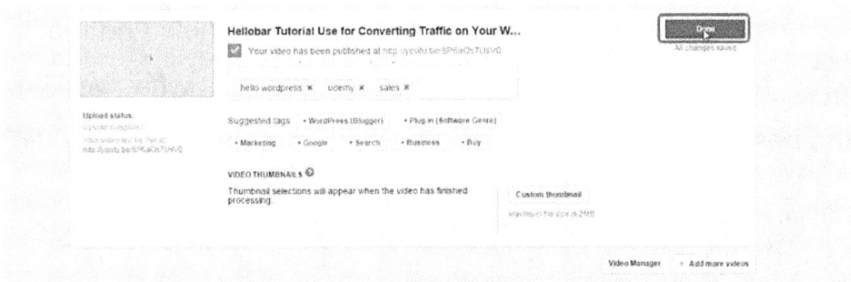

Thumbnails are important, but you can go back through and do a thumbnail any other time. My video is uploaded and then it is available on my channel now.

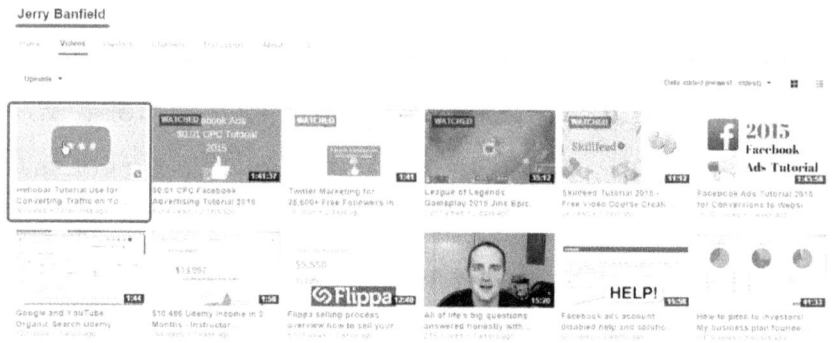

Even though there is no thumbnail, I have got the video up on my channel and I'm done with it. More importantly, when I go to upload a video, there isn't one video sitting there that hasn't been finished yet. So all I have to do is upload one video at the time.

I have got over *900* videos up on *YouTube* now and the way I have done that is one video at a time. It is what worked the best. You want to upload one video at a time like I just did.

Upload it and publish it. Get it up there.

You can always go back and edit things based on what's working, but what you don't want to do is to upload a bunch of videos at a time and then get stuck in this place where you have all these titles, descriptions and tags to do, and you don't want to do anything because you know you have got to go through and edit all those old videos and get them up.

So just do one video at a time, and you will have *900* videos up before you know it.

YouTube title optimization tips for *YouTube* search and *YouTube* suggested video

Optimizing your titles on *YouTube* is tricky to get just right because there are two key objectives you want to do. First you want to match your title exactly for search results as you type the suggested results up. This is often the easy way to figure out what you might want to rank on.

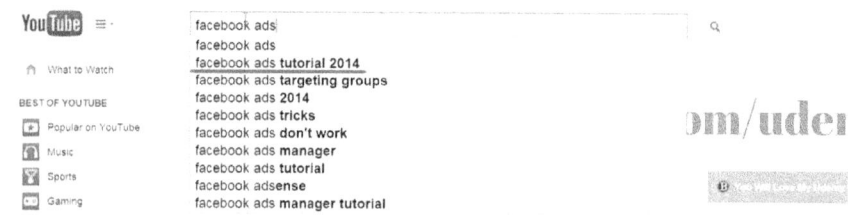

I'm in *Facebook* ads and I want to get on those very specific terms because I can always do more broad: *Facebook Ads tutorial* and then *2015*. I want to show up exactly on that term.

Here is what I have for the term: **Facebook Ads tutorial 2015**.

If you scroll down pass the ads, I have the first, second, and technically a third because that is my video someone else has uploaded, then the fourth and the fifth. I have utter domination on this term and that's what I want.

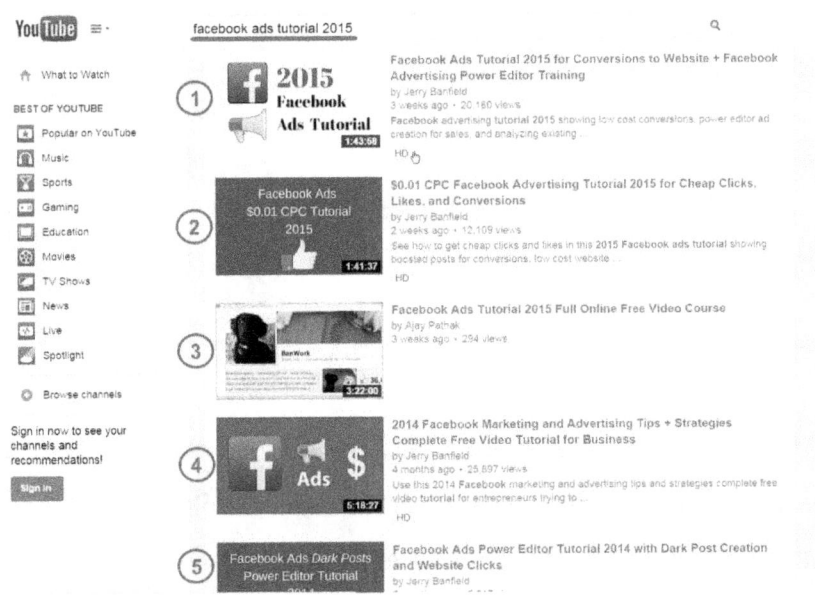

When someone searches for this term, they have almost no choice of anyone else to go except me. That's what you want and get with highly relevant recent terms in your title.

Now here is the challenge.

The challenge is to match these exact search terms with the most clickable suggested video terms. When you click on my video, what you get on the right side are suggested videos. You want to encourage people to click on those suggested videos too.

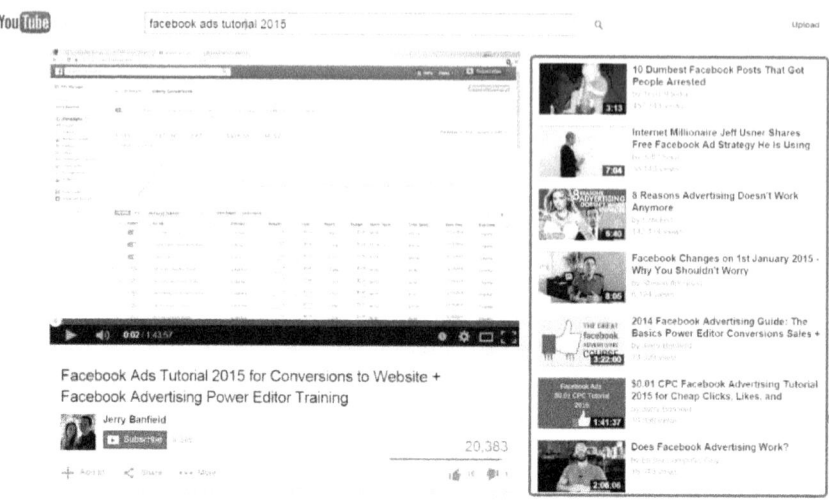

It is challenging to make a title that exactly matches the search results and then it is worth clicking on. So this video, both of these highlight what I have done to try and do both. I have put *"Facebook Ads tutorial 2015 for conversion to Website and Power Editor Training."* I have tried very hard to capture all kind of exact matches plus make my video worth clicking.

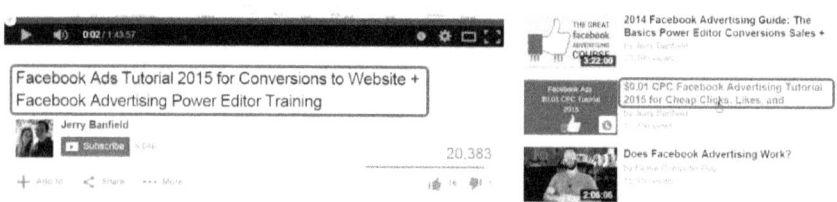

This is the same thing for this video at the right. What you can do is start out with something very attractive to click on like *$0.01 CPC*. That tends to do good to get clicks, but this video has also the actual words *"Facebook Advertising Tutorial 2015"* and it is trying to rank on a little bit farther out there.

So you have to just do your best to try to get the exact match terms you are trying to show up for and to get a really clickable title.

As you can see, *YouTube* thinks a few of these other videos will get clicked on suggested videos, this is another similar type of search ranking, but the value of having a title that gets clicked on is obvious. *YouTube* is showing the *"10 Dumbest Facebook Posts That Got People Arrested."*

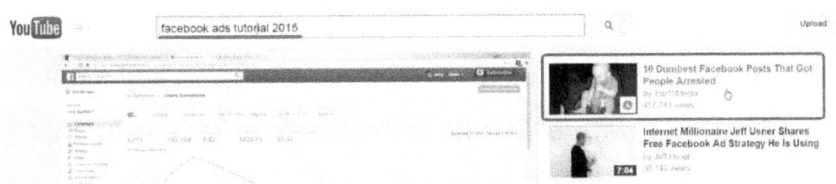

This video is not very likely to be exactly related to what I'm showing on my ads tutorial, but *YouTube* thinks people would click on this and is suggesting it.

That's the power of picking a title correctly and picking a good clickable title for suggested video, and you want to try and do both.

One way you can do both is to look at your analytics.

When you are in your **"traffic sources,"** look at the existing videos you already have and see what people are searching for.

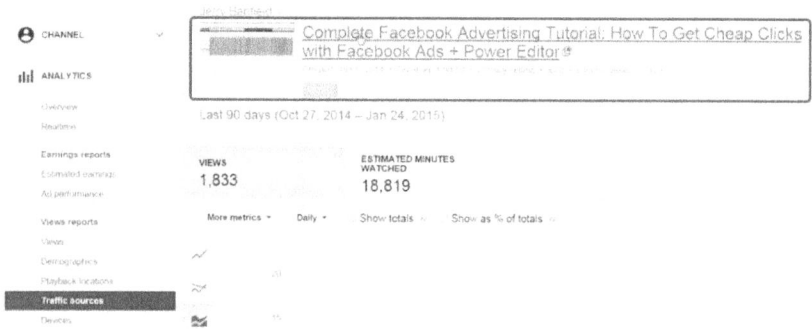

We are on my *"Complete Facebook Advertising Tutorial,"* video and this is how I figured out people were searching for *"Facebook Ads tutorial 2014."* In the *Traffic source* column, I found them searching for this term on this video.

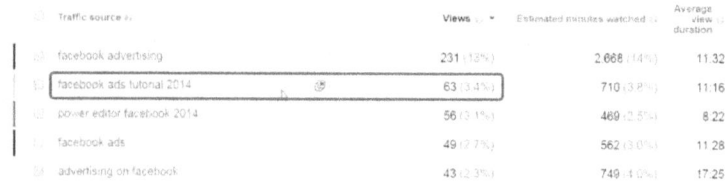

This is the same thing on this video, I have gone in and looked at the analytics, and then I optimized this video to get search results from that.

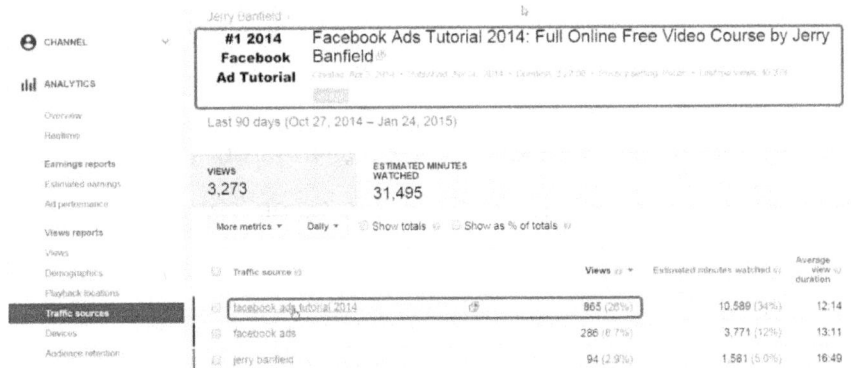

I'm getting search results from broad terms also, but I specifically went back and edited the title to put this exact term in: *"Facebook ads tutorial 2014."*

This video has done very well on suggested video because it is very clickable on suggested videos, and not as well on search because I'm only getting up on the terms *"Facebook ads"* and *"1 cent Facebook ads."*

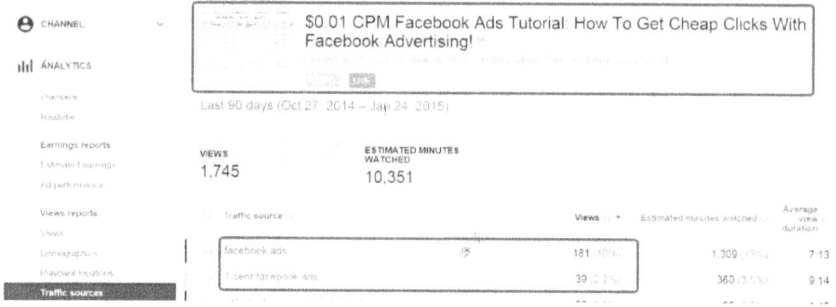

It might make sense to rename it to that, but this is working very well this way. While what you are doing is working well, you often don't want to mess with it too much in terms of breaking it.

If you have a title, a description and tags that are working very good, sometimes you risk losing more traffic.

The solution for that is always to go through and make new videos. That's exactly what I did with this one.

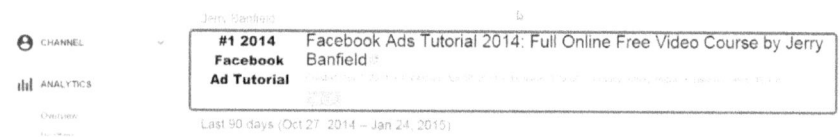

This video is working great on *"Facebook Ads tutorial"* for *2014*, so I made new videos to target *2015* instead of trying to edit this video and to getting those new search results.

I hope this detailed look at how to make a good title that both gets featured in search results and that gets featured in suggested video together, helps you to see exactly what you can do in order to maximize the return and *SEO* you get out of your *YouTube* videos.

YouTube tagging tutorial in depth for maximizing suggested video views

Now it is time to talk about tagging your *YouTube* videos successfully. What do you do to tag successfully? I will show you what I do, what other people do and the result. The objective of tags is to get views from *YouTube's* suggested video.

That's the primary objective of tags. *YouTube's* titles and descriptions do a lot for *YouTube's* search. Your tags can help *YouTube's* search, but the main objective is to get in those suggested videos.

This is where suggested videos are and this is one tagging strategy that you can use. It is narrow tagging. If you have got an established *YouTube* channel with a lot of viewers, lots of times you might want to just tag yourself.

When you look at the suggested videos below, you will notice that most of them are from the **Top 10 Media** channel.

Most of the videos showing are the same channel to start with and that's a very good thing because if you have a lot of traffic coming in already, when people go to suggested videos you want to keep those viewers on your channel.

However, I don't usually recommend this strategy because it limits your options greatly getting started. I do not do that strategy myself as I use a shotgun tagging strategy.

You will see on this *"Facebook ads"* video that's been very successful getting suggested views that I have put a bunch of different tags in it.

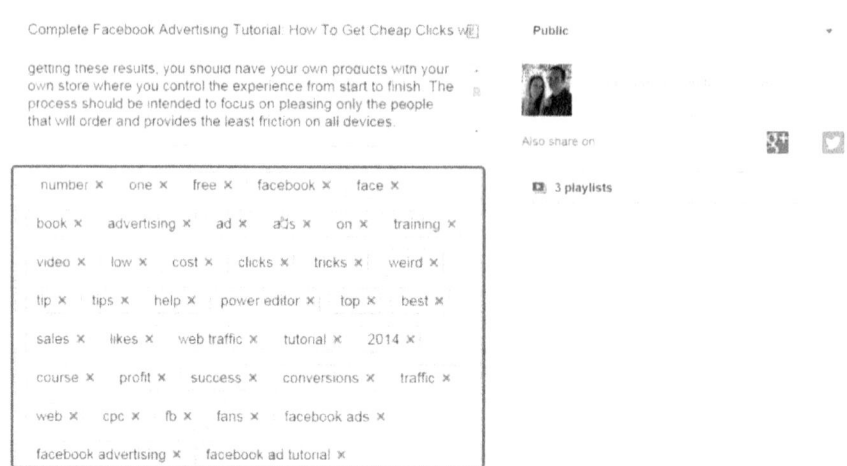

My video appears all over the place and if you go to the analytics, you can see the actual videos I'm getting views off of. I'm getting views off all kinds of other channels and my own, but the main video it got views off in the last 365 days is off someone else's channel.

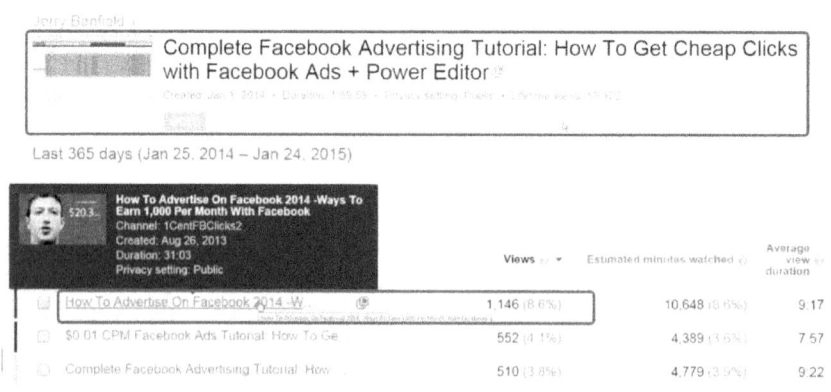

It means that I pulled a thousand views into my channel off their channel. That's what suggested video can do for you.

I'm looking through the *traffic source* and showing you, in order of most views, what suggested video views have come in, and this is telling me the referrer. Now, this second result, which is my own video, sent me views and that's good.

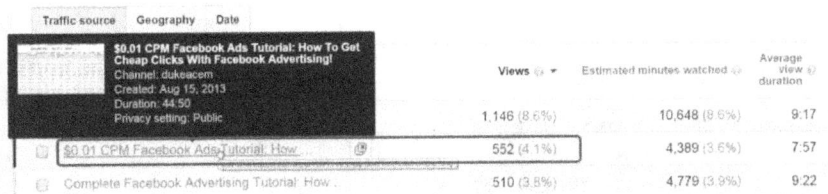

The third result is my own video and sent me more.

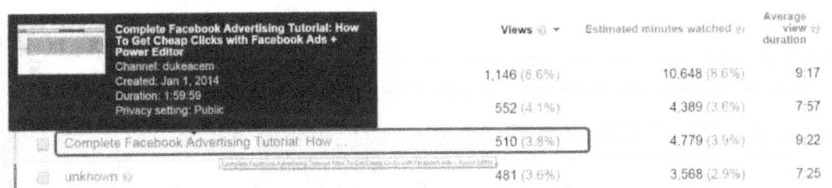

I want people consistently watching my channel.

Again, another *YouTube* channel sent me *426 YouTube* views to my one video.

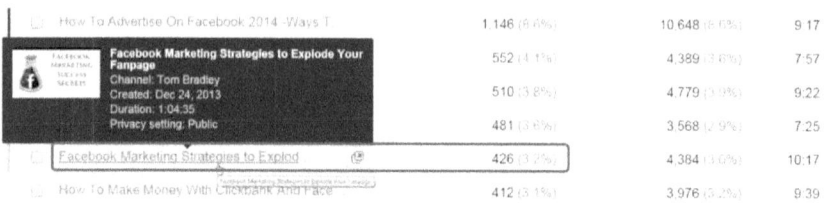

At a larger scale, this is what you want to do. You want to pull traffic off of other people's channels and that means though that you are allowing other channels to pull traffic off of you.

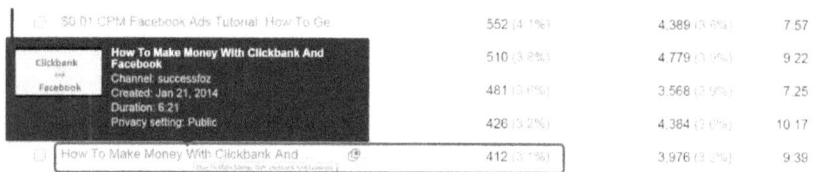

This is very cool to pull traffic off of other people's channels and if you look in my tags, I put a bunch of different tags to try and show up on all kinds of different videos.

If someone tags a video with *"advertising,"* my video has a chance to show up on it.

The best tags are more specific like *"Facebook advertising"* because whenever videos are tag with this term, then my video can show up with it. If you want to keep people on your channel you can create a tag which is just specific and that's secret. A tag that you are using that no one else uses.

I will show you the same thing on another video that I have done a little bit different strategy with. Again, this video is doing very well in suggested video, consistently getting an 8-minute view duration each, which is just about as good as search.

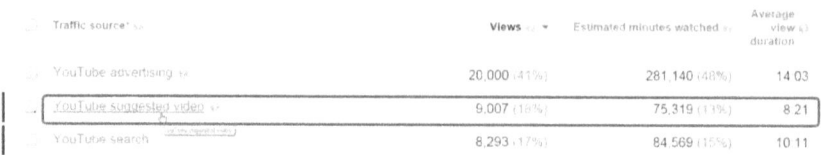

When I look at the details, I see another channel sending me views.

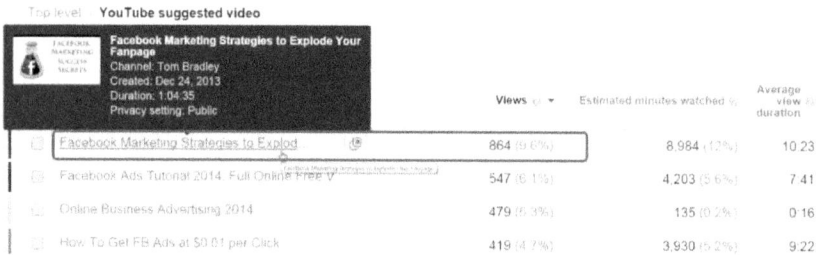

Then I'm getting views on my own videos and pulling views in from other videos and other channels. Now, take a look at how I have tagged this one. I have tagged it a little more intentionally to try to get traffic off of other people's channels.

I have intentionally matched *Life on fire TV* with what I see in my analytics. You can see then that I have got *LifeOnFireTV* right here sending me views on this video.

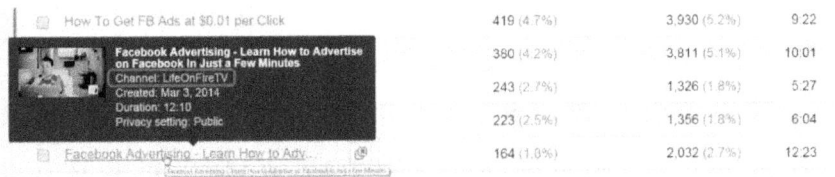

They are already sending me views on another video without tagging *LifeOnFireTV*. Do I necessarily need to tag *LifeOnFireTV*? No, not necessarily because I'm still getting views on all of these videos regardless of having tagged their channel or not. It can help sometimes though, but if you are going to do it, you want to make sure to tag the channels that are giving you the most views in your analytics and remove the ones that aren't.

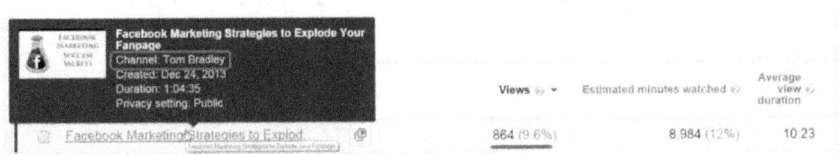

I can put in *Tom Bradley* because that is clearly giving me a lot of good views and I can intentionally target his videos, and take out tags that aren't working.

Getting tags done really well is an iterative process. You want to look at who is actually viewing your channel, and then optimize your tags so that you intentionally start targeting them. So from this, I might want *Facebook App Ninja* because I'm seeing a good amount of traffic come in from this guy.

So I put *"fbappsninja"* in the tags and then I can intentionally target his videos instead of getting in on simply related terms.

So now I have intentionally targeted his channel.

Then I can do the same thing with *"Facebook Mari."*

I already used the tag *"Mari Smith"* because she targets her videos like that, but then I can even add *"facebookmari"* for the exact channel.

At the same time, I can take out tags that are not sending me good things specifically.

That is how you just go through and iterate your tags over and over again until you get a good tagging strategy down. You remove tags that aren't doing anything and if you see a certain channel sending you good traffic, you add their tag.

The power of this is to intentionally target other people's channels and then shotgun approach the terms.

> advertising × facebook × fb × ads × on × #1 ×
> number × top × learn × how × learn how ×
> 2014 × tips × strategies × how to get ×
> cheap facebook ads × lifeonfiretv × keithkranc × moz ×
> how to start × facebook advertising ca... × ultimate ×
> guide × michelle pescosolido × jeff usner ×
> eli the computer guy × advanced × shopify ×
> mari smith × social media × experts × company ×
> business × teespring × spring × tutorial × free ×
> full × video × facebook ads × budget ×
> facebook advertising × tom bradley × fbappsninja ×
> facebookmari × robert davis ×

That way *YouTube* tries to share my video in lots of different places. It is a combination of just consistent effort going in and changing up your tags and matching them correctly with what's working.

I hope this *YouTube* tagging information helps you to more effectively tag your videos and get more suggested video views on your videos.

YouTube video description in depth. Long descriptions are way better!

Should you have a short or a long *YouTube* video description? The answer is that you want to go in depth. You want a laundry list of things in your *YouTube* description and here is why. This is a look at my videos by most views in the last year.

Top 10 Videos			
Video	Views	Estimated minutes watched	Total estimated earnings
Complete Facebook Advertising Tutorial: Ho...	56,528 (5.9%)	610,245 (6.6%)	$0.00 (0.0%)
Destiny Gameplay Xbox One Hunter Full Ga...	55,595 (5.8%)	603,158 (6.5%)	$0.00 (0.0%)
Facebook Ads Tutorial 2014: Full Online Free	49,378 (5.1%)	583,559 (6.3%)	$0.00 (0.0%)
Wolfenstein The New Order Gameplay Xbox...	42,305 (4.4%)	179,209 (2.5%)	$0.71 (1.8%)
$0.01 CPM Facebook Ads Tutorial: How To G...	37,876 (3.9%)	238,916 (3.4%)	$0.00 (0.0%)
How do you tell a girl you love her?	34,120 (3.5%)	23,999 (0.3%)	$12.38 (32%)

I have excluded these two video gaming ones and I have taken a look at the three top videos.

Complete Facebook Advertising Tutorial: How To Get Cheap Clicks with Facebook Ads + Power Editor

Last 365 days (Jan 25, 2014 – Jan 24, 2015)

So I click right here with you and then I will go to edit.

Now, take a look at this big long description.

The reason this works is because *YouTube* gets more data. *YouTube* can't actually see what's in your video, so it needs data. The only way *YouTube* knows what's in your video is by having text. The more text you have in the description, the more exact keywords you can show up on.

So for example if someone put in a long search term, a video like this is more likely to show up because there are tons of different terms in the actual description. This is one of my top videos in terms of views. So I will take you to another video.

#1 2014 Facebook Ad Tutorial

Take a look at this long description, but nearly not as long as the other one. I copied all kinds of terms that this video helps with and I wanted to show up on. It is like an extra place to use tags and it is actually better to write in exactly what you want to show up on and write it naturally. You just don't want to keyword spam, but if you can put it into sentence format like this, then you can count on getting good results.

Finally, here is one more of my videos and this one has more than *100,000* views on it.

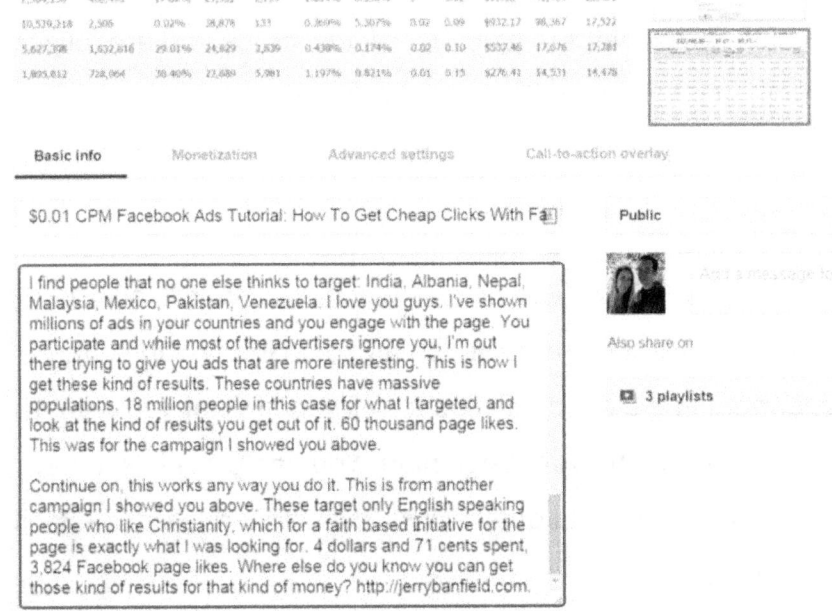

Look at the description on this one. Again, a long description with all kinds of individual words in it so that people can read the it and *YouTube* knows what exactly what to show up for.

In your description, you absolutely want to fill this entire box up, if possible, with natural writing related to what the video is. What I do with my newest videos now, I actually go in and use a transcription in the description so that what I'm talking about in the video is the description.

This is absolutely ideal for *YouTube SEO* because you are coming up all over the place for all the words you are talking about, and it is original content. They are my words and I didn't copy someone else's words and stick them in there. They are my actual words.

For *YouTube SEO*, and the description specifically, you absolutely want to get as much as you can. One thing that's important in the description is to reference what you want to show up for in the very beginning. You can put a link if you want, but you should put the first few words related to exactly what your title is.

You want people to click on your videos, so let's go to *YouTube* search and see how this actually shows up.

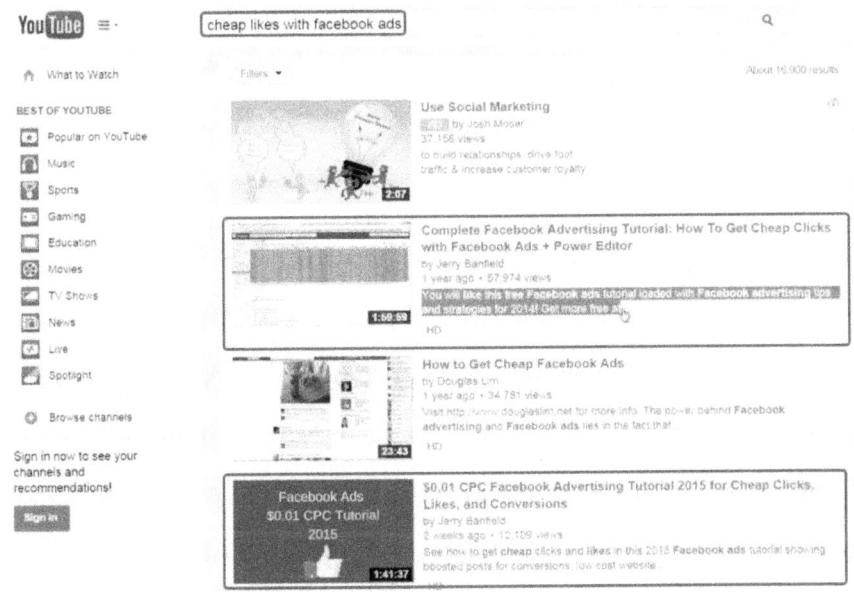

When I search for *"cheap likes with Facebook ads,"* you will see that my video comes up first on this, and then third and fourth. You can see that this strategy works too. This is a very exact term and my newest video using this is already up to third.

Here is exactly what you need to know about the description. In the description, you get this many characters that *YouTube* will give you. These characters are to sell clicks on the video and search.

That's the whole point.

You can do it with different things like a *URL*, but how often do you think people actually click that *URL* in the search description? It doesn't happen that often and on top of that if you put a *URL* that matches your search term, it will actually break it. You want to make sure that you put a sales pitch for why to click on the video in the first lines of the description.

This video above is ranking number one and you can see exactly what's going on with it: *"You will like this free Facebook ads tutorial loaded with Facebook advertising tips and strategies for 2014!"* The search terms are in bold: *like, Facebook ads, Facebook advertising tips* for exact match keywords.

This is the same thing for the other videos down the page. *Cheap, likes* and *Facebook ads* are bold for these exact terms.

The last video also has these terms: *Cheap, likes,* and *Facebook ads.*

All of this very clearly sell why the video should be clicked on and notice that the second result below starts off with a *visit link for more info.* That's not as good as converting clicks because it starts off talking about you first.

You want to sell why to click on the video first. If you want to throw a link in the description, you can put it back here.

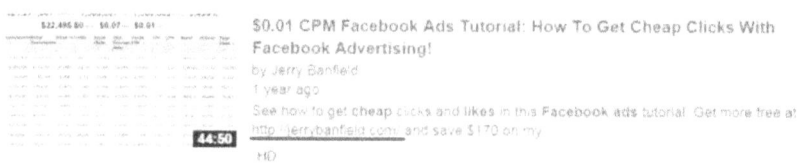

You can find out exactly how many characters are showing if you can just copy it…

And then paste it in *MS Word*.

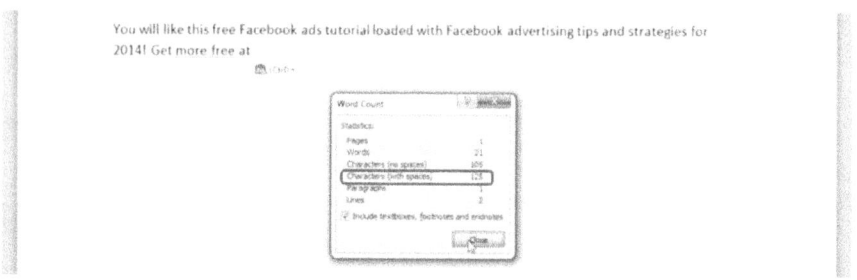

The count is *125* characters with spaces.

That's what *YouTube* will give you and these characters at the beginning of the description are the most important. Write these first *125* characters of your description having in mind that it is what will show up in search results.

You should put as much effort writing these first *125* characters as for the entire rest of the description. It should match your title closely and match your main search results closely.

You want to optimize the very beginning of the description to get clicks and if you are going to put a *URL* in it, put it in the very end of those *125* characters, not in the beginning.

Then you want a deep list, either in plain writing or you can put it in exact keywords you want to show up on, to get people to see those in search.

Before I close this section, find below the character limits for the title, tags and description.

YouTube title, tags and description character limits.

YouTube title: 100 characters.

YouTube tags: 500 characters.

YouTube description: 5,000 characters.

I hope this section for doing your description is helpful.

YouTube keyword tool for expanding your description and making a better title

Keyword research on *YouTube* is much easier today. You can just find about any keyword tool to use. Here is one I use: *keywordtool.io*. It has *Google*, *YouTube* and *Bing*.

What I do is I take a look at the keywords I'm working on. My title is *"How to Stop Hurrying and Feel This Moment!"*

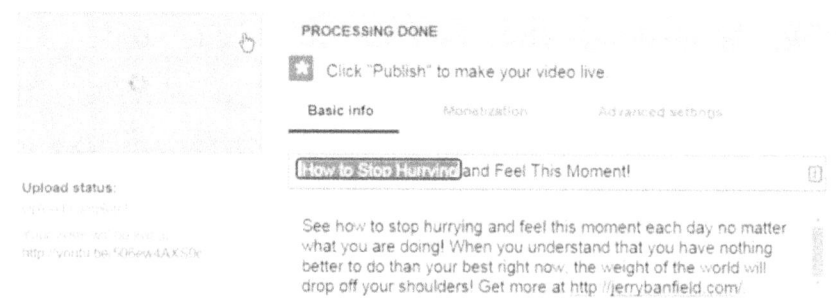

So I put in "how to stop hurrying," which is the beginning of my title for my new video and see what other keywords there are related to this that come up on *YouTube*.

These are the results.

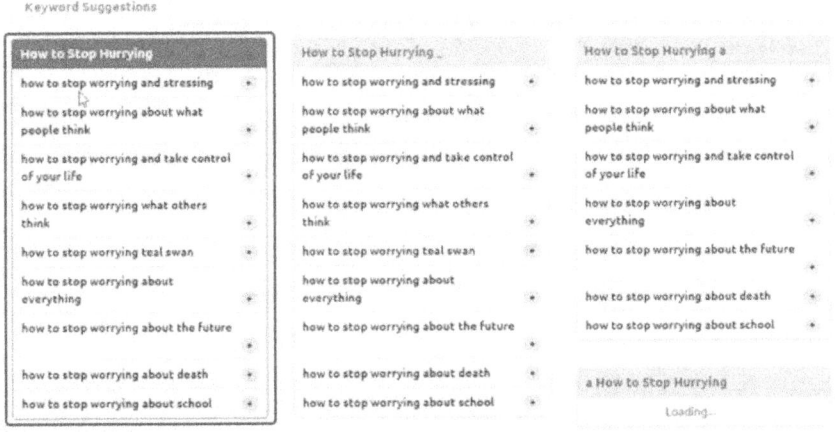

I can use *"How to Stop Worrying and Stressing,"* as that looks like a good keyword. What I will do is take away the exact keywords out *"How to Stop Worrying"* and retitle to *"How to Stop Hurrying, How to Stop Worrying and How to Feel This Moment."*

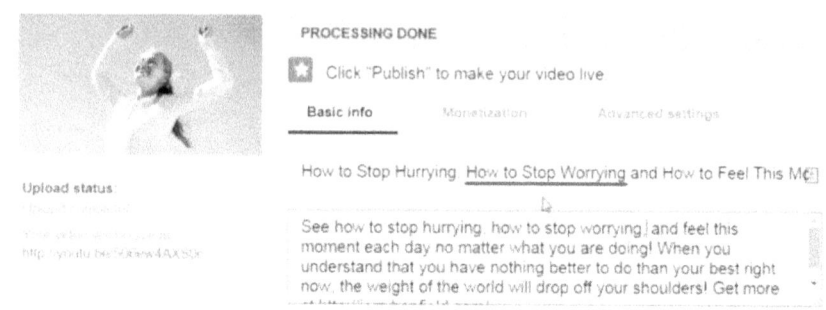

Now I have got several different phrases in the title that I can put in the description area and the tags.

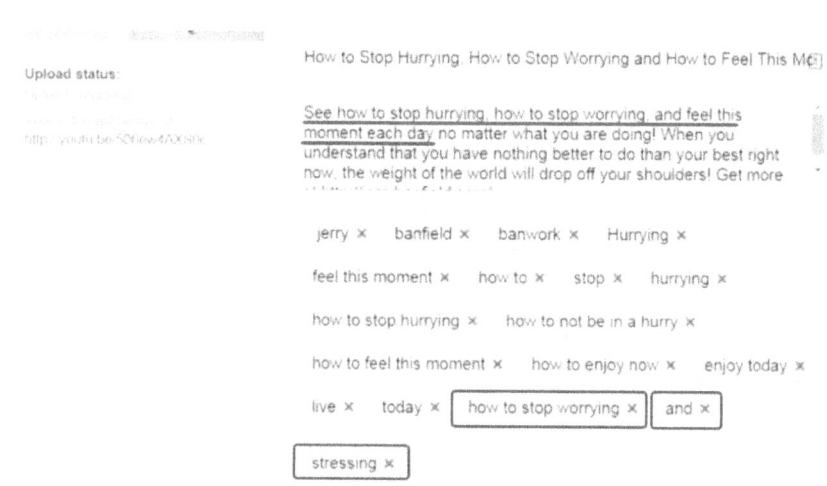

I have *"How to Stop Hurrying"* as the title, but as it turns out *"How to Stop Worrying"* is much more of an active keyword on *YouTube* based on the title, so I can now show up for all of these and I can put in the entire keyword too. I can also just put in things like *"and"* then *"stressing"* to shorten up the actual keywords I use.

I can use tags like: *"what others think,"* to get all those individual keywords in and other key-phrase endings: *about the future, about everything, about death* and *about school.*

I got now a much stronger set of keywords than I had in the original video with just *"How to Stop Worrying,"* and I could even change the order of the words in the title like this.

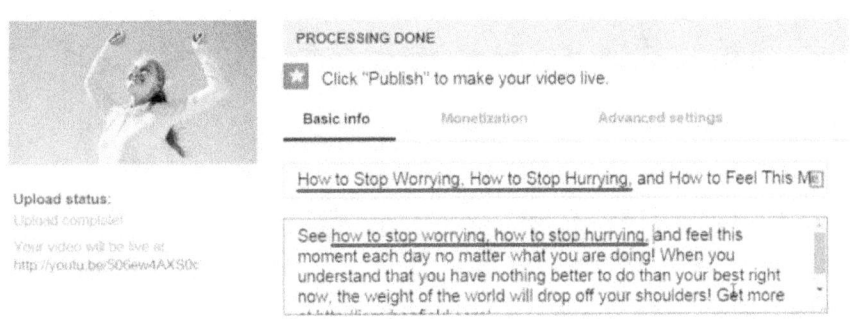

"How to Stop Worrying" is now first and *"How to Stop Hurrying"* second in the title and description, so that it is based more on what people are searching for. Now it is a much better video title and description.

What I can also do is grab all these terms in Keyword Tool IO and paste them at the end of the description like this.

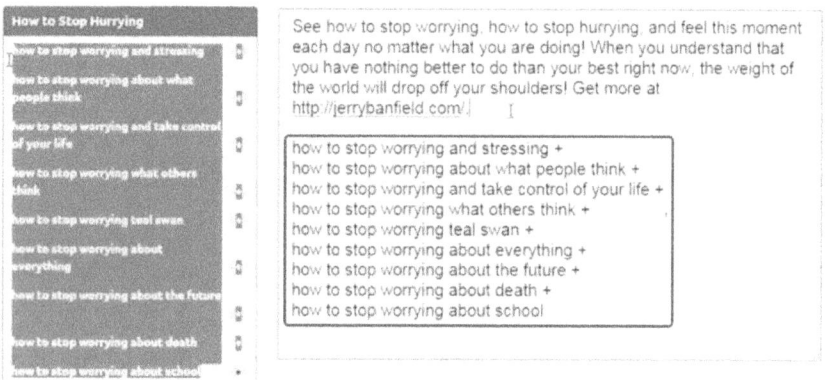

I have then to modify it a bit to make it more readable. I can say that all these questions are answered like this.

I probably don't want to put something totally irrelevant in there, so I cut one of these out.

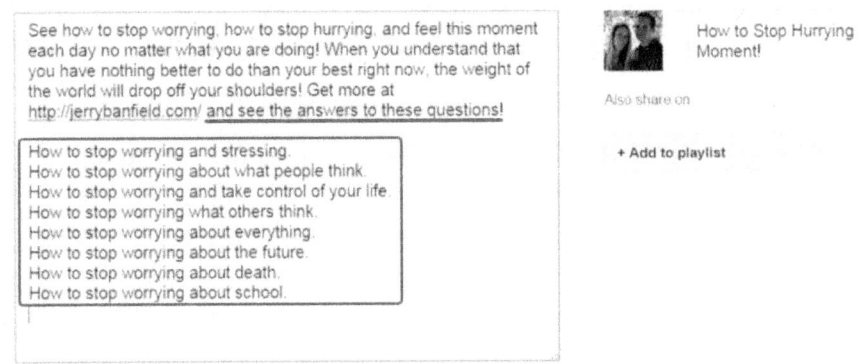

I correct them so that it looks like regular language and I can easily put a capital *"H"* at the beginning of each line.

All of these exact terms will come up in the search and *YouTube* knows now that this video deals with all of these basic subjects. I can go further then with *"Stop Worrying"* as the exact search results and see what comes back.

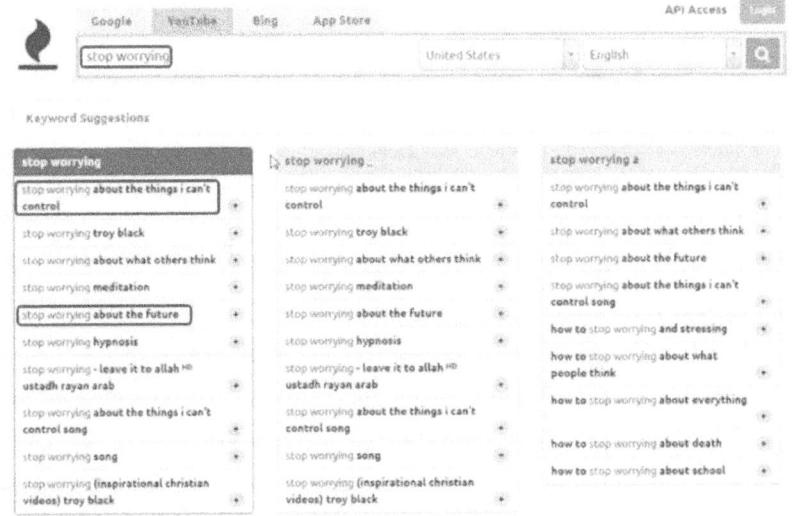

Then I can expand my description even more with phrases like *"stop worrying about things I can't control"* and *"stop worrying about the future,"* and make sentences like this.

I can continually go down in the keyword tool and grab more phrases relevant to my video and add them in my description. Now this description has got a nice set of keywords in it and I can even do something like *"Feel this moment,"* which is in the title, so that I got extra keywords.

Descriptions are the only thing *YouTube* has in order to figure out exactly what's in your video, so what I do is give *YouTube* as much data as to what is actually included in my video. Then later on, I can get actual video transcriptions in, so all what I say is included.

I also conveniently used the phrase *"feel this moment"* because that is an existing *Pitbull* song. I can tag it and when people are watching this video with the song, they are liable to be wanting to figure out how to *stop worrying* or *stop hurrying,* and then give me some suggested video views.

That's how you use your exact search terms to take advantage of what people are actually watching, and then you can extend with terms like: *"Feel this moment for life."*

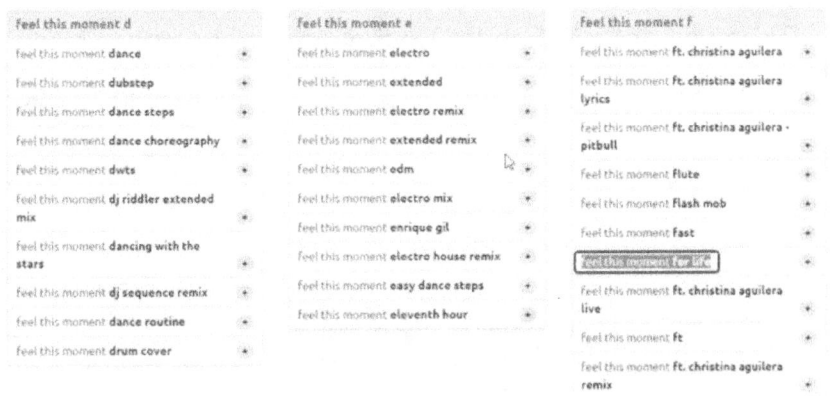

That's one more line in your description, *"How to feel this moment for life,"* and you can just continue to build up like that.

The idea is to take advantage of existing terms that people are watching on *YouTube* by using them in the title, and then you get a good list of questions your video answers.

When people make the exact search terms for what your video talks about, you are covered. You put these terms in tags and individual words.

Then you get a thumbnail up that encourages people to click on and you can always change it later if it doesn't work good.

You hit **Publish** and you are done!

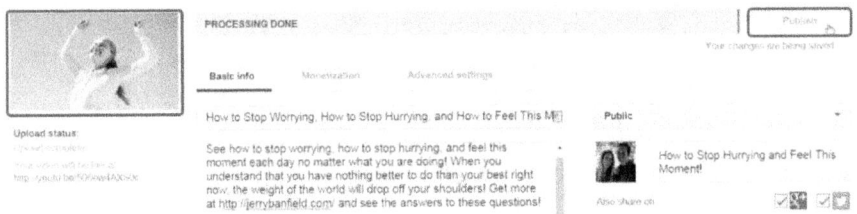

I hope this has been helpful for you in seeing a simple way that you can go grab some more keywords to put on your *YouTube* videos.

Proof these *YouTube* strategies are working rapidly

How did it actually work out for me showing you exactly in the previous sections what I did on optimizing my own channel? Here is exactly what's happened.

When I made my *YouTube* course (*jerrybanfield.com/product/youtube/*), it encouraged me to go through and apply the things I'm showing you more thoroughly on my channel. One of the areas I have shown was optimizing keywords. Look how huge of an impact this has made on my channel already.

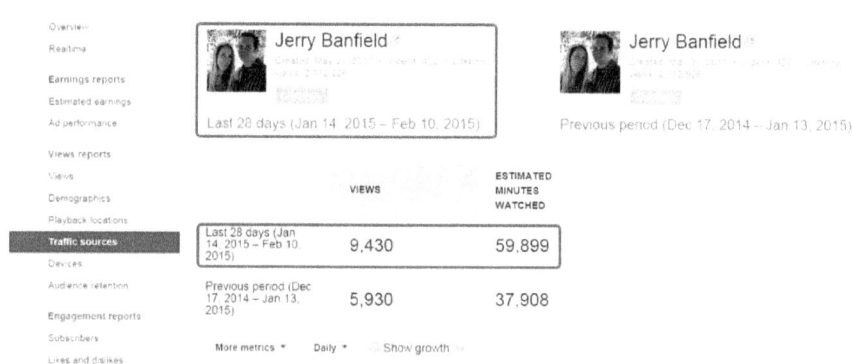

I'm doing a comparison between the last *28* days and the previous *28* days period, when I have applied what I have shown you.

These results are for suggested video only view. The suggested video is one primary method of discovery, and one that I focused on optimizing, especially when I talked to you about adding a secret tag to increase the suggested videos views and optimizing keywords.

Look at the amount of increase in these views.

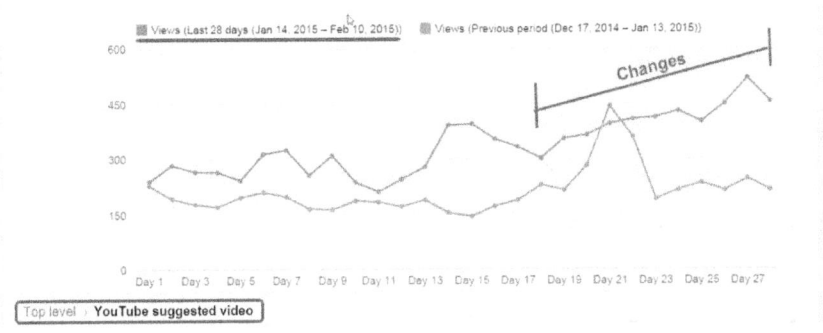

You'll note that it has been a consistent increase and this is where I made some of the changes, especially in this last few days on the blue line. This is when I made some of these changes and then I have seen huge improvements.

The first result is from a new video altogether, but what you'll notice is that my views are going up on nearly all of the videos.

Traffic source / Compare by rank	Views	Estimated minutes watched	Average view duration
$0.01 CPC Facebook Advertising Tutorial 2015...			
Last 28 days (Jan 14, 2015 – Feb 10, 2015)	233 (2.5%)	1,093 (1.8%)	4:41
Previous period (Dec 17, 2014 – Jan 13, 2015)	11 (0.2%)	126 (0.3%)	11:24
Facebook Marketing + Advertising Tutorial for B...			
Last 28 days (Jan 14, 2015 – Feb 10, 2015)	211 (2.2%)	1,161 (1.9%)	5:30
Previous period (Dec 17, 2014 – Jan 13, 2015)	153 (2.6%)	1,717 (4.5%)	11:13
Facebook Ads Tutorial 2015 for Conversions to...			
Last 28 days (Jan 14, 2015 – Feb 10, 2015)	193 (2.0%)	1,292 (2.2%)	6:41
Previous period (Dec 17, 2014 – Jan 13, 2015)	23 (0.4%)	229 (0.6%)	9:58
How To Get FB Ads at $0.01 per Click			
Last 28 days (Jan 14, 2015 – Feb 10, 2015)	181 (1.9%)	2,244 (3.7%)	12:23
Previous period (Dec 17, 2014 – Jan 13, 2015)	45 (0.8%)	265 (0.7%)	5:53
Beginners Guide to Facebook through this Vide...			
Last 28 days (Jan 14, 2015 – Feb 10, 2015)	159 (1.7%)	1,262 (2.1%)	7:56
Previous period (Dec 17, 2014 – Jan 13, 2015)	2 (0.0%)	2 (0.0%)	1:09

I'm pulling a lot more suggested video views off of that video with the secret tag.

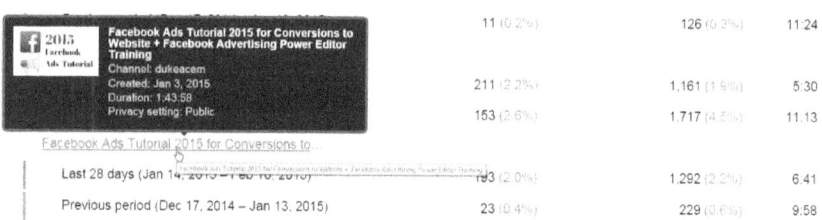

The existing videos I'm doing are pulling more off of other videos. This is a nice video they made and I'm getting tons of suggested views from it.

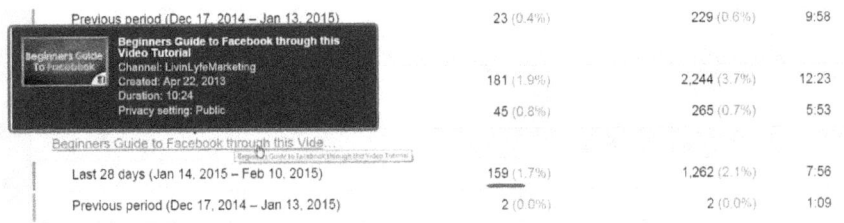

I'm getting more views out of the videos I already was getting views from.

This video dropped a little, but my minutes watched on it actually went up on average.

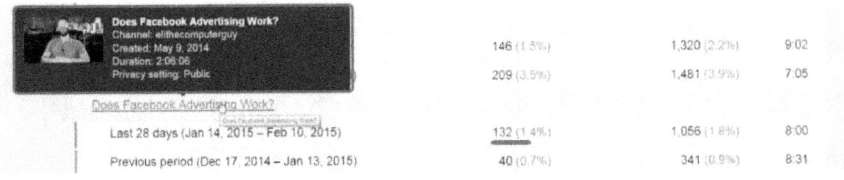

On this one especially, where I showed you how I found what keywords he was using, and put them exactly in on my video you will notice a huge growth.

I have the same improvement for this *"Facebook advertising"* video. I have nearly doubled on this one just from a few days of applying the new tags.

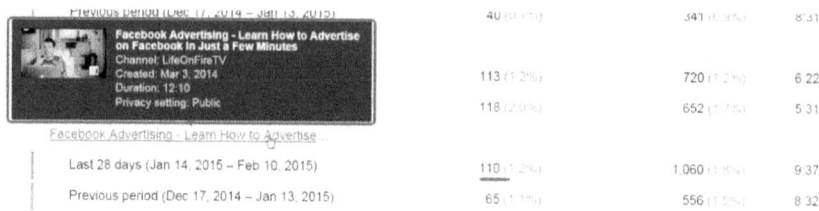

Huge increase in the amount of views for the *"Facebook Marketing"* video too.

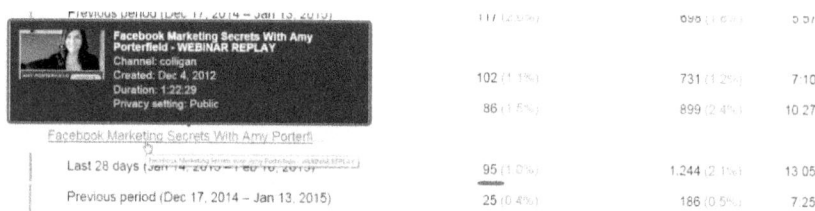

What I'm sharing with you in this section is proof that what I'm doing in the course of even making my *YouTube* course and further putting effort and time on my *YouTube* channel is working very well for me.

It is all about putting the right effort in the right places. If you do the things I'm showing in this chapter, you can get these same kinds of results.

	VIEWS	ESTIMATED MINUTES WATCHED
Last 28 days (Jan 14, 2015 – Feb 10, 2015)	9,430	59,899
Previous period (Dec 17, 2014 – Jan 13, 2015)	5,930	37,908

I hope that you have the same opportunity to get the same results.

CHAPTER 8

YouTube viral video launch process

How can you get a video go viral and compete with big channels? If you want an answer to this, this chapter is for you.

In this first section, I will show you a *YouTube viral video creation fast tutorial and overview* on how I launched my new gaming video "Call of Duty Advanced Warfare Exo Zombies."

What you want is to get results fast and this is my *YouTube viral video launch day 2 reviewing the ad campaign and initial views*.

What happened to this video after a year? See the *results of this video a year later. This made my next viral video happen* and this time I got more than a million organic views.

Read on…

YouTube viral video creation fast tutorial and overview

Do you want to see how to make a viral video on *YouTube* in a very hot and trending topic from start to finish? Here is exactly how to do that. I'm doing it right now on the new *"Call of Duty Advanced Warfare Exo Zombies."*

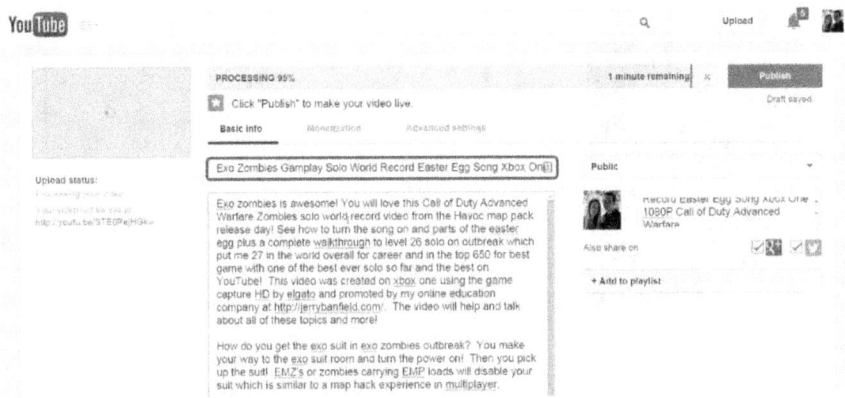

I'm putting my video up, which is about an hour long. I have gone through and have done everything on it to give you a little bit of background of what I mean.

Here are two examples on when I did this before. I mainly just did it to test out and see if I could do it.

The first one is *"Wolfenstein The New Order Gameplay XBOX One."* I got it right up there in *YouTube* search in second position for this very competitive term, and it has the lowest amount of views compared to the other videos in the top 5. This video is up against heavy hitters.

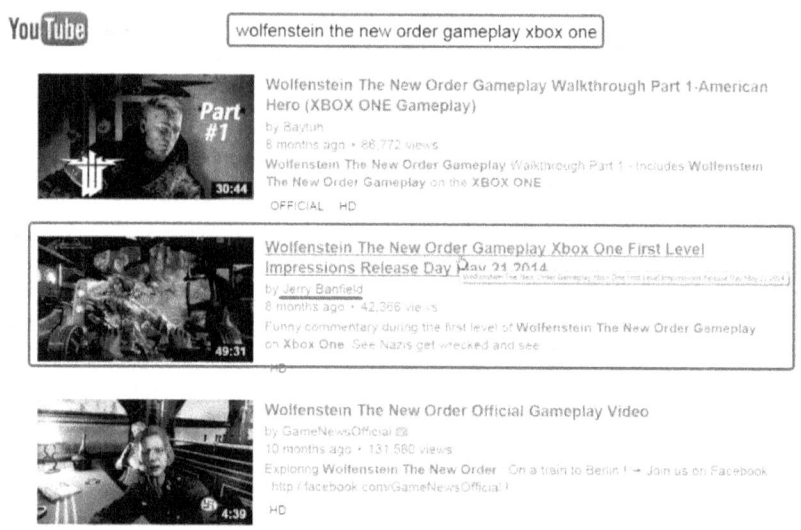

The second one is *"Destiny XBOX One"* and I managed to get it in top position in *YouTube* search for this term: *Destiny xbox one gameplay review.*

The Complete YouTube Book

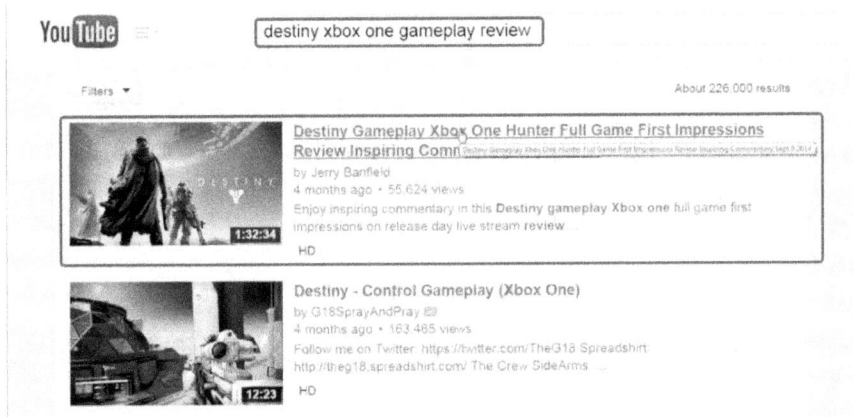

My video went viral, it got a bunch of free views right away, and I got thousands of views in total.

You can use this same things I'm showing you in this section to do this on any video game, trending topic or niche you want to get into on *YouTube*. If you are trying to do something timely, this is exactly perfect for it, but this will work even better if you have evergreen content.

Here is what I did.

I first filmed the video and I'm uploading it now.

You want to do that as well ahead of time as you can plan if you are doing something that may require repeat filming like a video game. I film all of my different shots individually so I made each game individually with no commentary.

Then I recorded the commentary with my *iRig HD* microphone while I watched the recording in *Camtasia Studio*.

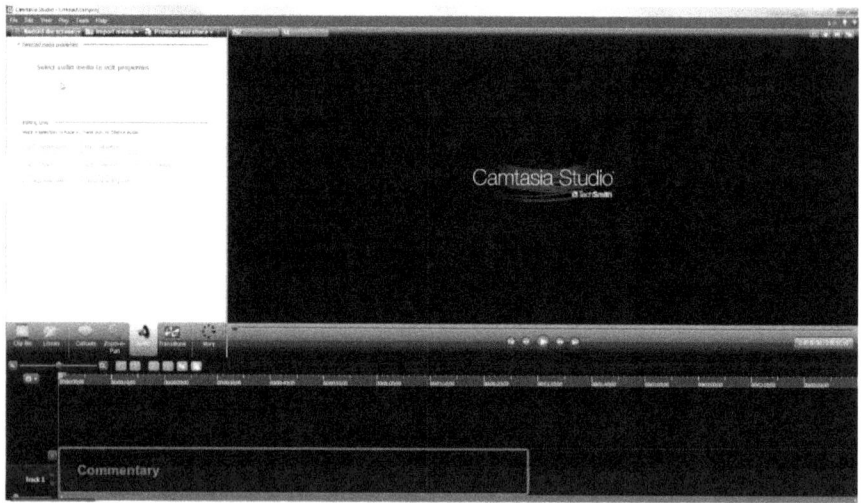

Then I dropped the audio in right on the timeline, saved it together with the video, and then uploaded it to *YouTube*.

I uploaded it to *YouTube* with all the keywords that I'm planning to put in the title including spelling *"gameplay"* properly. I put that as the file name which helps maximize *SEO*. I then went through and wrote a hell of a description, and tried to both write it useful and keyword stuffed with everything related to this video, answering very specific questions in the video, so that the description is useful all by itself.

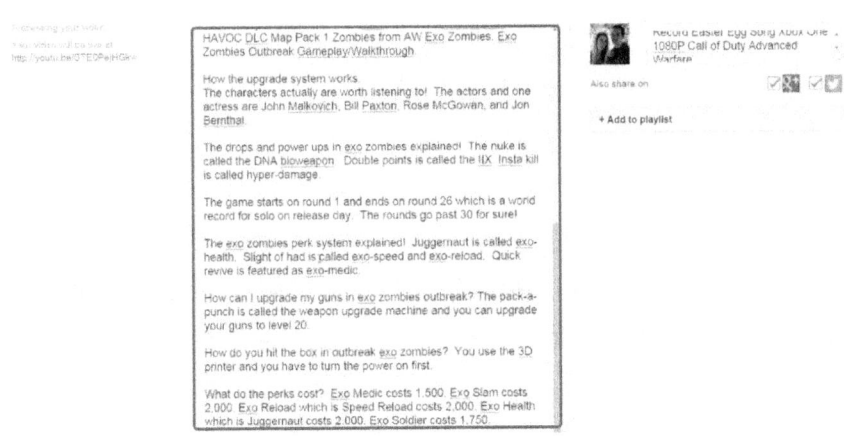

It has got a lot of niche keywords in it: if people search for who are the actors in the new *Zombie DLC map*, I have got that, if they search for very specific terms, my video has that. So *YouTube* is likely to pull it up more often.

What I can do that I haven't done yet is to actually include all of my links at the bottom of it. I can go to another window, go over to my existing home channel video and then copy the links that I have already done in another video.

I have already got some good links I can just grab and paste at the bottom down here because the video should have good links in on it.

I then took out a couple of irrelevant links and the *"subscribe to my YouTube channel"* is in down here too. I have got good links in at the bottom with several to my website and to my channel with a *Subscribe* button.

After doing all that, then I have shared it on social media when it went live. I have also got a custom thumbnail down here for it too, so that it will have a thumbnail that sticks out and is very noticeable.

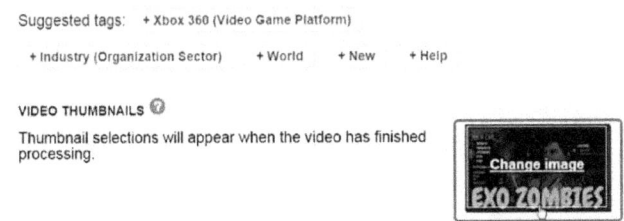

Just a couple of words on it *"Exo Zombies"* with one of the actual characters from it.

I went kitchen sink on the tags, I dumped all of the exact specific tags and I put in the relevant games, the relevant video game systems and related things. Especially if you can throw a little short tag in sometimes, we search for *WR* instead of *World Record* and that's very helpful.

```
Call Of Duty: Advanced...  ×    Xbox One (Video Gam...  ×
Video Game (Industry)  ×    exo zombies  ×
Xbox (Video Game Plat...  ×    1080p  ×    world record  ×
dukeacem  ×    easter egg  ×    tutorial  ×
exo zombies gameplay  ×    walkthrough  ×    world record  ×
wr  ×    tips  ×    tricks  ×    solo  ×    single player  ×    review  ×
mode  ×    official  ×    dlc  ×    xbox  ×    one  ×    xbox one  ×
exo zombies mode  ×    cod  ×    havoc  ×    reaction  ×
cod aw exo zombies  ×    exo zombies easter egg  ×    release  ×
exo zombies advanced...  ×    Call Of Duty (Video Ga...  ×
exo  ×    zombies  ×
```

I have uploaded the video and I have got it all up here. Then, I'm creating ads for it and launching it live.

YouTube viral video launch day 2 reviewing the ad campaign and initial views

Here is a review of the initial results of what I have done after showing you how I set up this video in the last section. After one day, the video has got *35,000* views mostly from ads, but thousands of organic views already. I have twenty-two likes on it and zero dislikes.

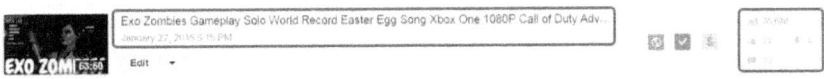

I'm very grateful because that's really good stats for a video getting started. I also have comments on it sharing that it is one of the only good videos on the topic. That's awesome, I'm grateful that the fans have received it that way. I have been ambitious and I have been taking a bit of a risk to put this video out there. I will get high enough now to rank organically and it probably hasn't had much time to get organic traffic because the ads just went up in the middle of the night.

So if you see, I have spent *$579* advertising this video already and I turned the budget down to *$50* a day from *$250* a day.

Campaign	Status	Budget	Views	Avg. CPV	Video played to: 25% / 50% / 75% / 100%	Total cost
Evil zombies	Serving	$50.00/day	33,710	$0.02	26% / 18% / 14% / 13%	$579.37
$0.01 CPC Facebook Ads 2015	(unclear)	$10.00/day	12,372	$0.02	14% / 9% / 7% / 6%	$209.98
Udemy Money	Serving	$10.00/day	2,023	$0.02	32% / 25% / 19% / 17%	$34.95

YouTube ads put *33,000* of those views on it and dumped a ton of minutes watched into it. *13%* of viewers watched all *50* minutes of the video. So, you know I have got an average watch time of probably close to *10* minutes on the video, which is really good. That's how it will really rank high. The video has got around *2,000* organic views already and considering the ads didn't get up there probably until the middle of the night, the real opportunity to see how it performs starts today.

I know this is scary, you might think, *"Oh my God! I wouldn't spend that,"* but I can tell you that if you want to get yourself out there, it involves taking risks sometimes. If you are trying to get to be a big journalist or you are just trying to get some recognition, or you want to get paid to play video games, you have got to put yourself out there.

If you are trying to get your brand noticed and if there is a timely opportunity you have got to go for it. Sometimes that might mean spending *$500* on *YouTube* ads to push your video up high enough in the search results to give you a chance.

What I have done is to get my video in the door. It gets it in with all of the biggest channels in the world on the topic it is up on. Now, it is as if I have got my video in the ring. I can see how it will stand up and I did the same thing for lots of my other videos.

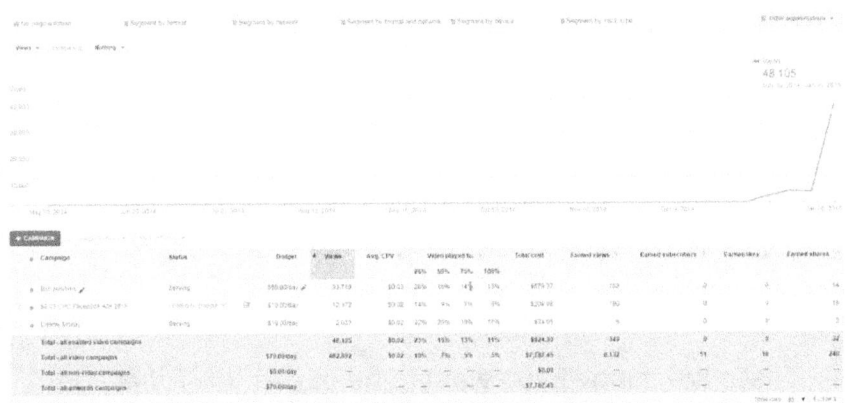

I learn and keep going. So this is an iterative process where I have spent more each time. On the other videos I spent maybe *$300* or *$400* and then on the first one I spent a couple of hundred. I consistently scale it up a little bit as I learned to make better videos based on feedback and the learning is very valuable in this.

You might think, well that's crazy, you only spent *$200* so far on your *"Facebook ads"* video and the thing with this is that

I'm continually spending money on this video. I'm going to leave that ad for a lot longer whereas the *zombies* video is mostly done. I'd probably turn the ad off tomorrow or the day after. I have spent most of the money upfront to get it ranked high.

Doing this kind of things are giving me the best chance to continue to grow and build an exceptional *YouTube* channel and there is alway risk involved in the things you do.

A guy I worked with named *Jordan*, started his business by buying several thousand dollars of websites on *Flippa*. He had a very successful business running *Adsense* websites and now he is changing to a different business model.

That's the thing, if you want to be big on *YouTube*, you have got to start out with ads today because there are too many other channels that are already big that would block you out for ever being seen, especially in the video gaming world.

So I hope this has been inspirational and useful for you. I like to show that I lead by example in everything. I would not ever tell you to do something, I wouldn't do myself. What I'm sharing with you here is what I'm doing that's working and how that's progressing.

I hope this is helpful for you in seeing what your best chances to get a video in the YouTube organic search rankings are.

Results of this video a year later. This made my next viral video happen!

I showed you how I launched this video on *YouTube* in the first section of this chapter, and showed you my results on day two. In this section I am showing you my results after over a year later since I released this video and first talked about it.

These are the results I got from this video.

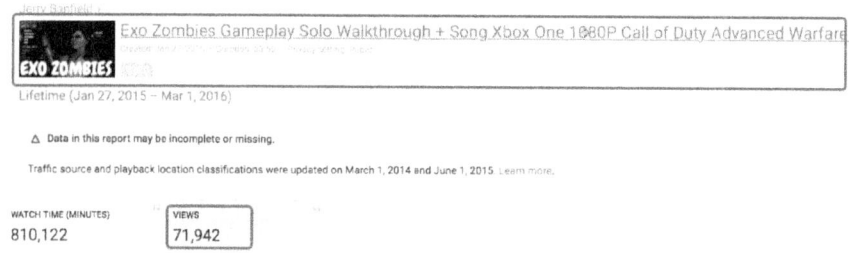

Seventy-one thousand views in total.

I go over to the subscribers section and you can see that I have got *74* subscribers in total, *69* net with *5* who unsubscribed and left.

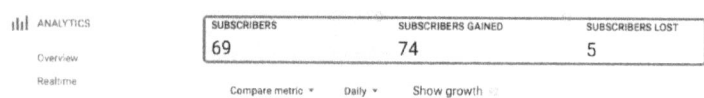

If I go on the *traffic sources* for this video, by views, you can see that most of the views came in initially from this ad; however, I have got a lot of organic views down there.

Watch time (minutes)		Views	Average view duration	Average percentage viewed
600,966 (74%)	YouTube Ad	38,365 (53%)	15:39	29'
161,055 (20%)	YouTube Search	27,632 (38%)	5:49	11'
27,225 (3.4%)		2,807 (3.9%)	9:41	18'
7,484 (0.9%)		944 (1.3%)	7:55	15'
4,865 (0.6%)	Other organic views	1,035 (1.4%)		
2,970 (0.4%)		322 (0.4%)		
1,847 (0.2%)		255 (0.4%)		
1,794 (0.2%)		259 (0.4%)		

I have *38,365* views from Ads and *27,632* views from *YouTube* search out of *71,942* in total. *33,577* views came for free and these free views are very valuable.

Now, you might say, *"Well that's not that great, you spent some money on ads, and then you get this amount of views on it."* Or you might say, *"Wow! I never had a video with that many views."*

I don't know what you might say about it, what I do know is that this same viral video launch process, this exact same process I used for this video, taught me how to make my next video.

Let me show you, I did this again on a different subject and the results are absolutely unbelievable.

This is a *Complete Hacking* course, beginner to advanced, and you notice that I did it just a few months after the zombies video, repeated the same process successfully to a video on the right subject that people really need.

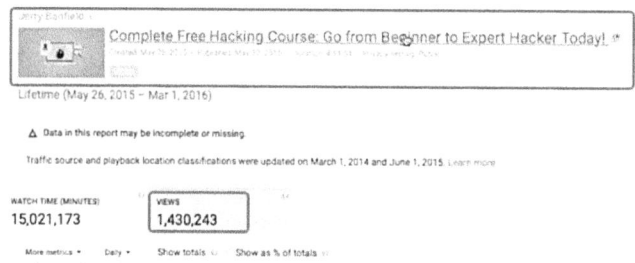

I have 1.4 million views on this video.

I ran a lot of ads in the beginning, but still today I get tons of organic traffic on this video.

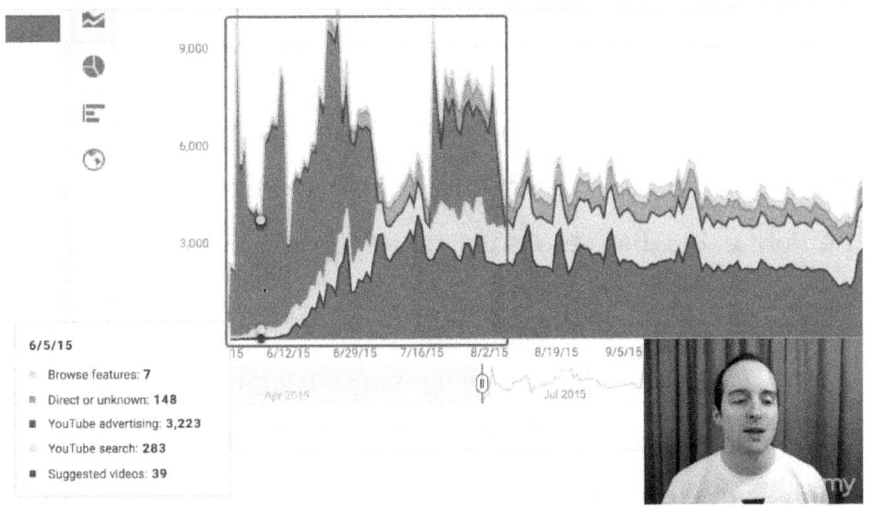

I show you the stats in detail now.

YouTube advertising has *233,658* views only for a total of *1,430,243* views.

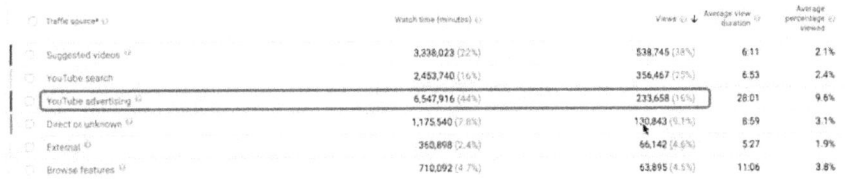

Suggested videos and *YouTube* search are bringing up the most views.

They are coming from everywhere, from *Direct or Unknown* and from *External*, which is often *Google* search.

That's a total of *1,196,585* organic views which are free.

What you do on *YouTube* is continually learn to apply the strategies and the system I give you, then when you do it with the right video, the results will be amazing.

The gaming video I put up was a good gaming video, but the difference with this *"Hacking"* video is that it gives a ton of helpful information, this is an educational 5-hour video that I did the same strategies on.

If you do this on the right subject, you can get incredible results. I have also made thousands of sales on *Udemy* and I have also given two other co-instructors the chance to teach full time on *Udemy* from using this video to sell the course.

The key in doing all of this is doing it on the right video and the only way to know if you have the right video is just to do this repeatedly across your videos that you think might be the right videos. At some point, you land on one that definitely is the right video, one that has a lot of traffic, one that you have done a really good job on.

CHAPTER 9

YouTube analytics are the secret to optimizing your *YouTube* channel for success!

This is a very important chapter if you want to learn how to improve your *YouTube* channel results based on your *Analytics*.

In the first section I will give you an <u>introduction to *YouTube* analytics including views, minutes watched + top videos</u>.

Then, you will have your <u>*YouTube* analytics traffic sources explained for *YouTube* search + suggested video</u>, which are the most important free traffic sources.

Subscribers on *YouTube* are absolute gold! This section is about the <u>*YouTube* subscriber analytics tab explained for how to know which videos get subs</u>. With this knowledge, you can make new videos that your audience want to watch and subscribe for.

If you are in the third or fourth position in *YouTube* search for a particular search term, I will show you how <u>*optimizing your YouTube video tags, title and description based on analytics*</u> can give you the top position.

Read on…

Introduction to *YouTube* analytics including views, minutes watched + top videos

If you want to have a successful *YouTube* channel, getting to know the *Analytics* is absolutely critical for finding what you are doing right and finding opportunities to improve.

Access your analytics from your *YouTube* dashboard located at *www.youtube.com/dashboard?o=U*

Then you go down and click on *"Analytics"* on the left hand menu.

Here is your basic intro analytics in your overview section.

You can't find out a whole lot more than the basics in this area, but it is important to get to know each individual part of the analytics.

1. Views

Views are simply the number of people that started watching your video, regardless of how much time they actually spent watching it. *Views* are a basic metric that now combines with *Minute Watched* to determine ranking.

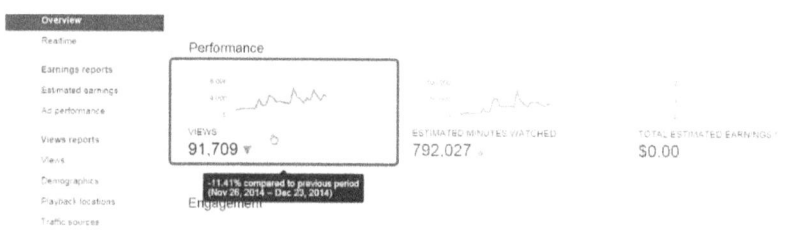

2. Estimated minutes watched

Estimated minutes watched are how many minutes *YouTube* thinks people actually spent watching the video.

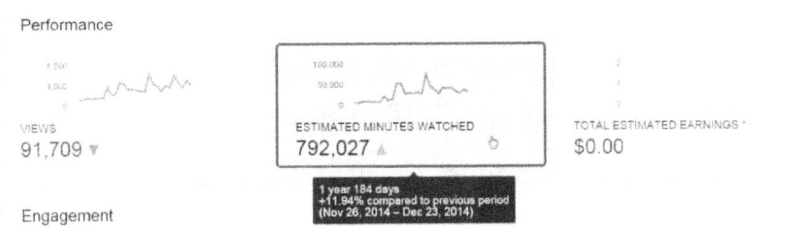

This combined with the *Views* is where you get the power of your *YouTube* channel.

Now engagement is also very good.

3. Likes and dislikes

You want people *liking* your videos, and even people *disliking* some of your videos tells *YouTube* that people are at least watching and noticing you.

It is funny to see some of the most popular videos in the world having many dislikes on them.

4. Comments and shares

Comments are exceptional too, especially when they are done through *Google* plus. *YouTube* loves to see *comments* and loves to see *shares* done directly through the *YouTube* sharing widget.

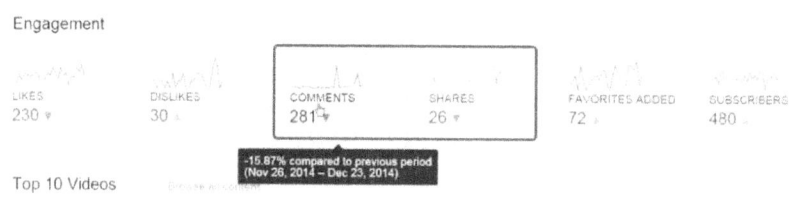

5. Favorites and subscribers

Favorites Added and *Subscribers* are also an excellent way *YouTube* knows if people like your video

Here is where each one of these metrics is coming from.

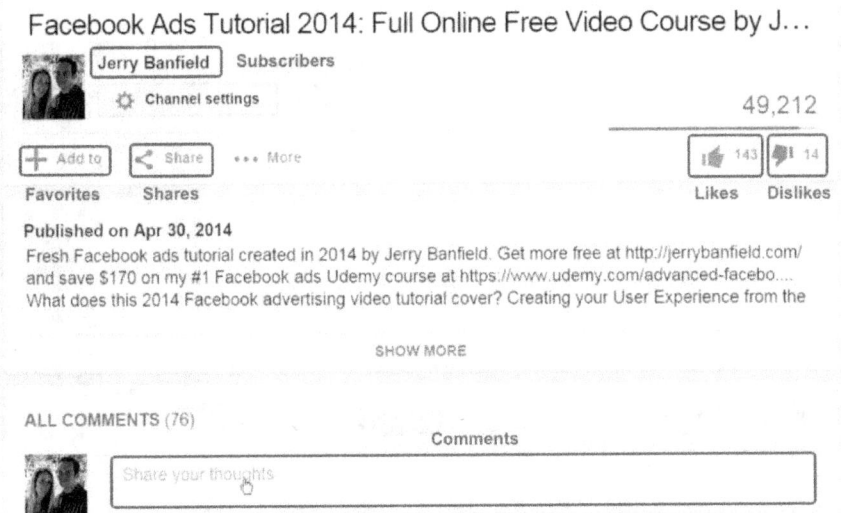

Likes happen when someone just clicks on the *"thumb up"* button and likes your video. The dislike button is the *"thumb down"* next to it and it is how you get your *Dislikes*.

The *Comments* are below the description and it is where people share their thoughts. Your *Shares* are tracked from the *"Share"* button. Your *Favorites* are counted from the *"+ Add to"* button.

Then, people can go to your channel to subscribe or they can do it straight from the upper right of the video if you have a watermark there, which I highly recommend you to have on your channel.

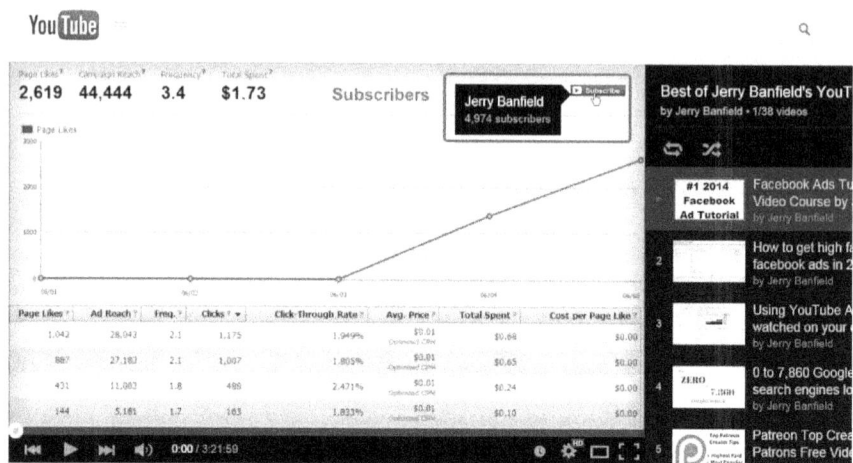

That's how all of these metrics are generated.

6. Estimated earnings

I have *Google Adsense* disabled and as you can see the *Estimated Earnings* do not show up.

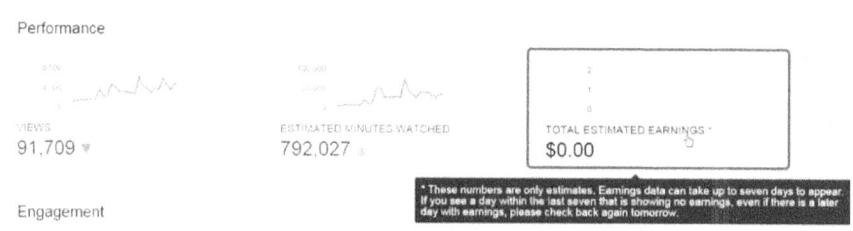

I don't have any of my videos monetized, but if you do have ads on your channel, then this is where your *Estimated Earnings* are going to show up.

Finally, in the basic analytics page, you then have your **Top 10 Videos**.

Video	Views	Estimated minutes watched	Total estimated earnings
Facebook Ads Tutorial 2015 for Conversions f...	19,709 (22%)	275,212 (35%)	$0.00 (0.0%)
$0.01 CPC Facebook Advertising Tutorial 201...	9,088 (9.9%)	162,005 (21%)	$0.00 (0.0%)
Buy bitcoin with cash at your local bank and s...	6,373 (6.9%)	29,316 (3.7%)	$0.00 (0.0%)
Flippa selling process overview how to sell yo...	4,686 (5.1%)	25,477 (3.2%)	$0.00 (0.0%)
YouTube SEO tutorial after you upload the vid...	3,710 (4.0%)	16,656 (2.1%)	$0.00 (0.0%)
How do you tell a girl you love her?	3,252 (3.5%)	2,268 (0.3%)	$0.00 (0.0%)
Facebook Ads Tutorial 2014: Full Online Free...	3,068 (3.3%)	27,930 (3.5%)	$0.00 (0.0%)
How I found happiness in life by seeing beyon...	3,002 (3.3%)	20,373 (2.6%)	$0.00 (0.0%)
How I Created 5 Udemy Courses in 45 days!	2,911 (3.2%)	17,582 (2.2%)	$0.00 (0.0%)
2014 Facebook Marketing and Advertising Tip...	2,833 (3.1%)	25,207 (3.2%)	$0.00 (0.0%)

They only show by views so if you are running ads on your videos, this makes it difficult to see which one actually is organically getting views. I will show you deeper in analytics how to do that. These are your top ten simply by views and all views are counted equal here.

Then you can sort by minutes watched if you click on it.

Video	Views	Estimated minutes watched	Total estimated earnings
Facebook Ads Tutorial 2015 for Conversions t...	19,709 (22%)	275,212 (35%)	$0.00 (0.0%)
$0.01 CPC Facebook Advertising Tutorial 201...	9,088 (9.9%)	162,005 (21%)	$0.00 (0.0%)
Buy bitcoin with cash at your local bank and s...	6,373 (6.9%)	29,316 (3.7%)	$0.00 (0.0%)
Facebook Ads Tutorial 2014 Full Online Free...	3,068 (3.3%)	27,930 (3.5%)	$0.00 (0.0%)
Flippa selling process overview how to sell yo...	4,686 (5.1%)	25,477 (3.2%)	$0.00 (0.0%)
2014 Facebook Marketing and Advertising Tip...	2,833 (3.1%)	25,207 (3.2%)	$0.00 (0.0%)
How I found happiness in life by seeing beyon...	3,002 (3.3%)	20,373 (2.6%)	$0.00 (0.0%)
League of Legends Gameplay 2015 Jinx Epic...	2,148 (2.3%)	19,882 (2.5%)	$0.00 (0.0%)
Complete Facebook Advertising Tutorial How...	1,923 (2.1%)	18,691 (2.4%)	$0.00 (0.0%)
How I Created 5 Udemy Courses in 45 days!...	2,911 (3.2%)	17,582 (2.2%)	$0.00 (0.0%)

Minutes Watched will help you see how much time people are actually spending on a video, which is helpful especially if you have really long videos.

Finally at the bottom you scroll down to the *Demographics* tab.

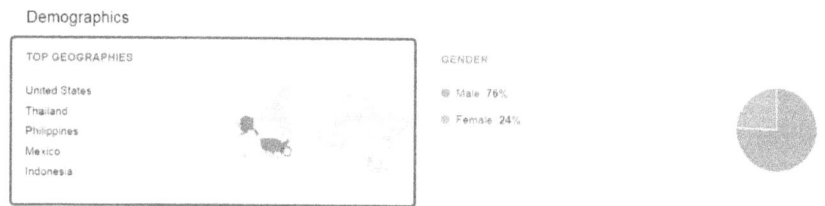

The *Top Geographies* shows you where people are watching your videos from. The *United States* is number one for me and that is almost all through organic search traffic and suggested videos.

Then you can see that I'm running ads in *Thailand, the Philippines, Mexico* and *Indonesia* to get really cheap views to buff the minutes watched on my channel, and then I'm getting organic search traffic from the *United States*.

In the *Gender* section, you'll note that most of my viewers are male, but that may be different for your channel.

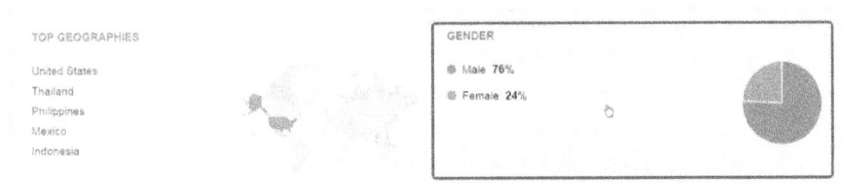

Top Playback Locations in the *Discovery* tab is a very important metric to see where people are actually watching your videos.

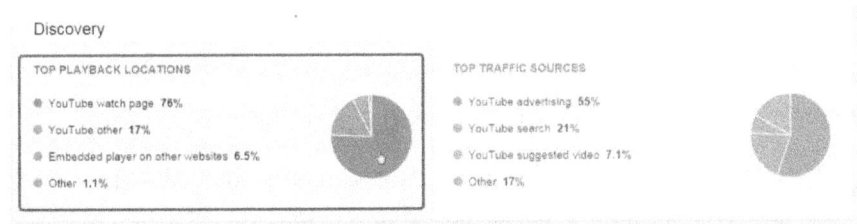

People are mostly finding my videos on the actual *YouTube* watch page because I am doing *YouTube* advertising. You may have different traffic sources like embedded players on other websites that are driving most of your videos or some other type of *YouTube* watch.

The Top Traffic Sources metrics are valuable for finding where you are getting people to watch your videos.

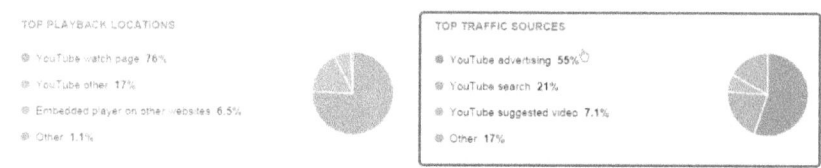

55% of my views are on *YouTube Advertising*, but I am only paying a couple of cents per view and I'm getting a lot of minutes watched, which resulted in this second metric, *YouTube Search*.

YouTube search and *YouTube suggested video* are the gold mine on *YouTube*. You want those search in those *suggested video views* because absolutely nothing is better than getting found in search and in suggested video for getting conversions through to your website, to getting subscribers and people genuinely interested in you and in what you are talking about.

This is an overview of the *YouTube* analytics and as you can see there are a lot more details you can go into from the left menu.

I'm going to go into those details with you in this chapter to show you that getting to know some of these reports can give you the chance to do some incredible things on your *YouTube* channel.

YouTube analytics traffic sources explained for *YouTube* search + suggested video

I think the most important part of *Analytics* are the *Traffic Sources* because they show you where you are actually getting views from. When I'm on my *Analytics* menu, I go down and click *"Traffic Sources."*

Now you can see where all of my traffic is coming from by source. If I scroll down here, this is where I'm getting the analytical value.

Traffic source	Views	Estimated minutes watched	Average view duration
YouTube advertising	50,754 (55%)	559,264 (71%)	11:01
YouTube search	18,838 (21%)	88,997 (11%)	4:43
YouTube suggested video	6,491 (7.1%)	39,863 (5.0%)	6:08
Unknown – direct	4,844 (5.3%)	40,315 (5.1%)	8:19
External website	3,906 (4.3%)	19,341 (2.4%)	4:57
YouTube Guide	2,071 (2.3%)	15,026 (1.9%)	7:15
Unknown – embedded player	1,772 (1.9%)	9,168 (1.2%)	5:10
YouTube channel page	1,617 (1.8%)	10,833 (1.4%)	6:41
External app	582 (0.6%)	1,447 (0.2%)	2:29
YouTube playlists	489 (0.5%)	2,811 (0.4%)	5:44
YouTube – other features	345 (0.4%)	2,461 (0.3%)	7:08

YouTube search and *YouTube* suggested video are free views, as well as *External website* and those that follow are also free views. *YouTube advertising* is not free views, but they helped all of the other metrics to get higher.

I want to isolate all of the other sources without *YouTube advertising*. I can select all traffic sources and uncheck *YouTube advertising* so what I can see here is how my traffic is growing just organically.

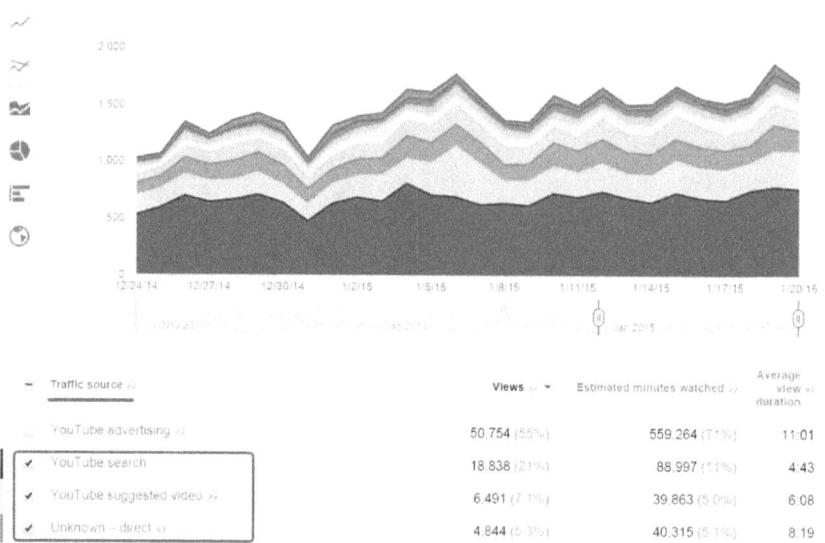

That's really powerful and you will notice that I just spiked up close to *2,000* views in one day organically.

What you want is this slow steady march to higher organic traffic because the organic traffic is where nearly all of the value is coming from. Now, as absurd as it sounds, these *50,000* views from *YouTube ads* are nearly useless in terms of actual conversions. Sometimes I get lucky and pull a subscriber, but most of the time I get absolutely nothing. The people who are watching ads are not in the mood to engage with me.

YouTube search is where all kinds of good things happen and since most *YouTube* channels don't run *YouTube* ads, all you have to do is run ads and *YouTube* will rank your video high enough to get found in search and suggested video.

Traffic source	Views	Estimated minutes watched	Average view duration
YouTube advertising	50,754 (55%)	559,264 (71%)	11:01
YouTube search	18,838 (21%)	88,997 (11%)	4:43
YouTube suggested video	6,491 (7.1%)	39,863 (5.0%)	6:08
Unknown – direct	4,844 (5.3%)	40,315 (5.1%)	8:19
External website	3,906 (4.3%)	19,341 (2.4%)	4:57

When you click on *YouTube search* then you get keywords across your entire channel. Now this is very limiting especially for long tail keywords.

Traffic source	Views	Estimated minutes watched	Average view duration
wolfenstein xbox one	408 (2.2%)	1,594 (1.8%)	3:54
how to tell a girl you love her	380 (2.0%)	280 (0.3%)	0:44
destiny xbox one	372 (2.0%)	1,642 (1.8%)	4:24
facebook ads tutorial 2014	342 (1.8%)	3,471 (3.9%)	10:08
facebook marketing	315 (1.7%)	1,841 (2.1%)	5:50
unknown	292 (1.6%)	1,007 (1.1%)	3:26
facebook ads	234 (1.2%)	1,950 (2.2%)	8:19
wolfenstein the new order xbox one	211 (1.1%)	852 (1.0%)	4:02
facebook advertising	152 (0.8%)	981 (1.1%)	6:27
xbox one destiny	130 (0.7%)	481 (0.5%)	3:41
jerry banfield	118 (0.6%)	1,150 (1.3%)	9:44
destiny gameplay xbox one	114 (0.6%)	495 (0.6%)	4:20
how to tell a girl you like her	109 (0.6%)	78 (0.1%)	0:43
twitter tutorial	105 (0.6%)	398 (0.4%)	3:47
wolfenstein gameplay xbox one	94 (0.5%)	598 (0.7%)	6:21
fiverr	91 (0.5%)	628 (0.7%)	6:54

You will notice that I have very few individual views on anyone keyword. Now, for my video gaming experiment with *"wolfenstein xbox one"* and *"destiny xbox one,"* I tested some of these *YouTube* video ranking strategies to limit, so those don't actually do much for me. But, for *"Facebook ads"* and *"Facebook marketing"* searches are huge.

facebook ads tutorial 2014	342 (1.8%)	3,471 (3.9%)	10:08
facebook marketing	315 (1.7%)	1,841 (2.1%)	5:50

This is where I'm getting conversions from, but the problem is that you can only see up to *25* results in the search at a time. So the actual search tab itself can tell you what you are doing right in a larger scale on your channel, but you are not going to find out much more detail than the top *25* terms.

Now my top *25* terms are important, noticing that *Facebook marketing* is one of my top *25* terms gives me a clear signal that I should be doing more *Facebook marketing* related videos instead of *Facebook ads* related videos.

After seeing this in my *Facebook marketing* search results and going in into more detail, I actually changed the name on my *Facebook* course to *"Facebook marketing and ads"* instead of *"Facebook ads and marketing"* because I'm getting more search results, more people are looking for things about

Facebook marketing compared to *Facebook ads*.

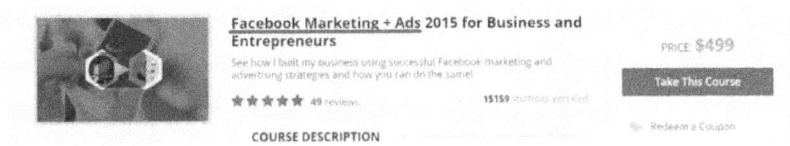

That's how powerful these *YouTube search* results are.

Another powerful thing is to go to *YouTube suggested video*.

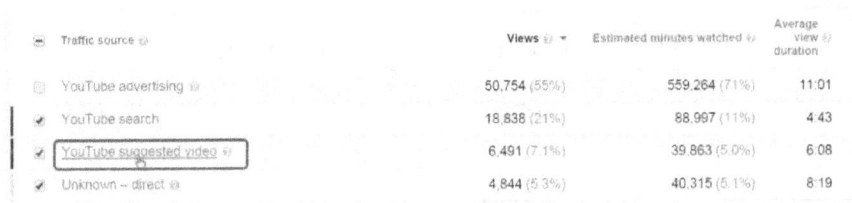

This gives you an idea of what videos are sending you traffic.

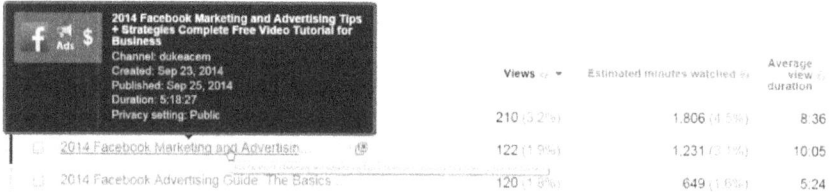

Now most of the time if you have a lot of videos, when you highlight the video like below, you will see your own videos.

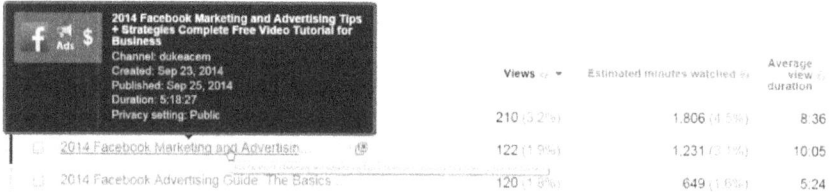

But what's really cool is when you see other people's video sending you traffic.

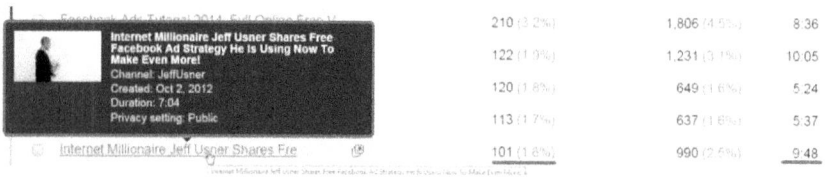

This video is from *Jeff Usner* and in the last *28* days it sent *101 views* to my channel with an *average view duration* of *9:48*.

How does that happen?

When you are on *Jeff Usner's* video look at what you have on the right side.

There are two videos by *Jerry Banfield* right next to his video in the suggested video section. Out of these six videos on the side, *YouTube* is suggesting two of my videos to watch and that's really sweet because it is giving me free traffic off of someone else's audience.

This is the same thing on this video.

Mari Smith has worked really hard to get herself an audience and then when someone is watching her video, they are going over and watch my videos.

Eli has an excellent large YouTube channel and it is the same thing.

I am pulling views off of his channel.

Then, all these other channels are also sending me YouTube views. It is really sweet to get to know these videos and figure out what your audience tends to like.

7 Steps to Facebook Success - Free Facebook...	62 (1.0%)	483 (1.2%)	7:47
Does Facebook Advertising Work?	52 (0.8%)	487 (1.2%)	9:21
How to Create a Facebook Ad to Get VERY Ta...	52 (0.8%)	527 (1.3%)	10:08
Facebook Ads Tutorial 2015 for Conversions to...	50 (0.8%)	385 (1.0%)	7:42
Facebook Ad Tutorial 2014	50 (0.8%)	365 (0.9%)	7:17
$0.01 CPC Facebook Advertising Tutorial 2015...	44 (0.7%)	281 (0.7%)	6:23
How To Start Planning Your Facebook Ads Tar...	43 (0.7%)	299 (0.8%)	6:57
How do you tell a girl you love her?	43 (0.7%)	23 (0.1%)	0:32
2014 Facebook Advertising Tutorial Focusing o...	43 (0.7%)	286 (0.7%)	6:39
Facebook Marketing Secrets With Amy Porterfi...	40 (0.6%)	655 (1.6%)	16:22
Free Twitter Followers (2014)- How to get follo...	40 (0.6%)	150 (0.4%)	3:45
How to Setup Your First Facebook Ad Campaign	40 (0.6%)	249 (0.6%)	6:13
Cheap Countries You Can Target With Facebo...	33 (0.5%)	145 (0.4%)	4:23
Facebook Ads Tutorial October 2014 for page li...	32 (0.5%)	215 (0.5%)	6:43
TEESPRING CRASH COURSE	31 (0.5%)	449 (1.1%)	14:29

Only top 25 entities available   1–25 of 25

My audience tends to like things about *Facebook Ads strategies,* of course, but they also like *"7 Steps to Facebook Success."* They are watching videos on how to get free *Twitter followers* also and about *Teespring.*

That's very valuable for me to know because if I know what else my audience is watching, then I can make those things for them. If they are wondering if *Facebook* advertising works at all, that is good for me to know because then I can make the same kind of video. *"Does Facebook Advertising work?"* I literally can use the same title if I wanted to.

That's very powerful and between the *Traffic Sources, YouTube search* and *YouTube suggested video,* you can get a ton of data that I'm going to show you how to dive deeper into.

One last thing on this section is *External website*.

Now, after I have clicked on that, what do you notice? *Google search* is up there on the top.

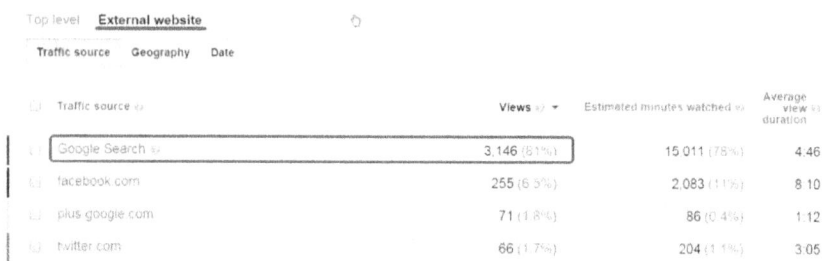

They are people putting things on *Google* search like "*Facebook ads tutorial 2014.*" When someone puts that in, *Google* is showing two of my *YouTube* videos in the top three results. That's sweet!

When people are searching in *Google* that is pretty much an ideal method to get found. If you look at this traffic, that's *3,146* views and *15,011* minutes watched in *28* days.

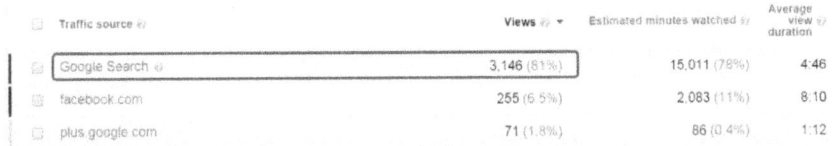

So *Google* is sending over *100* people to my *YouTube* videos for free every single day. If I had to pay for those in search, that will cost between *$1* to *$10* per click and I'd probably wouldn't get an average of four minutes watched per video.

The power of putting all of these things into practice is getting *Google* to give you free traffic. I click on *"Google Search"* to see the details of this free traffic.

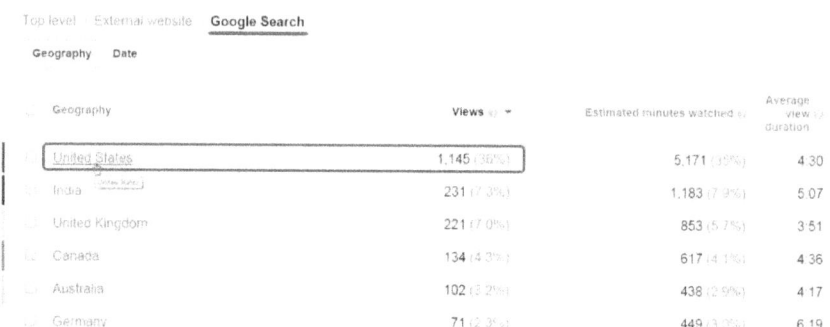

Over *1,000* views are from the *United States* and those are very valuable search traffic and results that I'm getting. They are also coming from all over the world.

118 countries found my *YouTube* videos in *Google* search.

You can set these things up all for yourself and that's how powerful this is getting to know these analytics and really understand all the things that are going on in your *YouTube* channel.

Traffic sources is where you find your return on investment on your *YouTube* channel.

YouTube subscriber analytics tab explained for how to know which videos get subs

If you want to learn about the value of subscribers on *YouTube* and how to analyze subscribers into *Analytics* to figure out which videos are getting new subscribers, this will be really helpful.

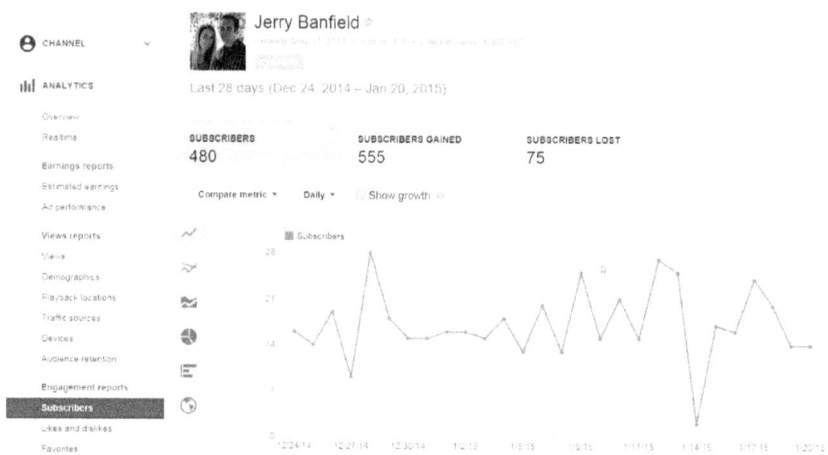

First, let's talk about the value of subscribers. I have almost *72,000* subscribers on my channel now, but had only *5,000* subscribers in *January 2015* when this screenshot above was taken.

That is really helpful for me because my videos get all kinds of free views from my subscribers every time I put a new video out.

Let me show you in the *Traffic Sources* how that works.

I hit *"Show only subscriber views"* when I'm in *Traffic Sources* under *Analytics*.

I had *5,000* subscribers at the time and those subscribers on average, watched a half of the video where *50%* of them viewed one video in the last *28* days, with *18,419* minutes watched. That is over *3* minutes on average watched per subscriber.

Subscribers are absolute gold on *YouTube*. How do they actually watch the videos? They watch them in the guide, the channel page, suggested videos, embedded in a website.

There are a lot of different ways they actually can watch videos.

The bottom line is that subscriber views are gold because they are totally free traffic. When you are making new videos, free traffic is gold for ranking.

Take a look at a guy who is really doing well on subscribers. He has got more than a million subscribers and *400 million* views. He is one of the biggest video gaming channels out there in the world.

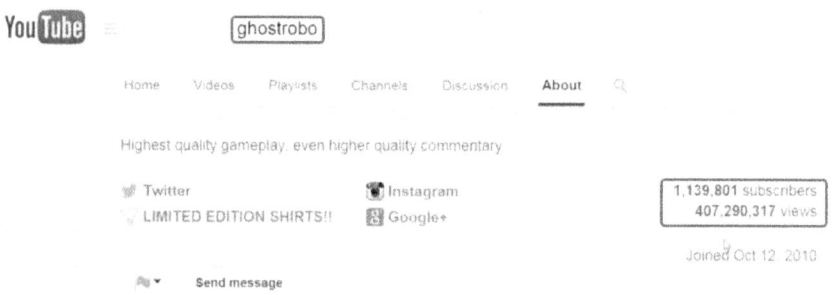

Every time he puts a new video out, it gets thousands of views for free from his subscribers. It then allows his videos to rank over the top of all other videos.

If you don't have that many subscribers, the only way you can rank higher than his videos is to get really lucky making a viral video, which you are not going to get most of the time, or spend hundreds, if not thousands of dollars, in ads.

Here is the thing though, if you have to pay for ads to go up against another channel who is getting them for free through subscribers, how do you think that is going to work out in the long term?

It is not!

Subscribers are absolute gold!

What I'm showing you in this section is how to figure out the value your subscribers are giving you and where they are coming from. If you don't know which videos are getting new subscribers, how can you know which ones people really like and make more of?

This is for the last *28* days and *Google* says some of the subscriber data was not tracking correctly around the *14th* where you can see a drop in the graph.

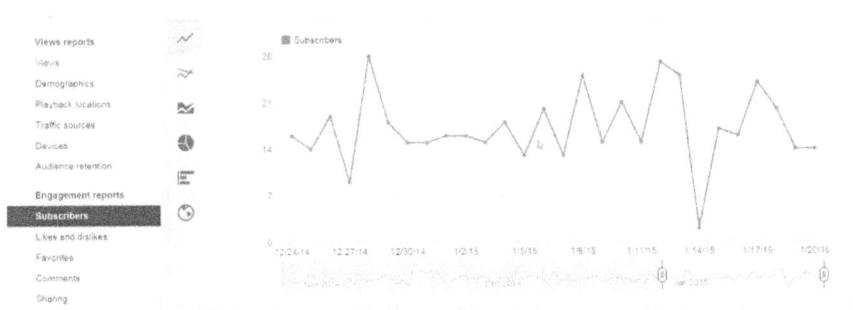

What's important in this tab is to see how your growth is going and how many subscribers you are getting everyday. Are you having days where you get a ton of subscribers or are you having consistent growth?

Let me show you my subscriber analytics over the last year. This is what's amazing: *4,084* net subscribers over the last year on my channel.

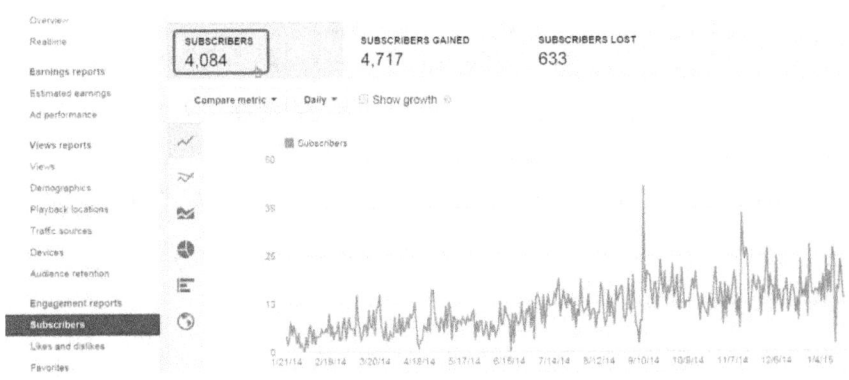

A year ago, I was getting about *5* subscribers a day and this year I'm getting around *15* subscribers a day. That's gigantic growth!

What I want to do is continue to get more subscribers every single day. Now, if you look back across the history of my entire *YouTube* channel, you will see that most of the first two years, I hardly got any subscribers.

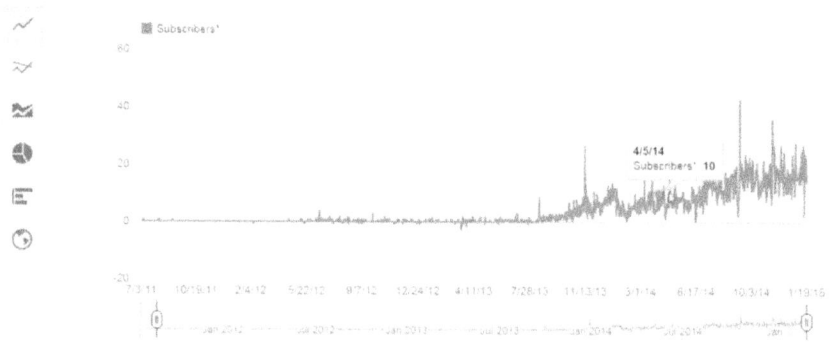

As I continued to put more and more videos up, I have continued to get more subscribers every day on average. If you want to grow your subscribers, that's how to do it.

Now, here is where I have got the most subscribers and this is what you want to find out. What videos are driving subscribers to your channel?

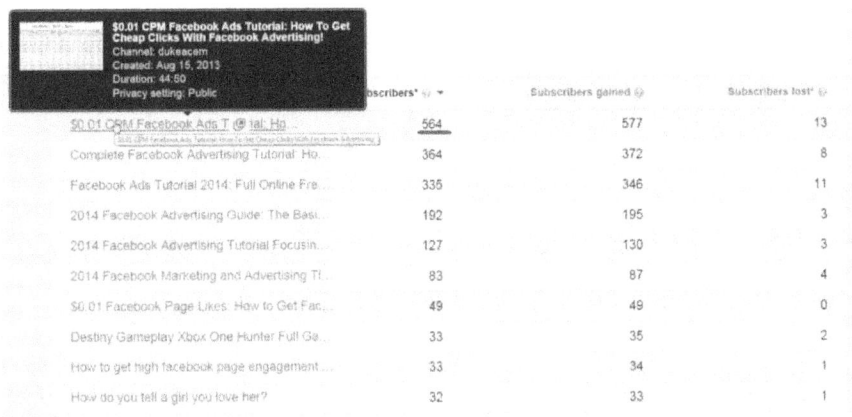

I have figured this out and I have been beating it to death. I noticed this was one of my first successful videos showing how to get cheap clicks with *Facebook* ads.

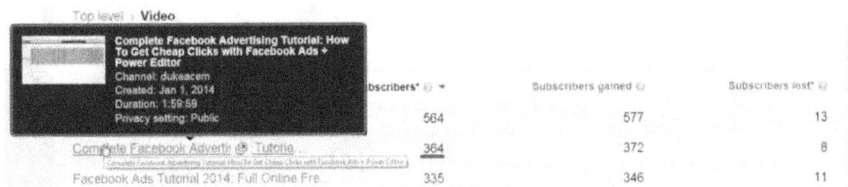

I got *564* subscribers from this one video alone. My next video in the same series produced *364* subscribers.

Guess what I did next. I made another one and another one, and much more. I continue to make videos about topics people subscribe on because getting subscribers is gigantic. When people are watching certain type of videos and subscribing, then I want to make more of them.

I did a test on a *video game* video and compared to the amount of views I got, I did very little subscribers.

So I'm not doing those videos anymore because they don't get subscribers. What I ultimately want are subscribers.

These *3* top videos were advertised and I have probably put about *2,000* views on each one with ads. Consequently, I ranked them very high and then they drew over a thousand subscribers.

If I look at just the last *28* days, the same video *"$0.01 CPM Facebook Ads Tutorial"* is now third even though it has got the most subscribers for all time.

Source	Subscribers	Subscribers gained	Subscribers lost
Facebook Ads Tutorial 2014: Full Online Fre...	24	24	0
2014 Facebook Marketing and Advertising Ti...	23	23	0
$0.01 CPM Facebook Ads T... ial: Ho...	21	22	1
Complete Facebook Advertising Tutorial: Ho...	16	16	0

The newer tutorials I have done are actually getting more subscribers now, and this brand new one I have done is pulling even more subscribers considering it has only been up for a few weeks and it hasn't been up *28* days yet.

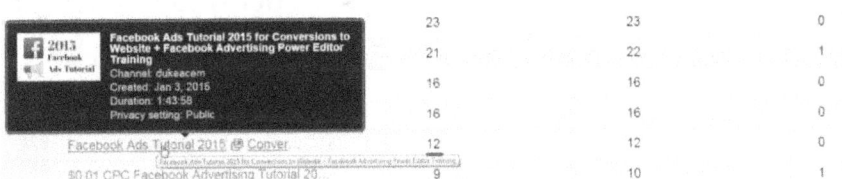

Having a lot of videos is really good to get subscribers. Even if you just get *1, 2* or *3* subscribers per video, you can get hundreds in total. You can see that I have got a lot of videos that have just a few subscribers on every month.

Source	Subscribers	Subscribers gained	Subscribers lost
Facebook Ads Power Editor Tutorial 2014 wit...	5	5	0
Izea Sponsorship Marketplace Overview for...	4	4	0
YouTube Channel Strategies for passive inc...	4	5	1
Destiny Gameplay Xbox One Hunter Full Ga...	3	3	0
WordPress YouTube Content Marketing Stra...	3	3	0
Youtube Advertising Tutorial 2014: How to C...	3	3	0
Twitter tutorial 2014 for 5,000+ free followers...	3	3	0
Udemy organic sales how I am promoting on...	3	3	0
How to get people to read your blog using m...	2	2	0
Facebook Ads Interest Targeting Audience O...	2	2	0
Facebook Posting Tricks with Ads to Get Ma...	2	2	0
How to Advertise on Twitter May 2014 Ad Cr...	2	2	0

The more videos I do, the more subscribers I get and it will be the same for you. The important lesson to remember is to look at your subscriber analytics and see which videos are driving you subscribers, and then make more like that.

When you look at the last *28* days, all of my top videos that are driving subscribers are about *Facebook* ads and marketing.

Source	Subscribers	Subscribers gained	Subscribers lost
Facebook Ads Tutorial 2014: Full Online Fre...	24	24	0
2014 Facebook Marketing and Advertising T...	23	23	0
$0.01 CPM Facebook Ads Tutorial: How To...	21	22	1
Complete Facebook Advertising Tutorial: Ho...	16	16	0
2014 Facebook Advertising Guide: The Basi...	16	16	0
Izea Sponsorship Marketplace Overview for...	12	12	0
	9	10	1
	7	8	1
	5	5	0
Izea Sponsorship Marketplace Overview for...	4	4	0
YouTube Channel Strategies for passive inc...	4	5	1
Destiny Gameplay Xbox One Hunter Full Ga...	3	3	0

The nine top videos are about *Facebook* and the tenth one is actually on a website I did looking at earning money with sponsored tweets.

I have done that on a basis of positive reinforcement so I get more subscribers. I find those top *20%* of videos that are generating the most subscribers, and then I make a bunch more of that exact same type of video.

The very last thing I want to show you is the *Geography* section for my subscribers all time.

Geography	Subscribers	Subscribers gained	Subscribers lost
United States	1,003	1,044	41
United Kingdom	152	156	4
Canada	112	118	6
India	98	103	5
Australia	80	83	3
Malaysia	71	73	2
Philippines	57	58	1
Brazil	42	45	3
Bangladesh	42	43	1
Egypt	41	41	0
Vietnam	39	39	0

You will notice the value in the subscribers, especially when you get a lot of subscribers from the *United States, Canada* and *the U.K.* Those are very valuable financially.

In total, *117* countries have sent me subscribers and you want to think global with your *YouTube* channel. A thousand *US* subscribers is great, but *2,428* subscribers tracked in total is a lot better.

Optimizing your *YouTube* video tags, title and description based on analytics

If you want to see how to take the first and second place when you have already pushed your video up to the third or fourth place, this section will be helpful for you.

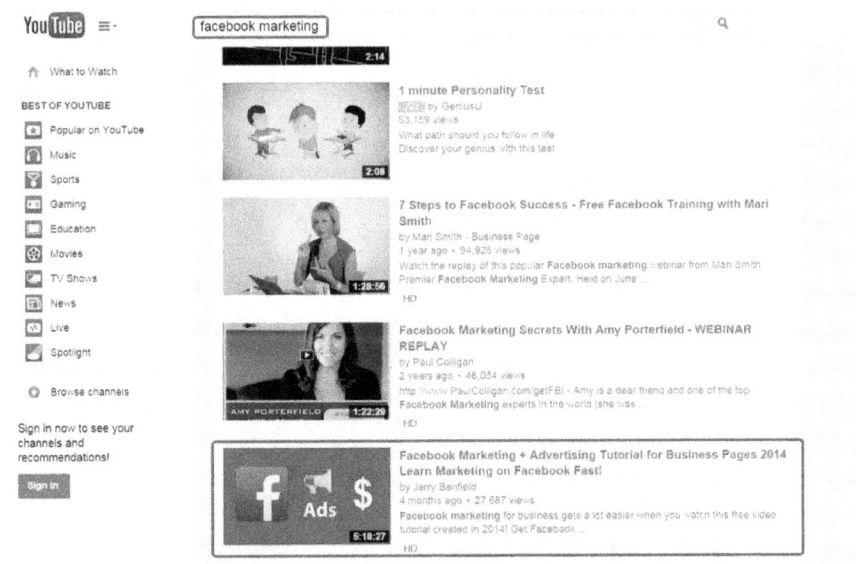

Here is what I'm actually doing to push up from 3rd and 4th into 1st and 2nd on terms that I'm already doing well on. If you look at some of these niche terms, I have already got a lock on both of these with 1st and 2nd position on both of these.

All I have to do now is push more on the general terms so that I can get up there and take the top. I'm searching around to see where I'm already at to make sure I don't mess up with what's already working.

I'd like to push higher on *"Facebook for business."*

What I'm going to do now is go back to just *"Facebook marketing"* and scroll down past the ads.

What I want to do is push up to number *1* and number *2* with these two videos that are 3rd and 4th. The first thing I should show you is that I'm already working hard on *Google Adwords* to push up there. I'm already in my *Adwords for video* account and I'm running a bunch of ad campaigns on these videos because there is simply nothing that substitutes for *minutes watched*.

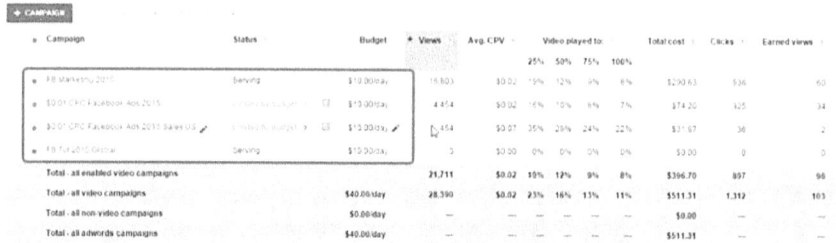

I'm running ads on all of these videos now and I'm pouring *minutes watched* in from the ads.

You will notice that the top ranking video and the second one have a lot of views.

7 Steps to Facebook Success - Free Facebook Training with Mari Smith
by Mari Smith - Business Page
1 year ago · 94,926 views
Watch the replay of this popular Facebook marketing webinar from Mari Smith. Premier Facebook Marketing Expert. Held on June ...
HD

Facebook Marketing Secrets With Amy Porterfield - WEBINAR REPLAY
by Paul Colligan
2 years ago · 46,054 views
http://www.PaulColligan.com/getFBI - Amy is a dear friend and one of the top Facebook Marketing experts in the world (she was ...
HD

So what I am going to do is quickly push pass these in the amount of views, and then I will push up higher. However, what I want to do in the meantime, is make sure my video is setup to rank high in the first place. One of the worst things that often could happen is you will have more views and see a video rank higher than you. If I do my tagging right, I can actually rank higher than these videos that are already up there.

This video is only a week old and for it to be 4th already is doing really good. So here is what I'm doing right, I have got *"Facebook marketing"* listed first on both of mine.

Then, what I want to do is optimize by the keywords that I'm seeing in my search results for my two videos.

I also want to optimize for the keywords I already took from both of the competing videos above me.

```
facebook marketing,facebook news feed,facebook
expert,mari smith,social media
marketing,facebook,facebook marketing secrets,amy
porterfield,facebook page,facebook promoted
posts,fbinfluence,facebook offers
```

Now what I want to do is see what I'm already showing up on. I want to make sure to get these keywords into the video as soon as possible. So I have opened this video up to edit it, and it looks like *"Facebook marketing strategies 2015 for business"* seems to be the strong point when adding keywords like *"strategies"* and *"business"* in the title.

My new title can be *"Facebook Marketing Strategies 2015 for Business: How to do Marketing on Facebook Successfully."*

That new title works better with *"marketing on Facebook"* and *"marketing strategies"* added.

What I want to do now is get the same keywords into the description.

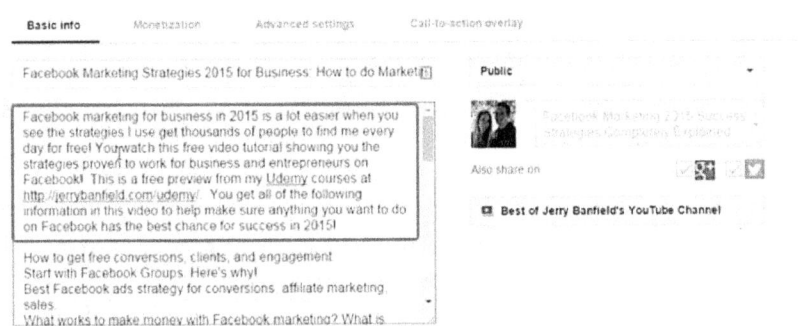

I want to mix the words up a little bit and I can change the beginning to:

"Facebook marketing for business in 2015 is a lot easier when you see the strategies I use to get thousands of people to find me everyday for free."

Then, I have a link to my website and I do not want to start with it because it can get broken in the search results. So I do not want it to show at all, but I still want it on the watch page like this.

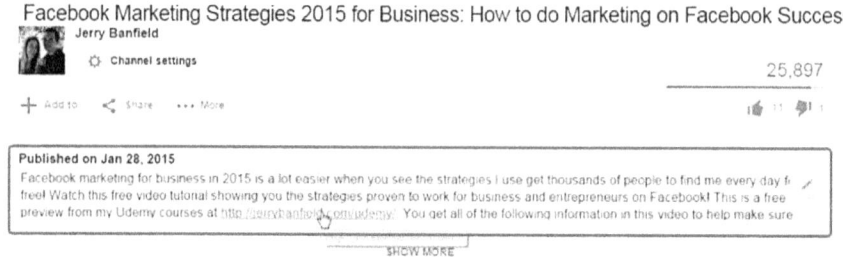

What I'm going to do now is delete all the tags I have for this video and replace them with new tags based on what's working.

When you first launch a video you can go straight from competitor tags as I have shown you how to do, but it is a bit easier sometimes to just throw your tags on it, whatever you think might work and see what actually happens. You don't necessarily know what people are going to like to watch.

I'm going to start my tags with what people are watching.

I select those terms that get me results and paste them straight in the tags section like this.

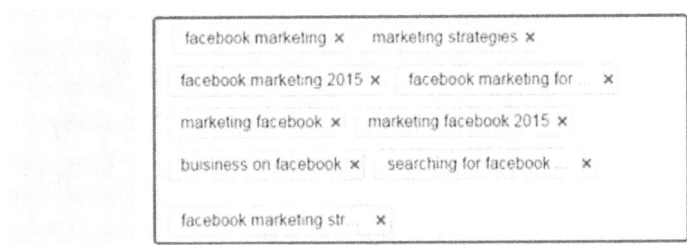

These are what people are watching and I want to make sure I'm exact tagged on the things people are watching. I want these exact tags because then I can count on getting the most minutes watched in search and that's what will help me rank the highest.

Now, I want to add the tags from the competitor videos.

Then I will save to make sure my tags are not too long. I also want to make sure to include my name in there and my company so that it shows up on my related suggested videos.

What I need to do now is put all of these tags into the actual search term description box because it can look like spamming, and *YouTube* will then rank the video lower.

Keyword spamming happens when you put keywords as tags that are not in your description. All I have to do is copy these competitors' keywords and paste them at the bottom of the description.

```
facebook marketing,facebook news feed,facebook
expert,mari smith,social media
marketing,facebook,facebook marketing secrets,amy
porterfield,facebook page,facebook promoted
posts,fbinfluence,facebook offers
```

Then I can capitalize *Facebook*.

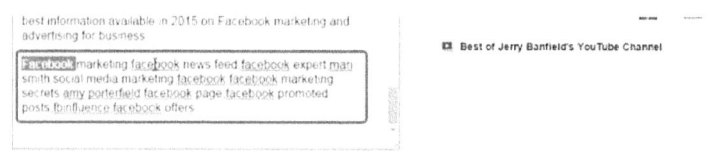

The next step would be to rewrite this so it is readable and appears like a natural organic sentence.

```
Facebook marketing by showing up in the Facebook news feed
makes it easy for anyone to be seen as a Facebook expert when
you use the social media marketing strategies on Facebook that I
explain in this video. Facebook marketing secrets,Facebook
page,Facebook promoted posts,fbinfluence,Facebook offers
```

I'm going to move the last section higher in the description and rewrite it as well.

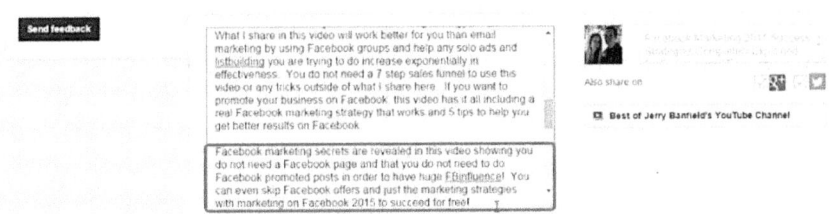

Now what I want to do is cross-check that I have got all these terms in the description as well. I do a search in my browser to highlight these terms on the page and add them if necessary.

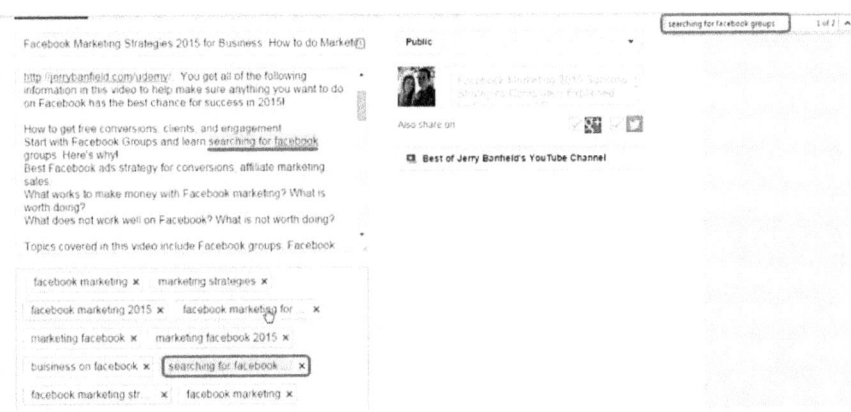

So now it looks like I have got everything completely delineated in *YouTube*. I have got a thumbnail on I'm already happy with and what I want to do then is encourage this to go up to the top.

I'm continuing to advertise this video on *YouTube ads for video* in order to get tons of minutes watched and consequently achieve the ranking results I expect.

CHAPTER 10

YouTube video ranking with Google AdWords for video

Google AdWords for video offers guaranteed views for your YouTube videos and can help them to get ranked higher.

In this first section I will give you an *introduction to Google AdWords for video*, which is used to advertise YouTube videos on YouTube.

My channel is growing today because of advertising my videos and you can do the same.

Making your YouTube ads with Google AdWords for video is the first step to get views to your videos and have a successful channel.

Choosing which videos to advertise can be overwhelming when you have hundreds of videos and this section will answer this.

Read on…

Introduction to *Google AdWords for Video*

Google AdWords for video offers guaranteed views for your *YouTube* videos provided on other people's videos online by *Google*.

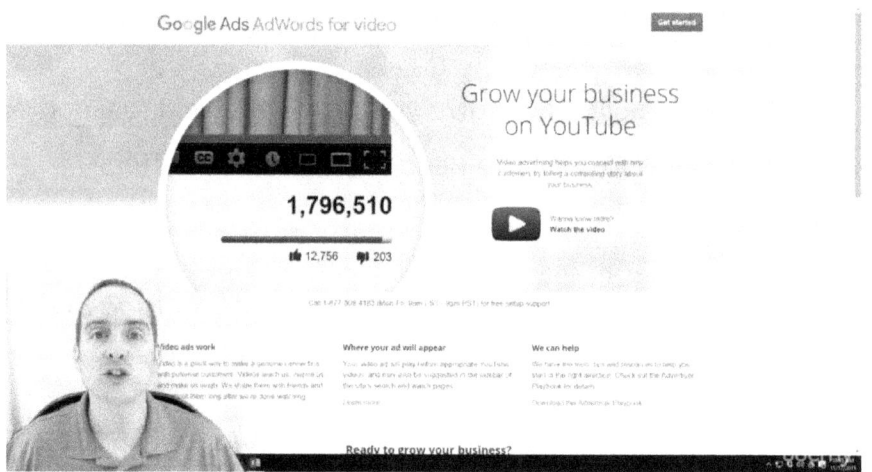

Google AdWords for video, (www.google.com/intl/en/landing/awv/) will make sure that someone actually watches your video. Getting started, having that idea that someone will really watch your video was huge. When I just put my channel up it was so hard to get anyone to watch my videos.

Using *Google AdWords for video,* you can have peace of mind that people will watch every video you make, and the cost can be as low as *1* cent each globally, or as low as a few cents each for views in the *US*, *Canada*, *UK*, *Australia*, etc...

Google AdWords for video is *YouTube's* advertising because *Google* owns *YouTube*. All of the ads you make are through *Google AdWords for video*. To use this you just need to sign up and have your *Google AdWords* account set up and then make video campaigns.

What I will do in this chapter is show you how it has worked for my channel and how to make your own ads based on making my own ads.

Let's talk *Google AdWords for video* aka *YouTube advertising*.

My channel is growing today because of advertising my videos

Over the last year on my *YouTube* channel, *YouTube* advertising has been the single biggest reason that my channel is growing so much.

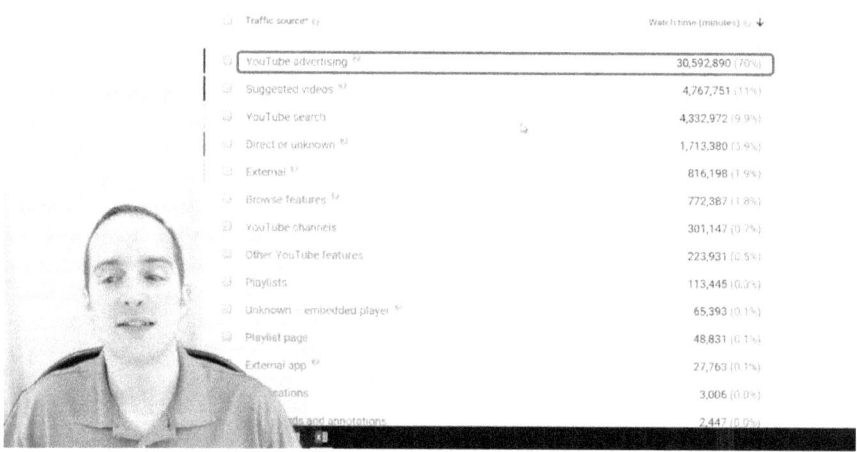

If you look above you can see that I have more than *30* million minutes watched on my channel because of *YouTube* advertising. Now is the key, most of these minutes down there would not have happened if it weren't for the organic ranking increase on my channel that came from using *YouTube* advertising.

The beauty of *YouTube* advertising is that you get a guaranteed organic rank boost because of all these minutes watched from the ads. You will notice that *70* percent of the minutes watched on my channel have come from ads.

Now here is the cool thing though, if you take out *YouTube* advertising, what you will notice on my channel is huge organic growth.

The more I have run these ads, the more my *minutes watched* have continued to grow without the ads running, and today I'm still running the ads a lot.

I am able to run the ads on new videos, promote them, get their organic ranking high, and then they get their own views from there. I don't have to keep running the ads on the videos once they are ranked well, so all I have to do is keep advertising my new videos. You can see the results from this over the last year.

When I switch it into views, then it makes a little more sense.

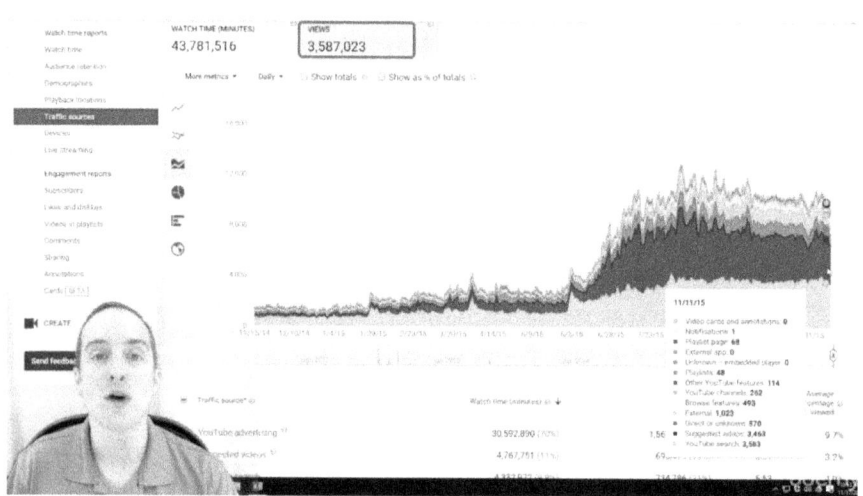

A year ago, when I was first about to make my *YouTube* course *(jerrybanfield.com/product/youtube/)*, I had less than *2,000* views a day on my *YouTube* channel, these are organic traffic sources. A year later, I have around *10,000* views a day on my channel. That's *5* times the growth in views and the main reason for that other than me uploading videos, is *YouTube* advertising.

I have advertised globally and I can show you on the *Geography* tab where people have watched from over the last year.

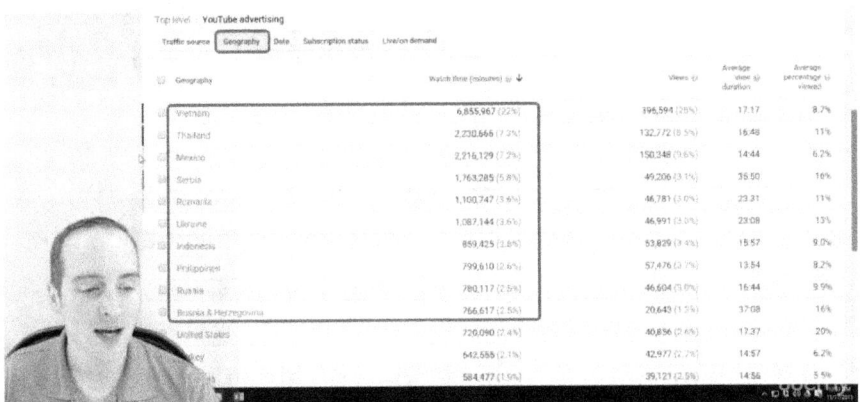

You can see that I have gotten a lot of views in *Vietnam, Thailand, Mexico* and I have paid for lots of views in the *United States* too. The beauty is that it doesn't matter where you get the views from because you still get the organic ranking increase.

Views in *Vietnam, Thailand, Mexico, Serbia* and all these countries serve you as they are all *1* cent each, and you can get views in the *US* for around *5* to *7* or *8* cents each. The views are so helpful for generating *this organic traffic increase* I showed you.

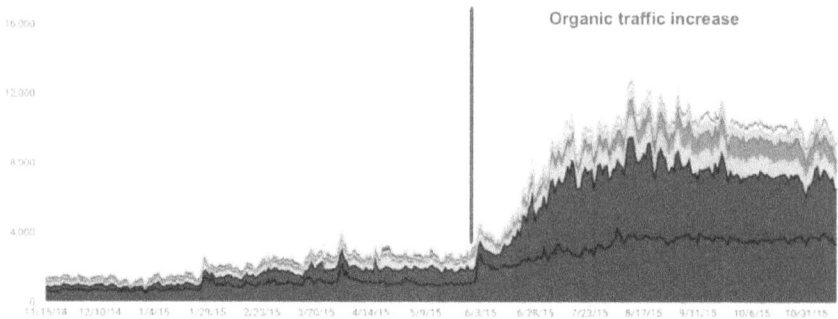

The organic traffic is just a gold mine on *YouTube* and it is amazing. I use *YouTube* ads to boost my organic traffic, which then does amazing things for my *YouTube* channel.

I will show you now exactly how I go about making ads for my channel and you can use this formula whether you have one or hundreds of videos. I will give you the system to make your own ads and to get the same kind of results.

Making your *YouTube* ads with *Google AdWords for Video*

To make your own *Google AdWords* ads for video with your *YouTube* channel and your *YouTube* videos, you go to: google.com/adwords

If you have a *Google* account, you sign in with it, and if you need to make a new one, you just sign up and get started.

Once you have signed up, put your billing information in and got your account ready by filling out your profile, then you are in your *AdWords* interface.

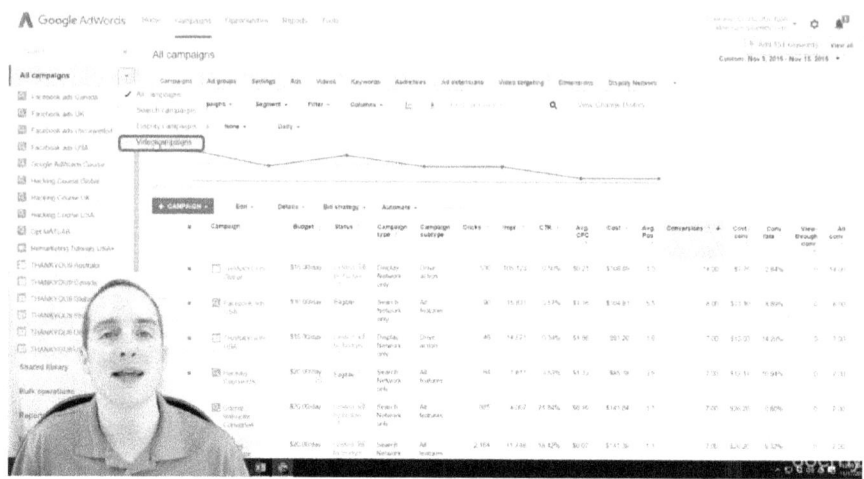

What you can see on the left side is the menu. I have got all campaigns and if you already have campaigns, you want to get rid of your search and display campaigns because you just want your *video campaigns*.

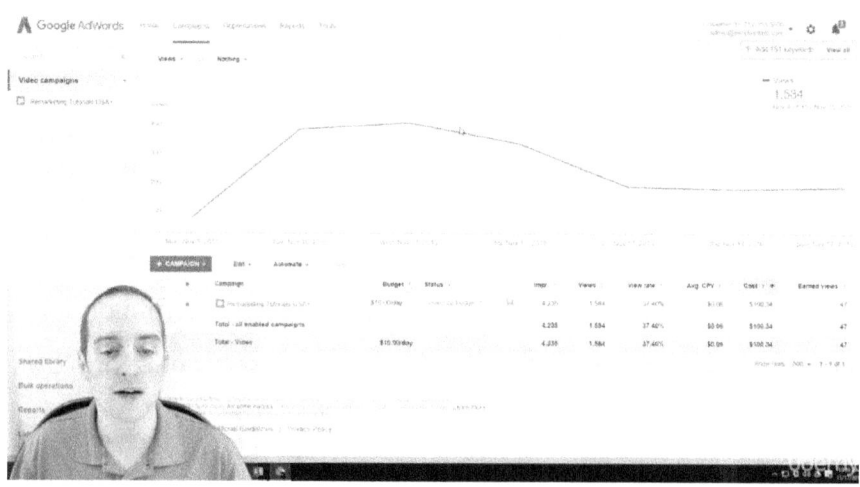

I have just started redoing my video campaigns in a new format to get even better results that I have already gotten. This is where your interface is and these are the ads I have got running right now.

If I show you all ads, you can see that I have made a lot of different *YouTube* video ads.

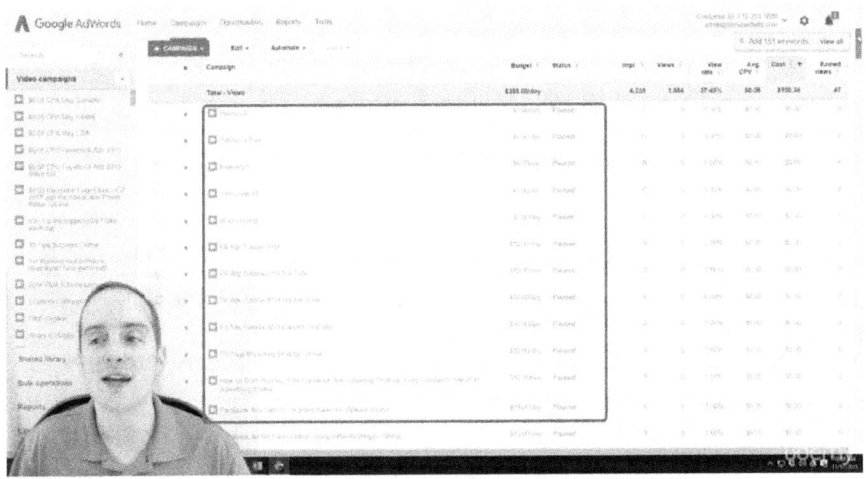

I can show you now my all time stats so you can see what experience I'm teaching from.

On this *AdWords* account, which has mostly been in the last year, I have spent *$24,500* on these *YouTube* ad campaigns.

I believed a lot in *YouTube* ads and you can see that I have done tons of different campaigns to promote now what are a bunch of viral videos online.

This works, it works consistently and it works if you work it. If you take the time to make the videos, put your ads in the videos, optimize based on the data you see, then you can get some really good results.

I have gotten *1.8* million views from the *$24,000* I have spent on ads, and I have got tons more of organic views that have led to all kinds of sales. These ads have produced anywhere from *2* to *5* times as much in sales over the long term, and a ton more in subscribers.

YouTube ads are amazing and that's why I'm showing you where to make them in the *Google AdWords* interface.

Choosing which videos to advertise

For doing your own *Google AdWords* ads for *YouTube*, it obviously helps to have a lot of videos. However, you can start from your very first video, just to get it out there and make sure someone watches it. I recommend that you have at least *10* if not *50* or hundred videos before you start doing much with *Google ads* though.

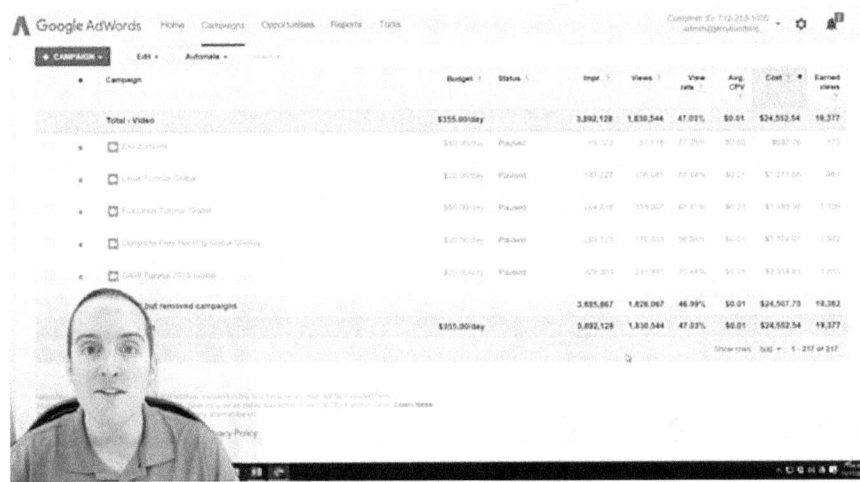

What I'm about to show you is how you look through your videos. I have *900 +* videos and I'm going to show you now how I pick which videos to advertise, and then put them into an ad campaign on *Google AdWords*.

I have run *217* ad campaigns for video on *AdWords* and this is something you do over a long time period, you do it repeatedly.

If you have a lot of videos, I will show you how I go pick my videos to advertise. I go grab my *Excel* spreadsheet to start with and I put the first video on just to warm this thing up.

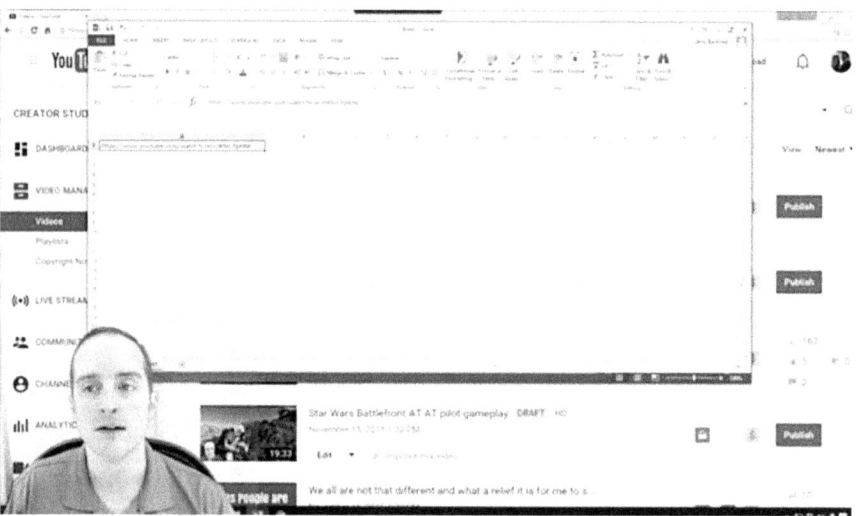

I have got my *Excel* spreadsheet ready and I have *655* videos to choose from.

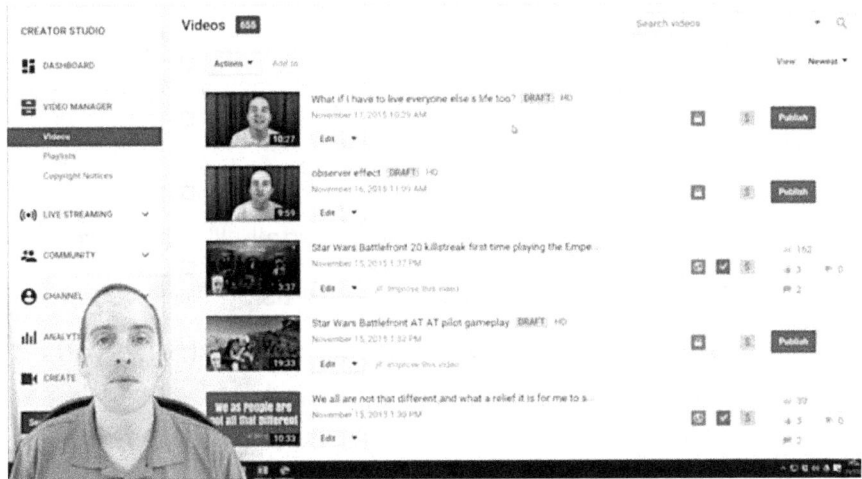

What I want to do right now is to advertise some of the daily inspirational videos I make for people who have already watched my videos.

The more videos you have, the more you can make specific objectives. Now regardless for how many videos you have, here is the basic process to select out which ones to advertise.

I'm in my *Video Manager* on the *Videos* tab where I'm doing this.

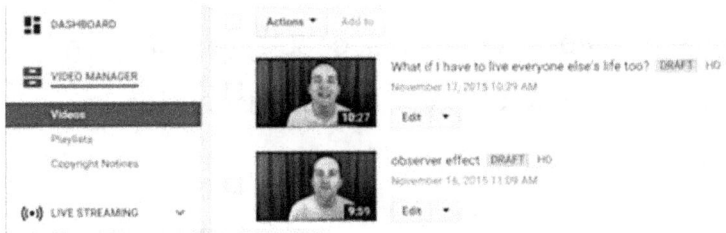

What I want to do is grab the link to the video, so then I can put that in *AdWords* quickly without having to manually go to each video.

I want to pick the videos that people really like to start with. So even if you just have *10* videos, advertising the ones people have already watched and really liked can give you an idea of where you can get the highest return.

After all I don't want to advertise videos like this one that has *one person liked* and *one person disliked*.

Probably better to advertise the other one, *17 people liked* and *no dislikes*. That's the first video I put on the spreadsheet earlier. What I will do now is just scroll through my channel and get some of my best videos that people have *liked* and *disliked*, and I'm going to get them together by subject.

The Complete YouTube Book

I'm not going to do a *Black Ops* video because that's a video game. Now here is one I can do: *"Avoiding Procrastination."* I right click to copy the link address, which gives me the video *URL* that I can paste in my spreadsheet.

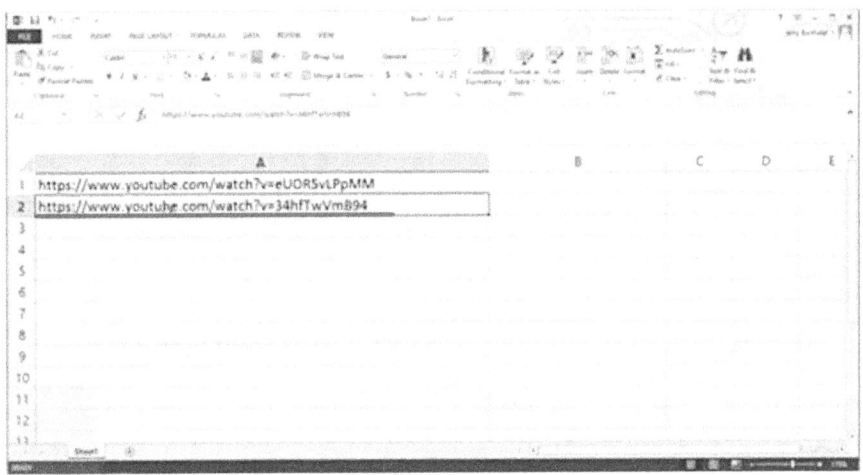

Now I have two videos and I want to grab about *5* or *10* of the videos that people consistently liked. Now you could look where to draw a line, *4* likes and no dislikes is pretty good. I have so many videos that I can scroll down and get some of the ones that are proven to be the best at this point.

If you have got less videos you can just be a little less choosy. The idea is that you want to get the ones that people definitely like to start with because they are the ones you want people to find. If you are doing remarketing, something like what I'm doing can be really helpful.

This one has got *8* likes and I can copy its *URL* to paste it in my spreadsheet.

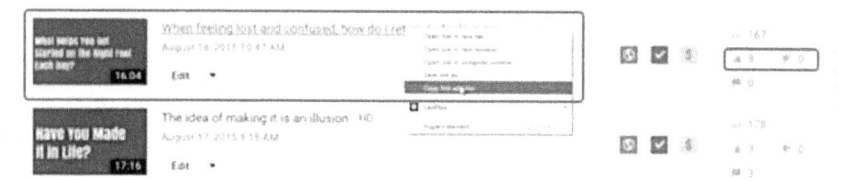

I'm going to keep doing this process until I have *10* videos I want to advertise.

When you want to make ads, it takes consistent work and effort in looking at your videos, and know which ones you want to use.

I have advertised videos like these a lot and then they receive a ton of positive feedback. That's where you get some of the really amazing things happening on your channel, and it just starts with grabbing a video and sticking it into an ad, and seeing what happens.

If you want to learn in details how to make these *YouTube* ads in *AdWords for video*, you may be interested in *"The Complete Google AdWords Course: Beginner to Advanced!"* at jerrybanfield.com/product/google-adwords/

CHAPTER 11

YouTube comments, engagement and community interactions

Engagement on your *YouTube* channel is very important to build your community of subscribers and grow a successful channel.

This first section is about <u>YouTube comments and engagement explained, and why it is valuable for growth</u>.

<u>I try to answer every comment on my YouTube channel</u> and you should do the same, especially if you have a new channel.

This is a Google feature that you do not want to miss. I will explain <u>how to add your biggest YouTube fans to a Google Plus circle with three clicks</u>.

Finally, a successful *YouTube* channel will give you many *Spam* and sometimes hate comments. Learn how to set-up your <u>YouTube community settings to block spammers and bullies</u>.

Read on…

YouTube comments and engagement explained, and why it is valuable for growth

Engagement on *YouTube* is important to build your community of subscribers. Your most enthusiastic subscribers will watch many if not all of your new videos, plus often they will be there to like and dislike them. Engaging with them is very important because you want to always get feedback right away when you upload a new video.

You can see on my *Video Manager* a lot of these likes and dislikes on my videos that are often from the most engaged subscribers.

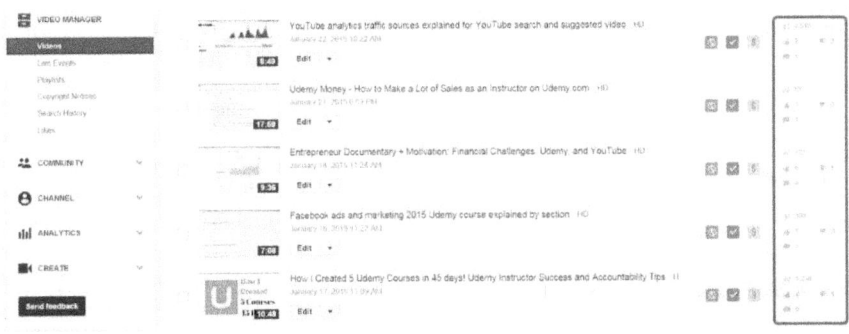

I get likes and dislikes from them immediately and that's very good feedback because what I ultimately want to know is what kind of videos I should make. Do I want to keep making the same type of videos?

I tried some *video gaming* videos, and then my subscribers, especially the regular ones, consistently end up disliking them. When I make a video like these tutorials on *Facebook* ads, then I get lots of good likes from my existing subscribers.

Subscribers are absolutely key for figuring out what videos are worth making because you ultimately want to make as many good videos as you can. Engagement happens through your community on *YouTube* and provides very valuable feedback.

The main place you can actually interact on *YouTube* when you are in your *Creator Studio* is in your *Community* tab under the *Comments* section.

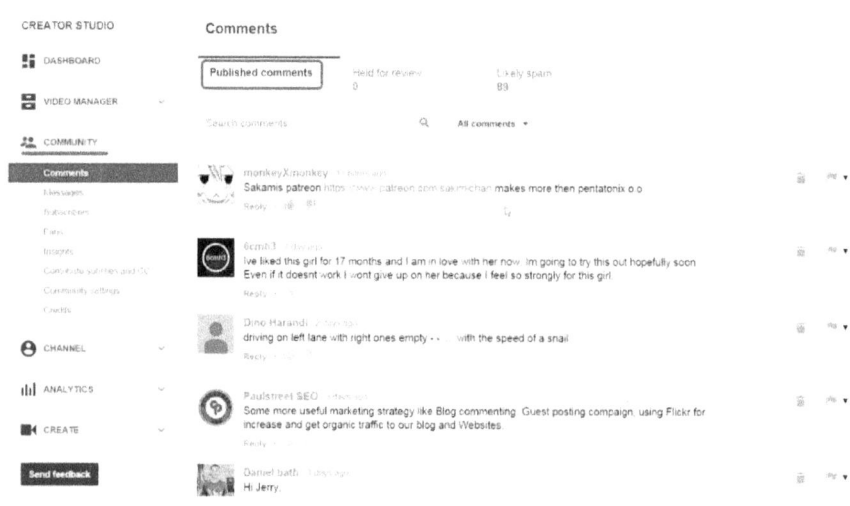

A lot of the comments are likely going to be spam, but that's ok. What you want to do is to interact and reply to as many of these as possible. It has been a few days since I have replied, but if you scroll down there are some of my replies.

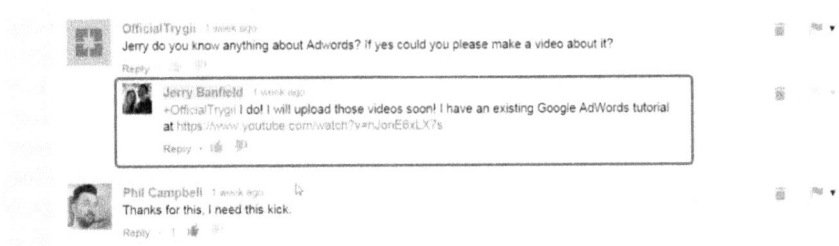

I update my comments about once a week. I go through the page and actually answer as many comments as I can because this is good not only for engaging with my subscribers, but it is very good for *SEO*. When this activity is happening on *Google+,* especially with different people's *Google+* accounts, then it is excellent for *SEO*.

You definitely want to use this community *Comment* tab, go through and reply to every single person, especially when your channel is young. The worse, the dumber, the more negative the comment is, the bigger the opportunity you have to make an awesome response that really pleases your subscribers.

What you want to do is make a response that your subscribers love and get people to see that you are really there to interact with. The worst thing that happens to most people in social media is that they get ignored, especially when engaging on bigger brand pages and people they are a big fan off.

How many times it has happened to you? You just love a page or love a brand and they never respond to you. I have been able to build a very active and enthusiastic community because people know I will talk back to them and that has been a big success to me in *YouTube*. It is just about getting and keeping these comments going.

I have got a lot of comments in the last week and they are loaded with valuable feedback as to what I can do in my videos that people like, what people don't like in my videos and what kind of person is following me.

Daniel Bath is from *Nigeria* and he is an excellent example of who I am trying to reach.

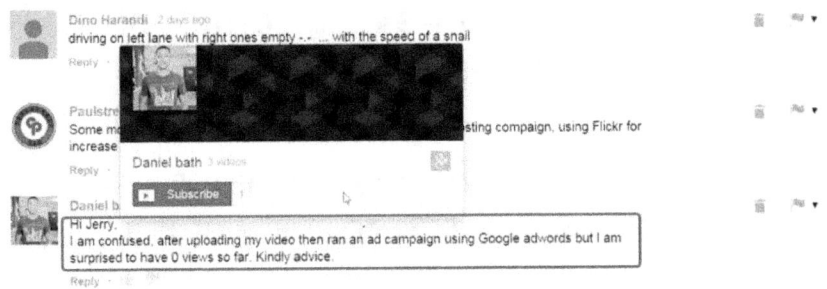

I found him primarily through the comments and interacting with him. He is in a country people ignore when they are trying to create content, and he is very enthusiastic about what I do, and checks every single day to see what new videos I have posted.

That is very valuable information and this is what you get out of doing and interacting with your community on *YouTube*, especially in the comments.

If you have got a channel up already, go to check your community and your comments now to see if you actually have anyone there to respond to.

I try to answer every comment on my *YouTube* channel.

The reason I try to answer every comment on my channel is for the *80/20* principle and because I love what I do. I want to connect with the people who most love what I do, or who have critical feedback that could help me.

Here is a good and detailed question.

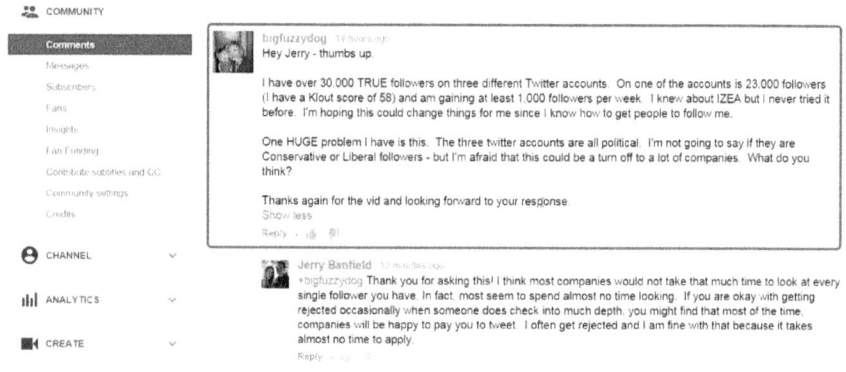

If people are willing to spend time to ask questions, these are likely some of the more enthusiastic people watching my channel. I have had millions of views on my channel and I have only had a few thousand comments. These are the top *1%* of people on my channel. It is very important to respond to these top *1%* with a genuine authentic answer.

How many times have you posted comments or questions on social media and you would have loved to have gotten a response.

Well, people love getting a response. If you have a *YouTube* channel it is critical to respond to every single comment you get. Not just for your love of what you are doing, and not just to get more subscribers, but to provide a genuine interaction to someone who spent time watching your videos, someone who has taken their time to watch what you have created. Give them something back with a comment. The longer and deeper your comment, the more it can be appreciated.

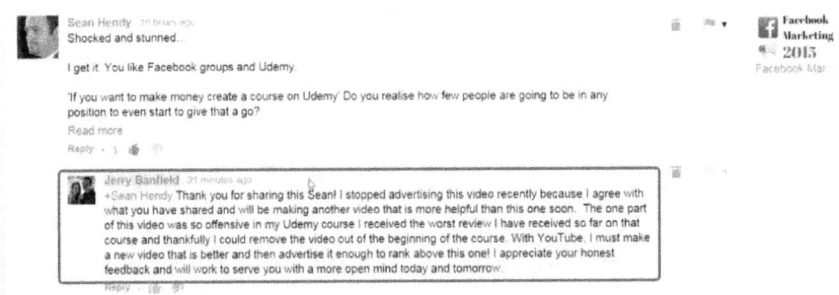

If you want more reason to do this, *Google+* notices all these comments. You will get your videos ranked higher on *Google* when they have interaction because *Google* wants people watching good *YouTube* videos.

Another reason you want to see questions like this, especially when someone posted some critical feedback, is that you want to be able to learn from what they share.

Sean has reinforced points I already have in mind about this video and encouraged me to make sure I don't just leave it out there without putting a better version of it on *YouTube*.

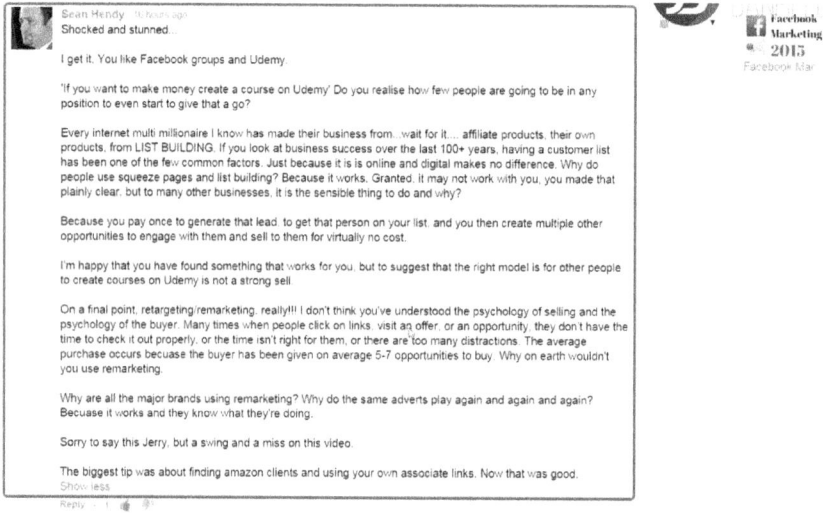

You want to see what people are thinking about your channel and the best comments are when someone shares a very personal comment, and it is worth it to take the time to share a very personal response.

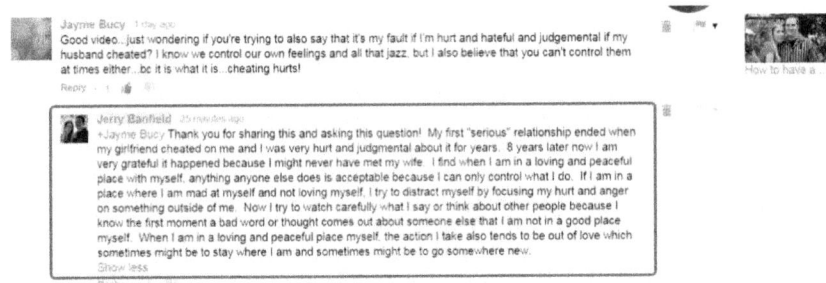

When you share yourself honestly and openly on social media, the best options you usually have will be to genuinely connect with people for real, not trying to put on a face, but to provide a genuine honest response. You have the chance to inspire someone and you have the chance to just be yourself without worrying about what people think.

I know that there are a lot of opportunities for fear. What if this happens? What if that happens? *99.9%* of the time that won't happen and the other *0.1%* of the time, you won't be able to have prepared for it fully.

So I just go through the comments and answer all of the questions as best as I can. It takes a lot of effort the bigger your channel gets to go through to answer and respond to everyone.

These are all just within the week and I have gone through and responded to all of these.

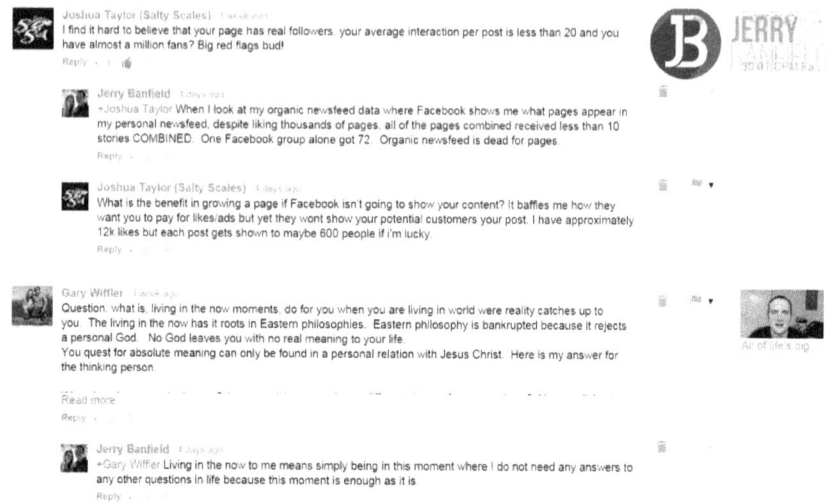

Now, sometimes I miss these follow up discussions, when the easiest response to give is just a *"thank you."* So at a bare minimum, you want to go through and see if you missed a comment.

Check your *YouTube* comments and respond to each one of them, if you have any. If you don't have any, plan on being willing to respond to the comments. Often you'll find that what you are trying to do in life produces a lot of unexpected results.

I just wanted to make a huge *YouTube* channel and I didn't realize how many comments I would then have on that channel. So no matter where you are at, you always will have work to do the bigger your channel gets. You literally could spend *10* or *15* hours a week responding to *YouTube* comments if you make a huge channel that can make you enough money to make a full time job.

You might be willing to respond to those comments if you could get paid, but the thing is that you aren't likely to get paid until you have responded to a lot of comments already. So if you want to get paid to make videos on *YouTube*, respond to all those comments or at least most of the comments.

You can get your most active fans engaged because most of the views on your videos will come from the same people watching them. You want to really cater towards that top *10%* of your audience who will sit there and watch every single video you make. You can find out who that is and get to know them. Learn what they want you to do and much more than that, all in the *YouTube* comments.

How to add your biggest *YouTube* fans to a *Google Plus* circle with three clicks

For engaging with your fans and getting your videos ranked high, *Google+* helps a lot because it often integrates directly with *YouTube* comments, which then *Google* counts as social sharing and will likely rank your video higher.

Growing your circles on *Google+* is often time consuming. However, *Google* offers a really cool function where you can add all of your biggest fans straight into your *Google+* circles. What I'm saying is when I am on my *Google+* page you can see below at *plus.google.com/+JerryBanfield/posts*, I can share all these things I created on my website.

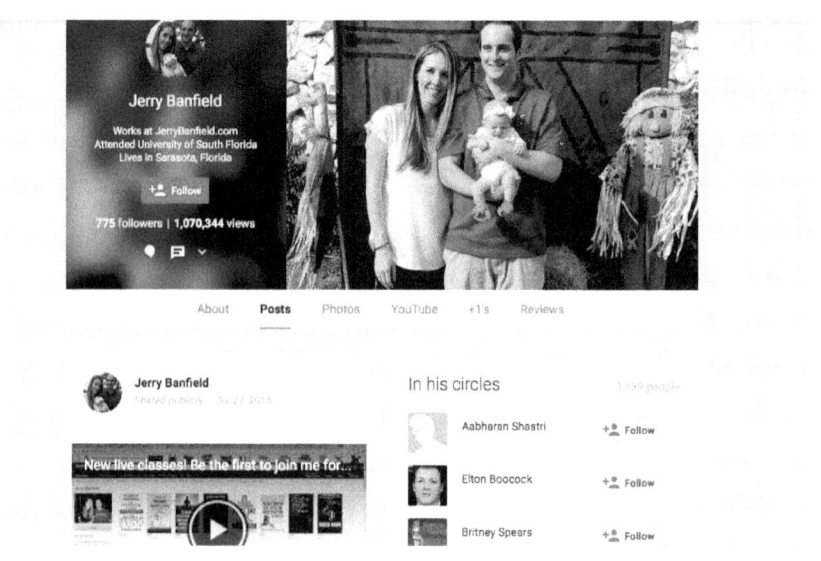

Then, I can get people off of my *YouTube* channel into my *Google+* circles, which helps massively with consistently growing my brand and my *SEO*.

You get there by going to *Community* on your *YouTube* channel when you are in your *Creator Studio*. Then, you go down to *Insights* where *Google* will offer you a top *YouTube* fan circle.

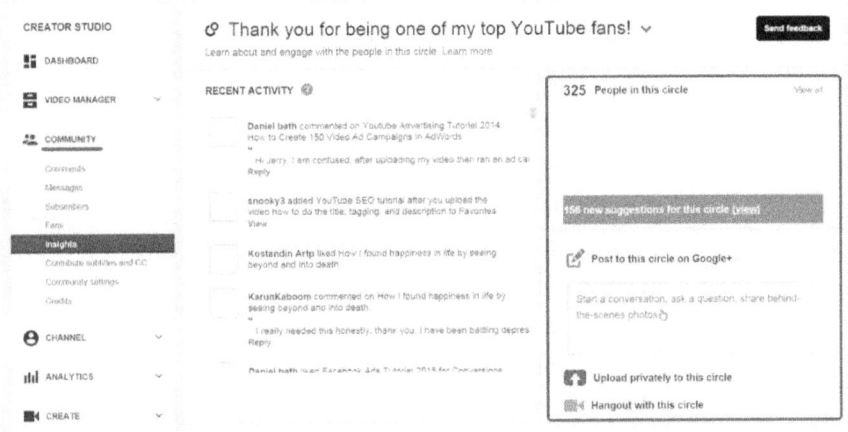

You always want to use this and what's cool is that you can also directly share or create with this circle to get more connected with those people. I'm grateful that I already have 325 people in this circle. Now, not all of them add me back and that's fine, and all I care about are getting as many people in this circle as possible.

The real sweetness of this is *Google* has *156* new suggestions for me. All I have to do is click on *"view."*

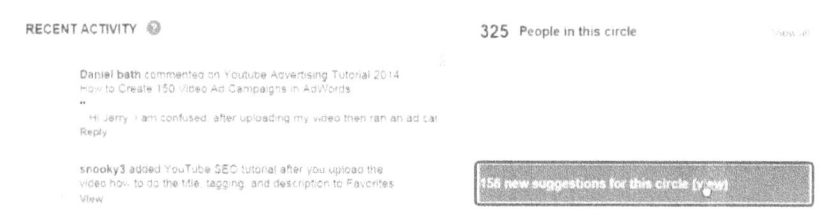

Then, I am shown the *Google+* page with all of my fans that it recommends for this circle. Now, I can click this one little button *"Add to circle."*

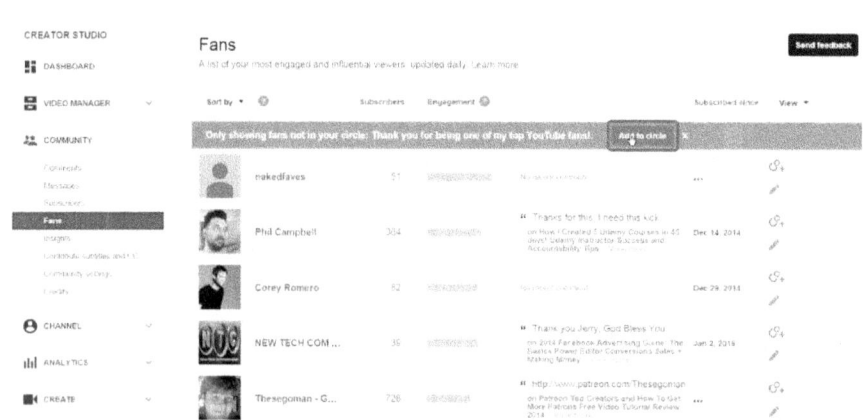

This new window shows and all *156* Fans are selected.

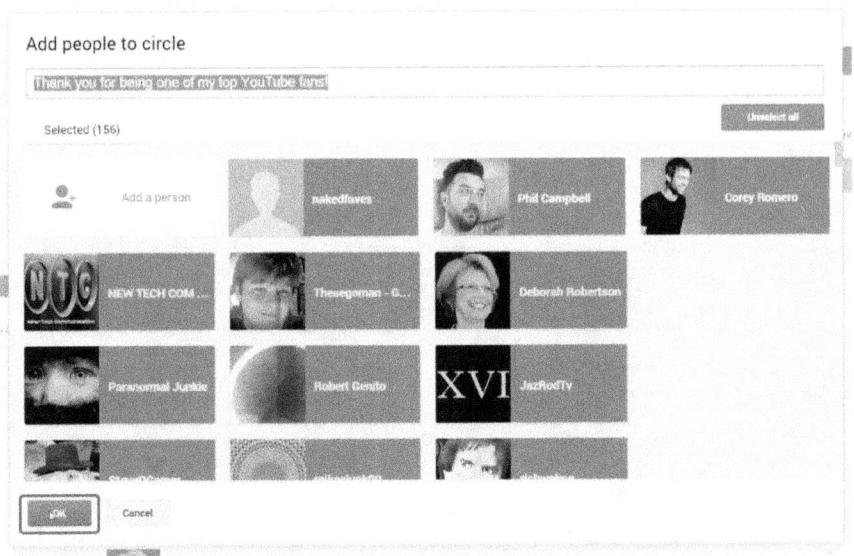

Then I click *"Ok"* so *Google* circles all of them at once.

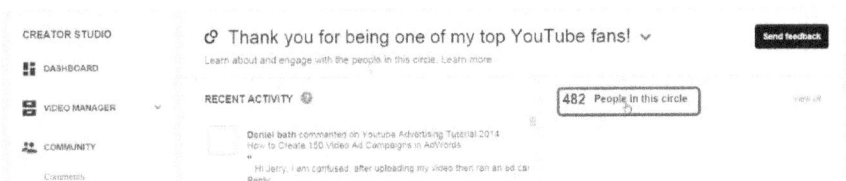

When you can take those bulk actions to add *150* people, especially on *Google+,* it is gigantically helpful.

The idea is to check this *Insights* tab within the *Community*, once every month or so, and you just keep building more and more people in this circle.

What happens when you look at my *Google+* page, is that more people keep circling me all the time and especially from these biggest fans.

They are the people that *Google* knows are the most interactive with my channel and are the most likely to circle me. I have now got *775* followers on *Google+*, which in the *Google+* world is pretty decent.

The idea is that I want to be able to share all of my links on my website, and share everything I create like my new online courses, with that core group on *Google+*, especially because I already need to do it for *SEO* anyway, so why not have them there on *Google+* too?

A very helpful feature *Google* offers, one you definitely want to take advantage of.

YouTube community settings to block spammers and bullies

If you have a channel that begins to be successful, you will soon have *Spam* comments of people advertising all kind of stuff, and bullies who don't like you and post nasty comments on all your videos.

There is a way to deal with *Spam* and bullies:

When you go to your dashboard, go to your *"Comments"* section.

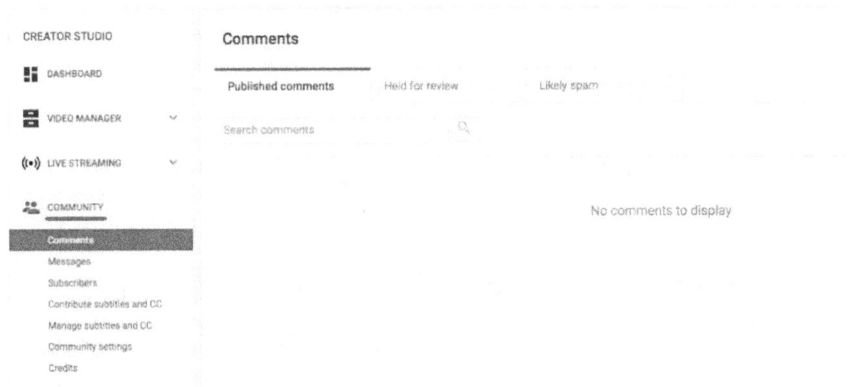

There you will see all your comments. The comment below is a *SPAM* comment as you can see.

What you can do is hide it from your *YouTube* channel.

Go to the *"Flag"* on this comment and select hide.

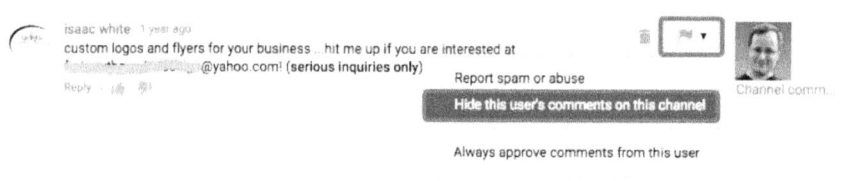

The beauty of doing this is that the comment will be hidden in your comment section below the video, but it will show to the *Spammer* when he is logged in. Believing his *Spam* is working he will spam, spam and spam until he is blue in the face… and waste his time.

If you click *Report Spam* or *Abuse* he might be removed too soon and it is not fun!

If there is a good commenter you may want to select *"Always approve comments from this user"* to approve them.

Go to your *Community Settings*.

There, you will see your approved users and your hidden users.

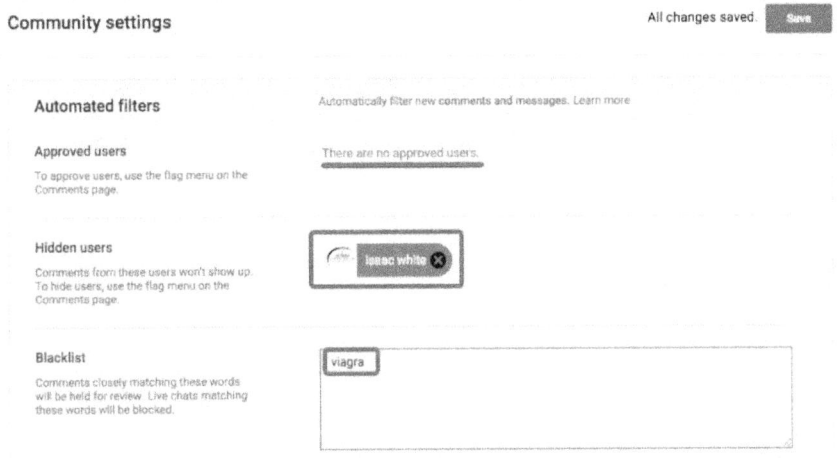

You can also type a list of words to blacklist.

The bottom section is the default you wish to have and I personally prefer to allow all comments as it can be quite a bit of work to review them one by one.

Default settings

Comments on your new videos
- Allow all comments
- Hold all comments for review
- Disable comments

Comments on your channel
- Allow all comments
- Hold all comments for review
- Disable comments

Creator credits on your channel
- Allow all creator credits
- Hold all creator credits for review

It is your choice of course, and at times it might be preferable to hold them for review to keep spammers and bullies at bay.

I hope this is useful.

CHAPTER 12

Ways to make money on *YouTube*

In this chapter you will discover four ways that you can use to make money with your *YouTube* channel.

In this first section, I will show you how this strategy made me *$660,000* and how you also can *start on YouTube and then work your way into making Udemy courses*.

This *case study of how to make new viral YouTube videos + earn with Google AdSense* will show you how you can have a very successful *YouTube* channel without filming a single video.

If you want to work as a freelancer and serve clients, this is the section for you. I will show you how I made *$2,500 per sale from YouTube tutorial videos with an "email for more help" link* and how you can do the same.

Finally, I will explain how *Patreon allows you to get paid to make YouTube videos and more!*

Read on…

Start on *YouTube* and then work your way into making *Udemy* courses

By far the best way I found to make money on *YouTube* is to connect and work with it into *Udemy*. I got started on *Udemy* in *2013* at about the same time I tried to get started making *YouTube* videos.

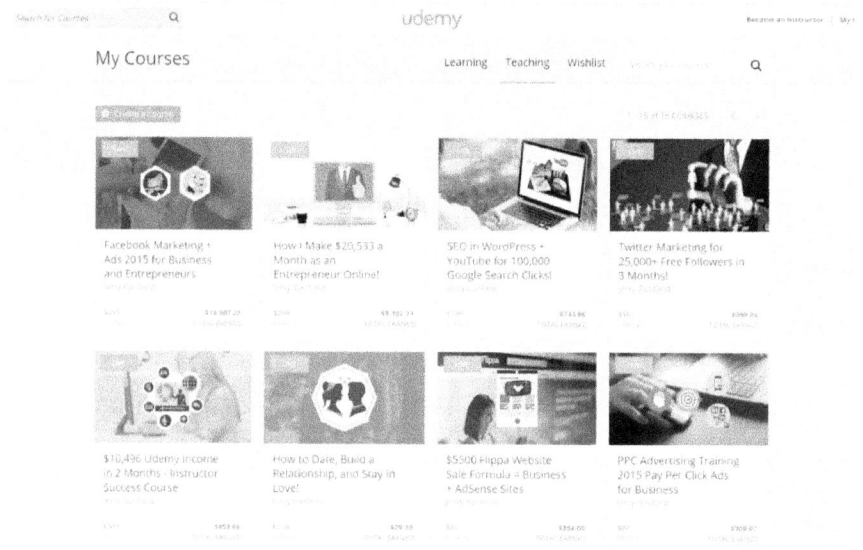

I did a very bad job when I first started on *Udemy* getting anything to actually happen. I will show you my revenue from *2014* when I really started.

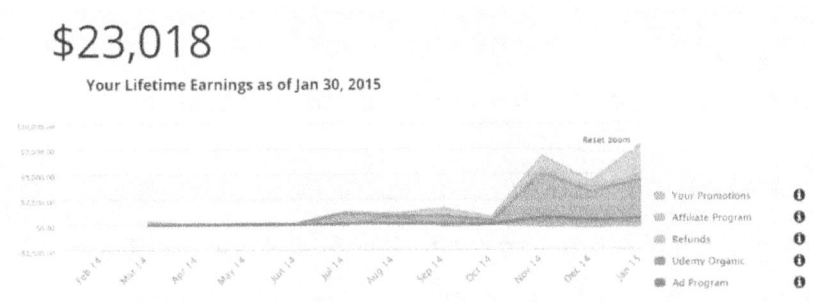

I made no money on *Udemy* for quite a while and then my *Udemy* sales took off thanks to my *YouTube* channel.

My *YouTube* channel was where I first started trying to make videos.

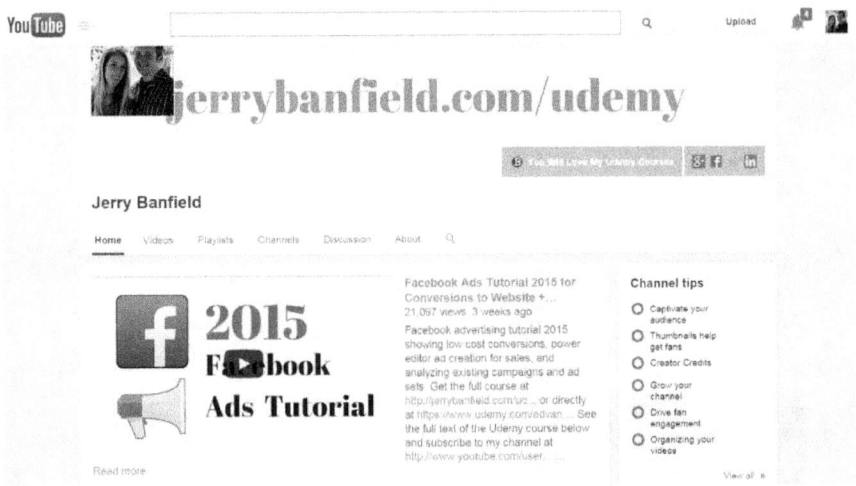

YouTube is a lot easier to get started on than *Udemy*. *YouTube* has almost no quality standards, except that you can't use other people's copyrighted stuff. That makes it very easy to just get started making videos. Then, the more videos you make, the better you will get at making videos.

You will get to know what people like that you make. You can figure out areas like *Facebook* ads, which for me is proven to be a very powerful area where I have a consistent and reliable traffic source on *YouTube*.

If you search for nearly anything related to *Facebook ads, Facebook marketing, Facebook Power Editor, Facebook ads tutorials* or anything like that, my videos are going to come up all over.

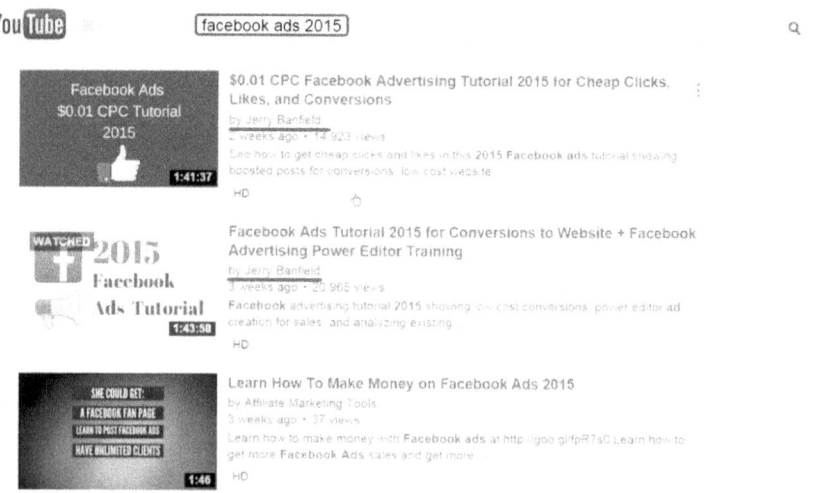

I discovered that on *YouTube*, but then I moved over to putting a course on *Udemy*. I just used my actual *YouTube*

videos when I first made my course.

Then, I went through and remade the entire course so that most of the course is exclusive to *Udemy*.

This course all by itself has made *$17,000* in around six months. I would never have done that or got to this point if I hadn't started out trying to make videos on *YouTube*, and got positive reinforcement from my *YouTube* audience saying: *"We really like these Facebook videos you're making. Please, keep making more of them."*

As I got better at making them, in *March* and *April 2014*, I was just starting to put serious effort into making more good *YouTube* videos and I started experimenting on *Udemy*.

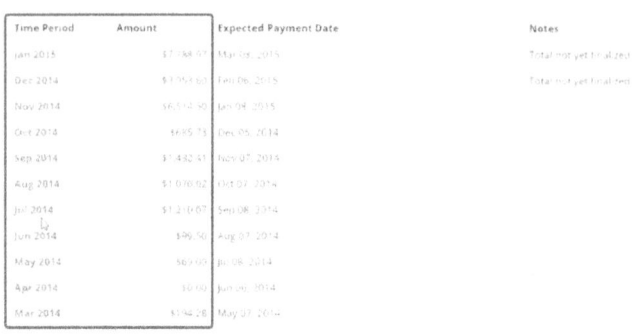

Since then, my income went way up on *Udemy*. I have made all kind of courses and in fact, I rarely make a native *YouTube* video now. What I do, is make courses like my *Facebook Ads* course (*jerrybanfield.com/product/facebook/*), which is loaded with all kinds of videos.

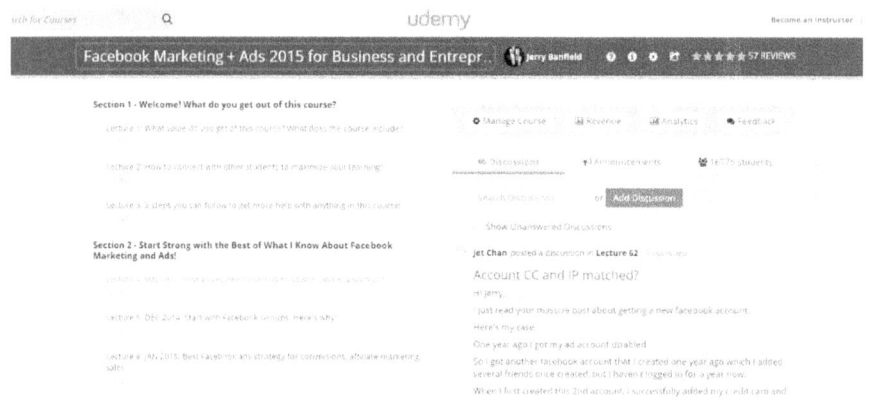

The course has *69* different lectures that are all unique videos and a couple of *PDFs*.

What I do now is make a small amount of these lectures available as free preview lectures on *YouTube*. When someone searches for *"Facebook ads 2015,"* they see these long videos and they are funneled back into my *Udemy* courses.

I give them a free preview using some sections of the course on a *YouTube* video, then they can see in the description where to buy the full course. That's how I have been able to consistently grow with *YouTube* and I do the same thing on my website at *jerrybanfield.com*. I funnel everything from it to *Udemy* too.

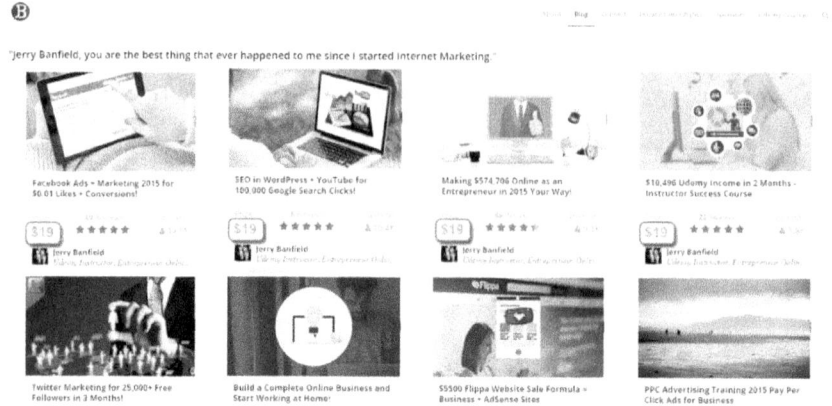

All of this started on *YouTube* and ultimately *Udemy*, which I believe is the most powerful way to make money online.

If you are trying to make money with *YouTube*, start to figure out what people like that you do and consistently get better at making videos. When you have polished what you are doing, and have videos you like to make and that your audience likes, then you can sit down to create a course on *Udemy*. You can make a bunch of courses on *Udemy* about the topics you enjoy.

I started with my *Facebook* course, but I continued to branch out with other courses, and created my *YouTube* course *(jerrybanfield.com/product/youtube/)*, from which this book is based on.

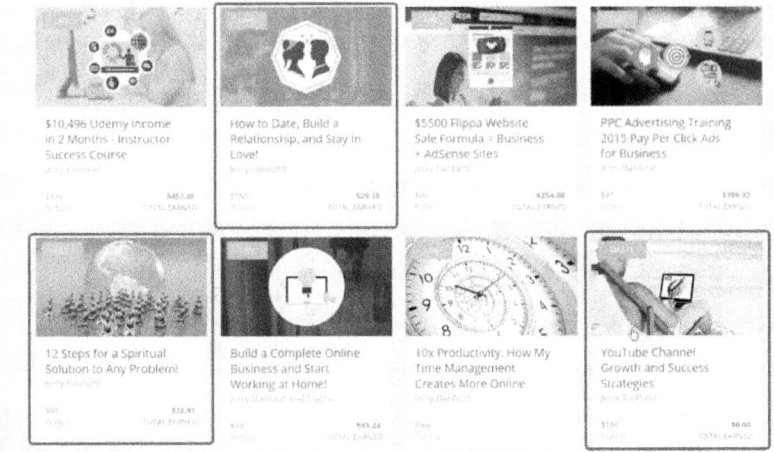

All of my courses on *Udemy* have made sales, even courses like my dating course and my spiritual course.

Udemy is very powerful, but *YouTube* is much easier to start. You can start on *YouTube* and work your way up to *Udemy*. Then, the bigger your *YouTube* channel becomes, the better you can funnel your traffic to your website to make sales on your *Udemy* courses, or you can funnel directly to your *Udemy* courses.

Finally, let me show you more history on my *YouTube* channel. These are my videos by most popular and I started out with all kinds of things like dating videos, I have got made by other people on *Fiverr*. My *"$0.01 CPM Facebook Ads Tutorial"* video was the first big successful video I made on

YouTube.

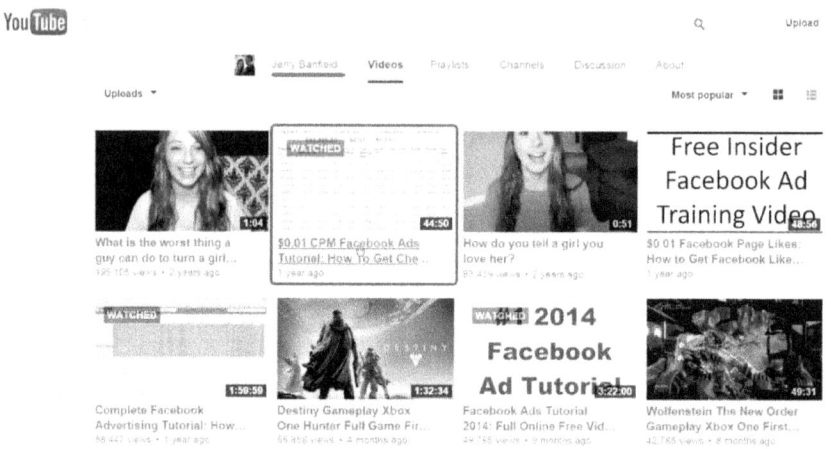

This video got more than *125,000* views and more than *260* likes on it.

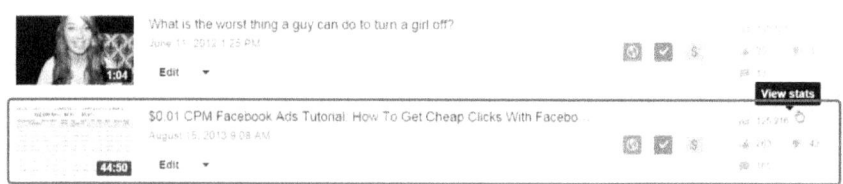

I got a bunch of clients off this video and this was the first video I put in one of my *Udemy* courses. If I never made this video, I doubt I would be writing this chapter right now.

When you make videos you care about passionately on *YouTube*, you can get a good chance to see how much people like your videos, then you can work your way into making *Udemy* courses, and from there monetize and sell your *Udemy* courses on your *YouTube* channel.

By *2016*, the *Udemy* courses I was teaching had made nearly *2 million dollars* in sales with me receiving over *$660,000* of that, reinforcing that the strategy I explained in this chapter works.

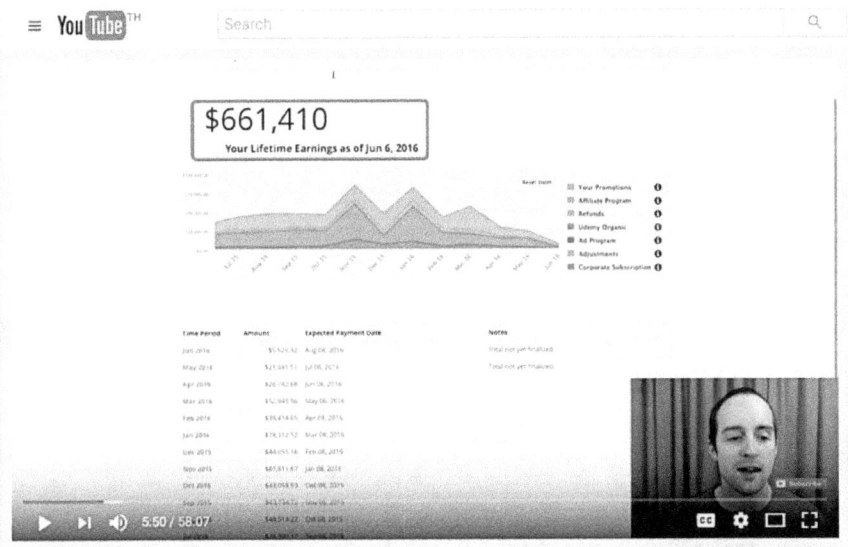

Things went so well on *Udemy* that they decided to launch a new pricing policy in *April 2016* that reduced sales by *80%* site-wide which encouraged many instructors to leave. Since I did not take the hint, *Udemy* chose to ban me based on what they said were policy violations *(youtu.be/-s51hrbg8VI)*

despite my best efforts to work within the rules.

I am now using the same strategy with *YouTube* to sell my courses directly on my website: *https://jerrybanfield.com*

This strategy will still work for you with *Udemy*, but also with other online course markets that popped-up on the Internet recently.

I hope this is useful for you.

Case study of how to make new viral *YouTube* videos + earn with *Google AdSense*

Here is a ridiculously easy way to make money on *YouTube* because you can do something you might already enjoy like making *top 10 funny dog videos*.

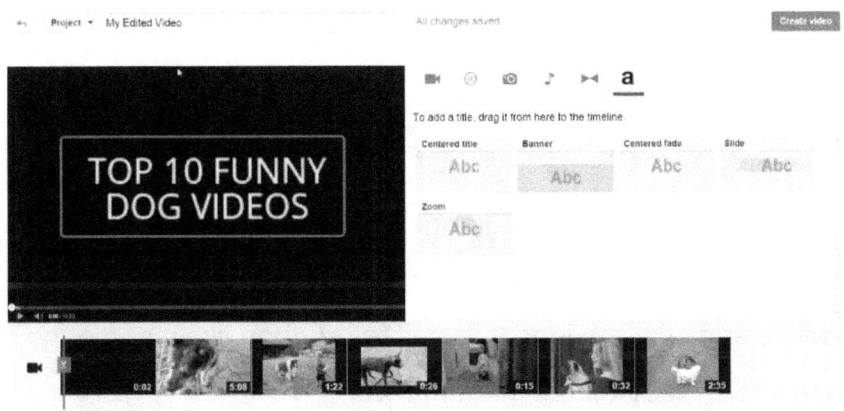

Here is a case study from a channel that's doing this right now. It is called **Top 10 Media** *(youtube.com/c/Top10Media)*.

It is a fairly new channel and they make videos about top 10 things like these: *10 Dumbest iPhone Apps, 10 Craziest Lawsuits You Won't Believe Are Real, 10 Most Embarrassing Mistakes in History,* etc…

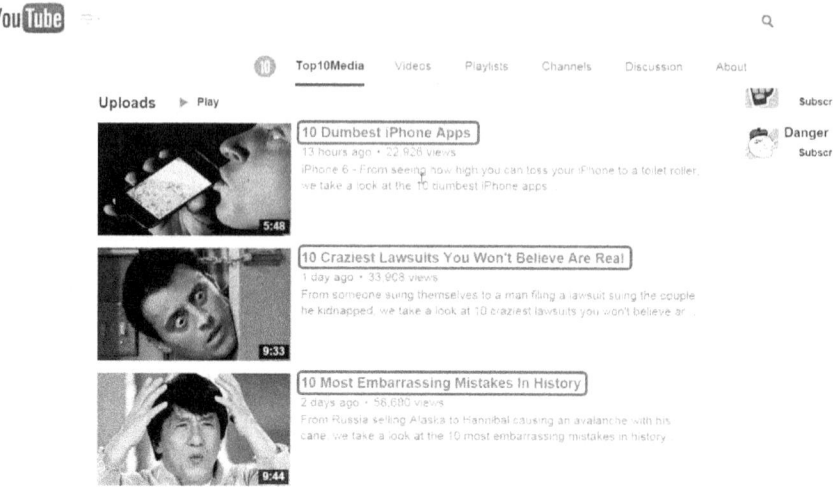

Let me show you the entire production process.

You can find videos or images you can stick into the video editor on *YouTube*. The best part is that you don't even have to come up with the idea yourself, more than likely someone else has already did all that hard work.

So here is a video on their channel, with *48,000* views: *10 Famous People Who Have Worked In Fast Food.*

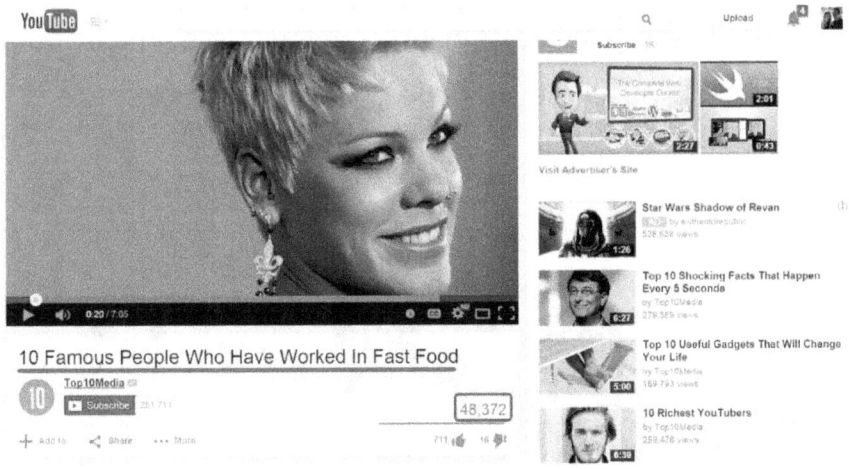

Now look, go to *www.therichest.com*.

Here is an article: *10 Famous People Who Have Worked In Fast Food*

You notice that *Barack Obama* is in the article, and if you scroll into the video you will notice, *"Hey! Barack Obama's in this video too!"*

If you go back to the website, you notice, *"Hey! That's Brad Pitt, right?"*

When you scroll back a little bit in the video, *"Look! Brad Pitt's in this video too!"*

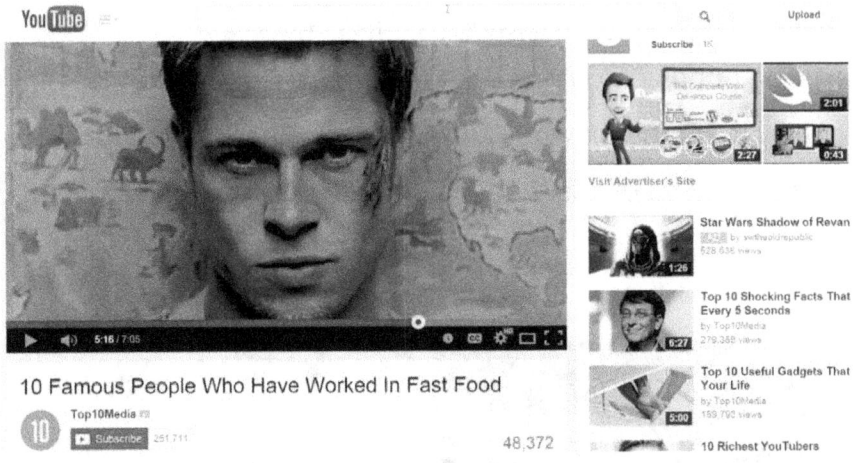

So, this is literally taken straight from an existing blog post and put into a video. Here is how much money that's making the channel:

An estimated monthly earnings of *$3,000 to $46,000.*

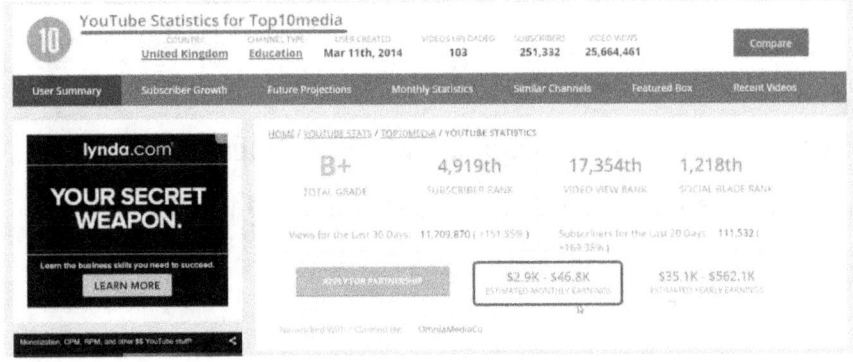

That's not exactly a very narrow range of income estimate but the fact is this channel is definitely making a good deal of money just by using *Google Adsense* on videos that are not original in terms of their content. They are taken from an existing popular blog, then the pictures are put in from whatever source they used. You can use the *YouTube Video Editor* to put all of this together without ever making your own video.

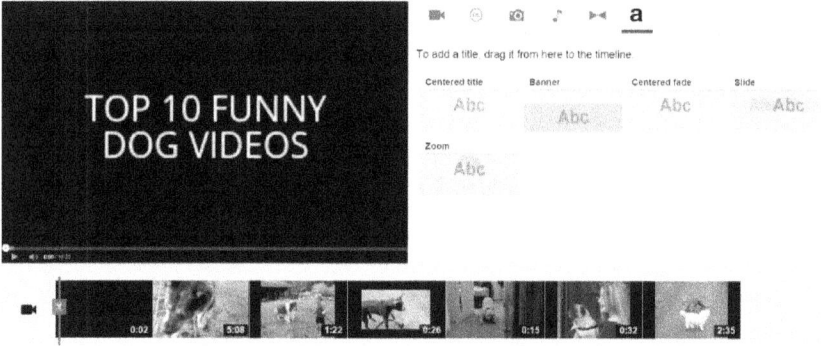

The one thing they do really good is the narration of the video.

In order to do that you need to use the *Video Editor* to create the video and upload it privately to your channel. Then, you will need to download the *YouTube MP4* to your computer.

Use a software to narrate the video, re-upload it with narration and you might want to delete the original.

That's what you can do to make a ton of money on *YouTube,* doing something you like to do, which basically could just be reading existing popular blog posts. Now, you'd only want to do this if you genuinely enjoy putting these kinds of things together and talking about them.

The idea is that you can simply go through existing content you already enjoy, narrate and upload it on *YouTube* using the *Video Editor*, put your own audio on it, so it is very personal and unique that way.

Then you can have the potential to be having hundreds of thousands of subscribers, making thousands of dollars on autopilot with *Google Adsense* every month, even if it is a new channel.

I hope that this powerful strategy to make money on *YouTube* that requires only assembling existing content, which is already available in the right way, will be helpful for you.

$2,500 per sale from *YouTube* tutorial videos with an *"email for more help"* link

My favorite way to make money on *YouTube* and that worked best for me is to put a *call-to-action email address* directly in the video description offering for more help. When I search for *"Facebook ads 2015"* and scroll down past the ads, you can see my videos.

What I would do is write, *"For more help email me…"* after the first sentence within the 2 lines, and place the email address later in the description so people have to click on the video in order to see the email on the video page.

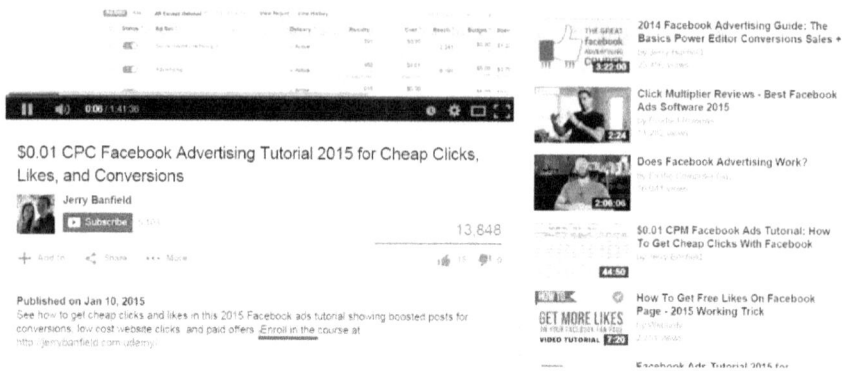

That worked great for *SEO* and once people clicked on the video, they read the description and emailed me for help. I would get emails coming in with no work consistently each day asking for more help, and then get new clients that way. I sold services as high as *$2,500* on the first order, a service with no cost associated with it because that was just a service fee for me. It didn't include any ad spend or anything like that.

The single most effective way I have found to make money on *YouTube* is to make a tutorial showing how to do something and then offer a service where you help out with what you are showing out of doing the tutorial. This works fast when you are able to show great proof in your tutorial that you are very good at what you are doing.

If you do graphic design you can put up a tutorial showing how to do something in *Photoshop* and that should be very good proof of your own ability to do good work. If you are trying to get people to visit you for any kind of service, you want to show that you can do a very good job yourself. Naturally, this works well for business services where people are looking for help with things.

Facebook ads was a perfect category to do this and while *99* out of a *100* people will continue trying to do it themselves, that one out of one hundred percent that sends an email is a potential client.

Now, there is a problem with this strategy because for every email you get that's a paying client, you probably get *10* emails from people who just want free advice. That's good too, especially if you are getting started. It is great for learning and it is great for growing in terms of building relationships.

You will notice that I do not have an email in my new videos now because I do not want people emailing me for help with *Facebook* ads. I have them going straight to my courses on my website *(jerrybanfield.com/shop/)*.

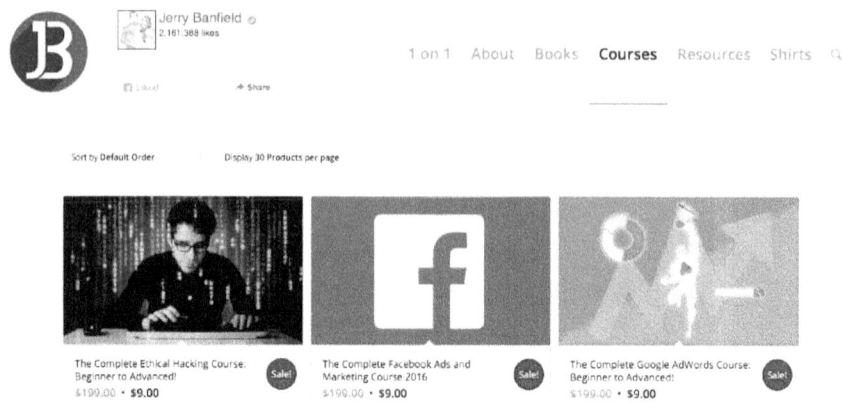

You can also put any other kind of link here and this is another ideal way to make money. This is what I'm doing now because it involves no work. When someone finds my video, clicks to my website and then buys one of my online courses, that doesn't take me any effort right now. My entire business is based on online courses and these videos are feeding people back to my website and to my online courses because it is completely automated income. I don't have to do anything for it and I don't have to respond to emails or take clients.

The description on *YouTube* is your chance to make money. The best way to make a lot of money is by offering people the chance to email you and build a personal relationship with you. However, if you have got a big enough channel on a big enough brand online, then you can try and push straight to product sales. If you don't, it is very hard to do product sales because of the trust factor. I'm often able to funnel people who have been following my channel now for a year into my online courses.

If you are just getting started, it is much better to use an email address in the description of your *YouTube* video and offer those people services, and build relationships using the strategy. I got two orders for *$2,500* services in one month last year using the strategy. Then, when I had the prices lower, I got tons of orders for *$199, $299* and *$399* services.

This is a giant moneymaking opportunity if you just set up a video showing proof and do it yourself help, and then offer your email address for more help.

People often are looking for help and they are not as defensive against being sold to when they reached out and invested their time with you. Use a conversion in the description to get people to invest their time with you, and then it can be very easy to make a sale.

I hope this is useful for you in figuring out a good way to make money off of your *YouTube* videos.

Patreon allows you to get paid to make *YouTube* videos and more!

You can get paid to make *YouTube* videos on *Patreon.com* and you can get paid to make many more things than that. Here is a quick overview of how it works.

Patreon allows creators and fans to connect in a place where fans become a patron of a creator they like. Then, the creator gets paid for every creation.

This is my *Patreon* at www.patreon.com/jerrybanfield.

I get paid for every video I make. The official payout status *$282.50* per video on *79* patrons paying me to make *YouTube*

videos. How sweet is that?

Patreon is a great environment to connect with people that will pay you to make videos. However, it is not quite that simple of course. You see that I have *79* patrons and it says that I get *$282.50* per video. What actually happens is that people can limit their contributions to monthly contribution. So what I actually get is around *$83.50* when I make more than *10* videos.

Before that, if you look at my charges for this month, every time I upload a video, then it gives me the chance to charge my patrons. So at the beginning of the month, I got *$257.50* pledged by *69* patrons.

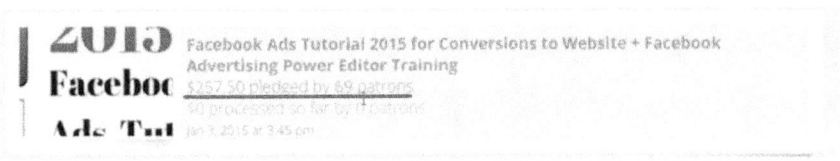

Then it drops consistently as I continue forward.

I have got *$111.50*, *$105.50*, *$114.50* and then down to *$87* and *$84* as I keep making all these new videos. The fact is that I get paid to make videos on *Patreon* by people who like my *YouTube* channel and want me to keep making videos.

The real sweet part about *Patreon* is that it is independent of *YouTube,* so you can make whatever you want on *Patreon*. You can make comics, podcasts, blog posts, e-books, and whatever you want to on *Patreon*.

This is how it works:

You put a video on your channel.

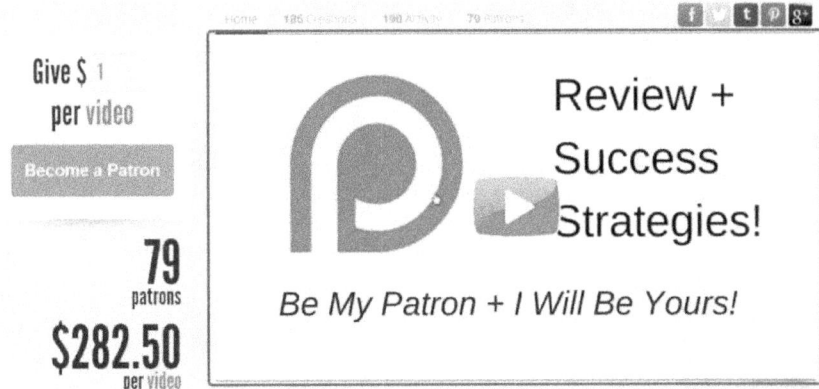

You set up your profile like I have done.

Be My Patron + I Will Be Yours!

What you give to me comes back to you and millions more!

- Getting started on Patreon is challenging and I work to help every Patreon creator have an easier time than I did getting my first 50 patrons. I asked my wife and my mom to be my first two patrons and worked hard to find more. I discovered that most creators on Patreon were working hard to get their first patrons too and that I really enjoy helping make it easier!

What you give, you will receive!

- When you join the more than 50 people already pledging $2/video or more to me, I will immediately pledge to your Patreon page! I do pledge for pledge on Patreon because the one thing all successful Patreon pages have in common is a lot of people supporting them.
- If you do not have a Patreon page, you can get linked on my YouTube channel and website to connect my audience with what you are doing.
- If you are on Patreon because you are trying to make more money online, I have 50+ free articles, podcasts, and YouTube videos on my

Then, you offer rewards.

It is like kick starters, except with monthly payments.

Now the caveat is that people love one time payments, but hate monthly payments. That means *Patreon* is very difficult to scale up. So the easiest way to do is just to do pledge with people to get started because no one wants to pledge for someone who has no patrons. Do pledge for pledge like I have done to get started, then it is a lot easier to keep building up.

If you want to see how much money you can make on this, have a look at my blog post about top *Patreon* earners *(jerrybanfield.com/top-patreon-creators/)*.

The table on the bottom have got lists of how much money people are making and how many patrons they have.

In the list below sorted by money earned, the first artist is making *$15,000* per video, the second guy is making *$15,000* per month to do a weekly podcast, and the third guy *$13,000* a month to do podcasts.

Then, a band is making *$13,000* per music video and the next guy who creates Internet videos and podcasts gets *$11,000* a month. The last one is a cool one, she has come up a lot recently and she gets *$12,000* per *"two weeks"* to make art, comics, paintings and tutorials.

How sweet is that?

Here is the catch, it says *$12,209.50 per two weeks*, but hers works the same as mine does per video. *Patreon* has two basic options, monthly and by unit, but all units can still be capped monthly.

So that's what happens:

A video is a unit I set.

Then, it is capped monthly.

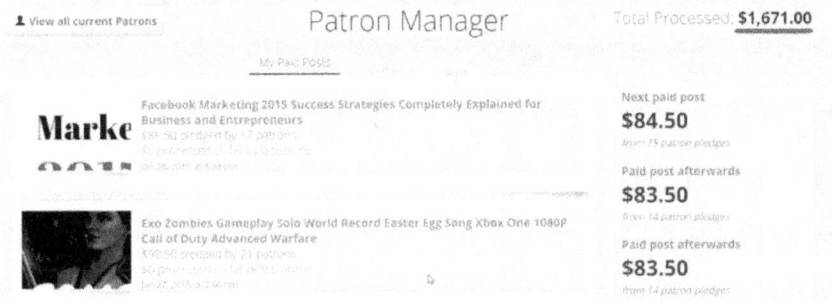

So I have made *$1,671* off of *Patreon* already. This has been a very good month, with a little luck I should make *$500* to *$1,000* this month off of *Patreon* after just getting started with it for a few months and not even having that big of an audience online.

So that's how powerful *Patreon* is.

This girl is having incredible success on her *Patreon*.

Now she gets a minimum of *$12,000* a month, but more than likely she is making about *$15,000* to *$20,000* per month off of her *Patreon*. She has one of the most successful *Patreon* accounts out there.

The thing is that *Patreon* is young and you can get in on this now, go pledge for pledge with people, and get started building your *YouTube* channel up.

You can see that these are all *YouTube* video posts I made where I have actually got paid to put the video up. Then *Patreon* emails all of my patrons every time. The sweet thing is that I get paid whether I make a video about *Facebook* marketing, *Call of Duty Zombies* or a *YouTube* video from one of my online courses.

I can offer free preview videos on *YouTube* for my online courses. I can actually make videos for my online courses, then I can use some of the videos, not more than 50%, as free preview videos. Then I can get paid for them on *Patreon*.

It is just incredible how many different ways you can get paid to make videos if you have got a clever set up, and *YouTube* and *Udemy* are great foundations to do that with.

I'd love to have you come by my *Patreon* page at www.patreon.com/jerrybanfield and become a patron.

CONCLUSION

Thank you for reading this book!

If you want to be successful with *YouTube*, you might also be interested to take **"The Complete *YouTube* Course: Go from Beginner to Advanced!"** which has already served *12,000+* students.

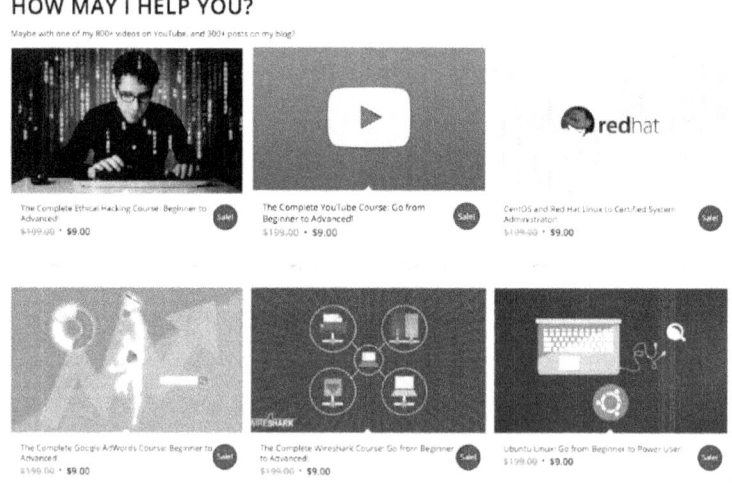

START LEARNING NOW

https://jerrybanfield.com/product/youtube/

You can read more books written by me at *https://jerrybanfield.com/books*.

I appreciate the time you spent reading this! If it has been helpful for you, I hope you will let others know that in a review at *http://jerry.tips/kindle10jb*

Jerry Banfield

https://jerrybanfield.com

LEGAL NOTICE

The Publisher has strived to be as accurate and complete as possible in the creation of this book, although he does not warrant or represent at any time that the contents within are accurate.

While all attempts have been made to verify information provided in this publication, the Publisher assumes no responsibility for errors, omissions, or contrary interpretation of the subject matter herein. Any perceived slights of specific persons, peoples, or organizations are unintentional.

In practical advice books, like anything else in life, there are no guarantees of results. Readers are cautioned to reply on their own judgment about their individual circumstances to act accordingly.

This book is not intended for use as a source of health, legal, business, accounting or financial advice. All readers are advised to seek services of competent professionals in health, legal, business, accounting and finance fields.

www.ingramcontent.com/pod-product-compliance
Lightning Source LLC
Chambersburg PA
CBHW070221190526

45169CB00001B/37